THINKING BIG

The Education of a Gambler

SOL FOX

THINKING BIG

The Education of a Gambler

Atheneum   NEW YORK   1985

Library of Congress Cataloging in Publication Data

Fox, Sol.
  Thinking big.

  1. Fox, Sol.   2. Gamblers—United States—Biography.
3. Compulsive gambling.   1. Title.
RC569.5.G35F694   1985   616.85'227   [B]   84-45620
ISBN 0-689-11551-2

Published simultaneously in Canada by McClelland and Stewart Ltd.
Composition by Westchester Book Composition, Inc.,
Yorktown Heights, New York
Manufactured by Fairfield Graphics, Fairfield, Pennsylvania
Designed by Kathleen Carey
First Edition

To my wife Carol Fox,

a gambler in a class by herself, with loving
appreciation for the advice, encouragement,
and support which made this venture possible.

F O R E W O R D

Among the baggage I carried out of childhood was a philosophy which my growing-up friends called "license"—the idea that you must pay your dues for the right to do something of special interest or importance.

We were strict about the requirements of license, seldom more so than in relation to our ritual roasting of potatoes salvaged or stolen from peddlers and cooked in bonfires blazing on vacant lots in our Williamsburg neighborhood of Brooklyn. Everyone was welcome to take part in these cookouts, but each was required to show license— to provide warmth or nourishment by bringing wood for the fire or extra potatoes for those who could bring wood but not spuds.

Although the principle of license seldom was applied to anything more serious than our potato parties, it remained part of my thinking about more important matters. Sometimes as a help, sometimes a hindrance, the issue of license has been present whenever I have considered whether I should go ahead with a project for which my credentials might otherwise be uncertain.

That was true in particular of an issue which for many years has held my interest: the whys and wherefores of gambling, and the ways of life that lead people to gamble, so many compulsively. Experience had made me especially curious about the condition of compulsive gamblers and why things are as they are for that class of people.

Free from the requirements of license, I would have tried to satisfy my curiosity long ago. But I was held back by the presence of licensed authorities—psychoanalysts, psychologists, and sociologists—at work in the field. Their explanations didn't satisfy me, but I questioned my license to seek answers that would make sense to me. Eventually, curiosity overcame other considerations, and I went ahead with my search.

Now, having completed my exploration, it is for others to judge whether my efforts have produced warmth or nourishment. But on the matter of license, I am satisfied. I believe I have paid my dues. I have lived this gambling life.

A C K N O W L E D G M E N T S

My work was made easier, and more pleasant, by several people for whose contributions I am grateful and whose assistance I am pleased to acknowledge.

The shape and texture of this work was influenced by the constant and constructive criticism, ideas, and encouragement of my sons Ted and Nick Fox, my friends Ronnie and Bob Wacker, and my brother Rube Fox. Any deficiencies can only be the result of my failure occasionally to heed their invariably sensible suggestions.

I am indebted also to a former colleague and long-time friend, Lydia Moss, for her careful reading of the manuscript to minimize error and remove other faults.

I am indebted to my good neighbor Jim Michelman for a constructive job of proofreading that helped enrich my work.

And I am pleased to express my thanks for the careful, dependable work of Roberta Langhans, who typed the manuscript.

PART ONE

FRAME OF REFERENCE

1.

IT was a rare spring day, the life-promising kind of day on which only good things should be expected to happen: Tuesday, my good-news day. I was at Jamaica, my lucky track. And I had just made the biggest bet of my life: seven hundred dollars, which in that less inflationary time was as much as I took home for six weeks' work as a rewrite man in the New York bureau of United Press.

I made that move confidently. But as I walked from the pari-mutuel betting booth to a place at the rail near the finish line, my mood changed from euphoria to dread.

More than ten thousand times during fifteen years as a horseplayer I had placed bets without experiencing anything like the malaise which now overwhelmed me. I was confused and frightened by a depression that felt like death. With only a minute to post time, I didn't know what to think or how to calm the panic draining me of every feeling but fear. I could only wait for the race to start.

I had made the play with the best of intentions. Having been at this exasperating business since I was nineteen, I had decided to call it quits, get married, and start a new life. I was in love, and the thought of a future with the woman I loved pleased me greatly. However, I was in debt for three thousand dollars, half a year's pay, and believed it would be irresponsible, not to say dishonorable, to burden a marriage with such an obligation. I planned a final supreme effort to win just enough to clear my debt, so I could move unencumbered into the future.

Each day for weeks I had spent hours studying past performance statistics, searching out sure things that would help me get rid of my debt. But there had been little movement, up or down. Then, the day before, I had parlayed fifty-five dollars into more than seven hundred dollars of betting money. Now, on this good news day, I had returned to press my luck.

I came to make one bet: five hundred dollars to win on the favorite in the fourth race, the only horse on the program worth a bet, in my judgment. My plan was to hold two hundred dollars in reserve for future action if bad racing luck should befall a horse which looked unbeatable.

The fourth race favorite stood at three to two in the morning line. If that price held up in the actual betting, I could expect to win seven hundred and fifty dollars, which, with seven hundred in hand, would be about half of what I needed to bring my debt to zero.

I would have preferred a one-shot opportunity to make a clean sweep of the debt. But I was being sensible. Since my analysis showed only one horse worth a bet, I comforted myself with the understanding that it is better to win with one short-priced horse than to lose with any number of bets at longer odds. With what I thought of as good sense, I assured myself that I could win the rest of the money I needed on another race, or races, on another day, or days.

Often I had bet on a dozen or more races a day with bookies who accepted bets at tracks across the country. There had been an empire-building, sun-never-sets sort of excitement in following time on its westward course, opening with action at any of half a dozen tracks in the east and ending with races in California three hours after the eastern tracks had called it a day. Betting that way had allowed little time to study the form of the horses on which I bet, so it had been necessary to rely on my memory of their past performances and the advice of handicappers in the racing papers. At some expense I had learned that this was no way to beat the horses. Experience had taught me that my best hope of winning, or at least cutting my losses, was to pick my spots—to bet only when my own careful analysis of speed ratings, class, and in-the-money performance led me to a horse with a distinct probability of winning. The favorite in the fourth race was such a horse—a standout, if not a sure thing—by my calculations.

However, before I could do what I had come to do, some other things happened. I got to the track early, fifty minutes before the fourth race, twenty minutes before the third. That left me with too much time on my hands and only one thing to do, despite every reason to do nothing. I thought I might as well take another look at the third race.

That morning, as every morning, I had conducted a thorough study of all the day's races. Buoyed by my win the day before and refreshed by a good night's sleep after my work on the UP night shift, I had taken extra time for the examination, almost three hours, before deciding that there was only the one bet to make.

One other race—the third—had attracted my attention. There were two good-looking horses in that field, the favorite and the second choice. However, neither had enough of an edge on the other to signal a bet, and in these conditions my handicapping strategy required me to pass the race.

Now, glancing at the tote board showing the total money bet on each horse in the third race and the odds reflecting each entry's share of the total betting pool, I saw something that didn't seem right. The horse which had been the second choice in the morning line for the third race at five to two was on the board at nine to one. I couldn't believe my eyes.

There is nothing sacred about the morning line. It is merely the track handicapper's forecast of probable odds, a guide at most. Bettors often ignore that guidance to establish substantially different odds. But this seemed too much. It wouldn't have been unreasonable for the betting to move a point or two either way from the early line. This was something more. In my opinion, odds three and a half times as much as the morning line on one of the two horses in the field with a chance to win could only be considered an overlay— offering odds substantially higher than normally would be expected.

To the horseplayer, a perceived overlay is an offer that shouldn't be refused without careful consideration. But it is a difficult call to make. Often, it is wishful thinking rather than an objective evaluation. Also, what is an overlay to one bettor is merely a long shot to another. The bettors whose money determines the final odds usually know what they are doing. Still, mistakes are made. As I read the tote board, this seemed such an error. The bettors were ignoring the true chief contender, putting their money in large amounts on the favorite and on two other horses that, according to my calculations, didn't have a chance. As a result, the odds on these three horses were being forced down unreasonably, while the odds on the real contender were going sky-high.

By itself, the chance of a potential payoff much greater than it should be is attractive to horseplayers, who are accustomed to having their payoffs discounted by fourteen percent or more to provide taxes for the state and operating funds and profit for the track. The crucial question, of course, is the overlay's chance of winning. A loser at any odds is a loser, and the favorite did seem to have an edge over the horse that now stood at nine to one. I knew that. I also knew I had come to the track to make just one bet, in the fourth race. Still, my mind lingered on the overlay.

There had been no change in jockey, weight, or equipment, any of which might affect the betting, and I knew of nothing else to explain the seemingly inflated odds. If my handicapping was correct, then nine to one on a horse with an even-up chance of winning was an overlay.

What happened next I still find painful to remember. I became aware suddenly that the underbet horse was a gray, a rare color for a horse. Most come in shades of brown. In the past, I had thought of gray as my lucky color and had sometimes bet on grays without bothering to check their form. I became aware also that this gray was to start from post position three, my lucky number. And there was another three: the third race. The combination of coincidental superstitions, time on my hands, and the unyielding belief that the gray was an overlay broke down what remained of my resistance. The final straw was another change in the odds. As the horses came onto the track for the post parade, the gray moved up to ten to one.

There were only nine minutes to post time.

Without further thought, I decided to bet one hundred dollars on the overlay. That would leave intact the five hundred dollars I had come to bet in the next race, as well as one hundred in my reserve fund. If the gray won, I would have an additional one thousand dollars, seventeen hundred in all. I could parlay that onto the fourth race favorite and win more than enough to pay off the outstanding balance of my debt.

On my way into the gloomy underbelly of the grandstand, where the row of betting booths was located, it occurred to me that if I bet three hundred on the gray and won, I would have more than enough to repay all I owed without having to bet on the fourth race or any race ever again. Best of all, losing wouldn't cause any great damage. I would still have four hundred for the fourth race.

Too often in the past, I reminded myself, there had been other situations of this kind and I had behaved hysterically. Now, before I could bet the three hundred on the overlay, I called a time out to demonstrate that I was in control and to think things through calmly.

Eight minutes remained to post time.

I spread *The Morning Telegraph* across the top of a trash can and spent what seemed a long time, but cannot have been more than two minutes, reviewing the figures I had studied so carefully that morning. It was as I remembered. The gray had shown consistent good speed in six- and seven-furlong races against the kind of cheaper horses that made up most of this field. He had made strong stretch runs in three of his last four sprints, winning one and coming close in two. He might need a longer distance, maybe the mile and an eighth of this race, to make his best showing. That is sometimes true of hard-driving sprinters. It is also true that the extra two or three furlongs of a race like this is often too much for them.

The favorite was the class horse in the field. He was stepping down after some promising though losing performances against better horses in races of this kind, and his speed rating at longer distances was a bit better than the gray's times in sprints. The issue was whether the gray would find the distance he might need in this race, or whether the favorite could give a winning account of himself against cheaper horses, only one of which, the gray, seemed to have any chance to upset him.

It could be said victory was possible for the gray, probable for the favorite. The issue had been too tight for me to call with confidence. But I had felt after the morning study that, forced to choose, I would have bet the favorite. Only the overlay made the gray attractive now. The gray was a wish; the favorite, a likelihood. I gave silent thanks for the great restraint I had shown in forcing myself to take a second look. Then—after rejecting the thought of splitting my money between the two—I decided to switch my bet to the favorite.

Only four minutes remained until post time.

Before I could change course again, I hurried to the fifty-dollar window, thrilled as always to be doing business where the high rollers did theirs, and bought four tickets on the favorite. That left safe the five hundred dollars for my planned bet in the next race. But, now, that didn't seem so smart. This favorite was as likely to win as the one waiting for me in the fourth race. Logically, I should bet as much on one as on the other. I hadn't completed a turn away from the betting clerk before I turned back to add three hundred dollars to my bet.

My choice stood at even money. A win would give me five hundred dollars more to bet on the fourth-race favorite. I began to feel as though that had already happened. Another possibility came to mind. If I bet all of the seven hundred dollars and won, then parlayed the fourteen hundred dollars on the next race and won, that two-step would give me all that was needed to pay off the debt threatening my future. I could go home free at last of any need to punish myself in this way.

I turned back to hand over the remaining two hundred dollars to a betting clerk I thought of as a savings bank teller accepting my money for interest-bearing safekeeping. I took several deep breaths and started toward the rail to watch the race, only to be attacked by the sickening feeling that, win or lose, I might have done something terribly wrong and foolish.

Panic seized me. I wanted my money back. I was stopped from asking by the knowledge that parimutuel betting operates on a no-refunds, no-exceptions policy and that it would be bad form to make such a request in any case. Instead, feeling that by my hysterical behavior I had surrendered any claim to respectability or good sense, I made my way to the rail, hoping that no one else had noticed my loss of control during the past few minutes.

Unable to feel or think anything else as I walked to a place at the rail just past the finish line, I thought, "Oh, my God. Oh, my God." Then I stood frozen, waiting. If someone had screamed in my ear,

"The world has come to an end," I wouldn't have heard or cared.

The track announcer's call, "And they're off," released my eyes and my brain, and I concentrated both to observe the field break like a herd from the starting gate. Within seconds, the eight horses had formed themselves into an uneven file with the gray in front, as might be expected of a speed horse. Presumably, his jockey was going to try to run the other horses into the ground and stay in front all the way. The favorite was in fourth place, three lengths behind the leader. That also was to be expected. His jockey apparently was rating his horse, keeping him close to the early pace, but saving energy for the final run in the stretch after the gray should have burned himself out.

The file of horses raced toward the far turn mechanically, uneventfully, as though on a carousel. Then the horse that had been running third fell back, and the favorite moved up to narrow the gap between himself and the gray to two lengths. There was a burning in my belly and chest.

My excitement rose as the field swung around the long turn toward the stretch and the horse that had been running second faltered and fell back. The favorite moved up on the heels of the gray. Now it was happening as it should. The favorite would catch the gray as they straightened out for the last three hundred yards of the stretch run, then fly past him to the finish. I remained silent, expressing nothing of my hopeful, frightened, prayerful excitement.

In the stretch, my horse continued to gain, running on the outside while the gray was held close to the rail to save ground. At the eighth pole, with about two hundred yards to go, my horse caught the gray and they ran head and head, as though yoked, using up ground, with neither able to gain an advantage.

I could see the jockey on the gray whipping his horse. The jockey on the favorite wasn't using his whip. I tried to shout at my jockey to whip the favorite, to whip him into a final burst that would carry him past the gray. But nothing more than a groan got past my lips before the horses crossed the line together.

I thought bitterly that only a tiny fraction of an inch on the photo of the finish would now decide the winner of this race. Around me, bettors debated whether "the three horse" or "the two horse," the favorite, had won. I expected the worst, and wished that another horse could be declared the winner. Somehow, that would have relieved me of the guilt and, curiously, the embarrassment I felt over my hysterical behavior.

When the order of finish was posted, one man nearby jumped with glee. All the others I could see turned glumly from the tote board. I stood fixed, staring, as the result was declared official. The overlay had won and paid twenty-three dollars and eighty cents, almost eleven to one. I would have won eight thousand three hundred and thirty dollars if I had bet the seven hundred dollars on the gray instead of switching to the favorite.

As that calculation worked itself out in my mind, I thought of crashing my head into the steel rail or, better, smashing my neck down upon it and thus beheading myself. I turned my face to the sun and tried to open my eyes to it, to draw in enough of its rays to blind me and burn my brain.

Reluctant to leave the scene of the disaster, I remained fixed, hoping someone might discover that a terrible mistake had been made in the posted results, hoping I might discover that the horror of the last twenty minutes had been a bad dream. When I could no longer hide from the reality of the results, I walked slowly back and forth, unable to drive from my mind the knowledge that if I had bet three hundred dollars on the gray, as at one point I had so firmly intended, I would now have had enough to repay all my creditors. If I had bet all of the seven hundred on the overlay rather than the favorite, I would not only be free of debt, I would be rich.

I knew I must clear my mind or go mad. Still, I continued to abuse myself. I thought of what I had done as criminal. I had violated my rules, lost control, and, the worst crime of all, I had acted stupidly. Even though no one else could see, I stood naked. And *stupid*.

Eager to make the most convenient atonement, I accepted losing as a just punishment for sins too numerous to call to mind, but most simply summed up in the word "horseplayer." And with that thought I finally touched bottom, and started moving very slowly back to normal. I didn't really want to die. There were other things to do; not least, to show up on time for work.

But, first, there was yet another betting decision to make.

I was in the habit of leaving some cash at home or at the office before going to the track, to be sure of dinner money in case I lost. This time I had brought the in-case money with me. I had twenty-four dollars and thirty-six cents. That was three times the cost for a taxi to the office and a decent dinner. I could bet twenty dollars on the fourth race, the race for which I had come to the track, lose, and still have enough for the taxi and dinner of a sandwich and beer.

The bugler sounded the post call for the fourth race. The horses were coming onto the track. The favorite, the horse for which I had come to the track, looked frisky, full of run. A twenty-dollar bet could salvage a little something from the ruin of the day. But I had no stomach for further action. I decided to stay for the running of the race, but not to bet. That was the one time I can remember watching a race in which I had an interest and money to bet, yet had not bet.

That turned out to be my one winning decision of the day. The horse I had thought of as the best of the program, the horse that was my reason for being at the track, finished out of the money.

For reasons I didn't understand, that outcome disappointed me even more than the events which had preceded it. I had expected my best bet to win, if only as a further, fitting punishment. This result demonstrated only that nothing I had done had mattered. If I had been able to avoid the third race, almost surely I would have bet, not only the five hundred dollars, as planned, but all of the seven hundred, on this race. And I still would have lost. It was all pointless, absurd, too much to think about. And it had been this way for too many years.

On that day, it didn't occur to me to wonder why.

IF my experience is typical, gamblers think a great deal about what they are doing, but seldom about *why*. In action, they would consider it a waste of time and energy to stop and think about the broader implications of their behavior. Only afterward, when the battle is done, does it become convenient, for those so inclined, to ponder questions more complex than how to bet and where to borrow.

Even after I began to think seriously about withdrawing from action, my attention was concentrated on ways and means of getting out, not on what I would have considered idle thoughts of why I had become a horseplayer in the first place. Years later, when I had begun to feel safe from the furies and had begun to see how different life could be without gambling, my mind turned back to that other time and questions arose. Then I began to wonder why I had behaved as I had on that good-news day at my lucky track, and on so many other good- and bad-news days, and why anyone should behave that way.

Compulsive gamblers don't do anything by halves. Once my curiosity was aroused, I found myself responding with a compulsion stronger than any which had driven me during my years as a gambler. I became involved in a period of reflection which occupied me for more years than I had spent as a horseplayer.

To begin my search, I did what I had been trained to do as a journalist when confronted with a question to be answered. I consulted the authoritative sources, in this case the reports of sociologists, psychologists, and others who have studied the issues raised by compulsive gambling. But, to borrow a term that used to describe a losing ticket in lotteries, I drew a blank. The research reports were better at describing than explaining, and there wasn't much in the gambling literature beyond some interesting historical material, several on-the-surface behavioral reports, and a few questionable theories. Two researchers who reviewed the gambling literature as part of a study financed by the National Science Foundation concluded that the available studies were "insufficient to answer many important questions about gambling behavior and its consequences."

I was surprised and disappointed to be stymied in my efforts, but, unwilling to be left at the post, decided to make a run for the truth on my own. I decided that my hope of arriving at understanding might best be satisfied by combining and comparing my personal experience with the information I found in the gambling literature. Thereupon I proceeded to reexamine my life as a gambler and to evaluate my perceptions against the findings of the scientific research.

My review began at a point described by one researcher. A study of fifty-five compulsive gamblers, members of a Gamblers Anonymous chapter in New England, found that, typically, those studied had grown up in the "facilitating atmosphere" of "permissive" communities where gambling was "part of the accepted round of activity." The report appeared to be describing towns and neighborhoods in and around Boston (traditionally a horseplayer's town, with the action centered at Suffolk Downs, Rockingham, and Narragansett race tracks). But the description just as well fit the Williamsburg slum of Brooklyn, where I grew up during the hard times before World War II.

Enough people gambled in Williamsburg to allow me to remember that everyone in my neighborhood bet on something some time— even grownups who lectured us on the evils of gambling, and gave us to understand that what they were doing (usually playing pinochle or seven-card rummy for pennies, or risking other pennies in the numbers game) was not really gambling. It would be easier for me to remember Williamsburg without its candy stores, than it would be to remember the old neighborhood without gambling—much of which took place in the candy stores.

Napoleon, enchanted by the Piazza San Marco in Venice, called that palatial space "the drawing room of Europe." On a much less grand scale, I have come to think of candy stores as the drawing rooms of Williamsburg. Few of my neighbors had living rooms more attractive than the often shabby little stores which were pleasantly dressed by the warmth of the people who gathered in them.

A great deal of community life took place in those social centers. At a time when work was hard to find, job leads were exchanged, politics was discussed, gossip communicated, and advice dispensed. Critical communication was maintained through telephone service that was provided by the candy-storekeepers to those who could not afford their own phones. On our block, only the Klamkins and the Schecters had telephones in their tenement apartments.

More important for the romantically inclined, encounters between young men and women were made convenient in these places where all were welcome, regardless of whether they had money to spend on the eats and drinks that were dispensed in these establishments. On the menu were a hundred kinds of penny candies; fat, salty pretzels; roasted sunflower "polly seeds"; and hard-shelled brown Indian nuts. And, better than fine wines to accompany them, small glasses of seltzer, memorialized as "two cents plain"; egg creams made of chocolate syrup, milk, and seltzer, but no eggs; and rich, thick malted milks.

Still more attractive to certain candy-store customers were two commonly available gambling opportunities. As a public service, some storekeepers provided drops for Solly, the numbers runner, who came every morning but Sunday to pick up bets on the numbers game which had been left for him by bettors hoping to win five dollars for each penny bet—actually, six dollars, less a dollar tip for the runner. He returned in the evening if there were any lucky winners to be paid off. By that time, storekeepers would have made available battered but durable wrought-iron chairs, marble-topped tables, and well-worn decks of cards for customers who wished to play pinochle or rummy. Anyone could use the tables and chairs free of charge for non-gambling purposes until card players appeared. Then, the rules of the house dictated that the gamblers had immediate priority, since each player paid five cents an hour for the privilege, cash in advance.

Generally, the rules limited action to games such as pinochle and rummy, which did not require the players to keep money on the table. Only Phil's, on Bushwick Avenue between Moore and Siegel Streets, permitted poker and blackjack and drew a profitable trade from the sports who preferred those money-on-the-table games.

What I remember of the Williamsburg candy stores is recalled mainly from my experiences in two stores my mother owned for eight years, one before and the other during the Depression. In the first, a busy little place on Grattan Street opposite the bustling Long Island Railroad freight depot, my mother refused to permit any form of gambling. Her one exception was a punchboard at Christmas from which, for a nickel, customers could push out folded tickets entitling winners to boxes of fancy candies. Economic necessity and popular demand persuaded her to let down the bars and allow card games at two tables in her second store, on Siegel Street.

With exceptions such as Phil's, candy store gambling was small-time and public. Those who desired more privacy or faster action went elsewhere. Some of our more enterprising neighbors, who otherwise would have had trouble paying the rent, made their apartments available for poker and other card games from which they "cut the pot," taking a specified share of the betting on each round.

Others made their homes available at no charge for more or less friendly games in which they participated, and a good deal of the at-home gambling was the kind we called "pastime"—engaged in for modest stakes no more valuable than matchsticks. One such game which began after World War II involved four men who have continued to play pinochle every Friday night for more than thirty years, with infrequent interruptions. Losses are limited to ten dollars in any one night and losers may play without cost after reaching that limit. Winners contribute to a kitty which finances fishing expeditions for the men and dinner-and-theatre evenings with their wives.

Store-front social clubs, or social-and-athletic clubs—the latter adding various sports activities to the sexual opportunities and gambling available at the former—were popular with our older brothers.

The sex consisted almost entirely of self-defeating, incomplete, clutch-and-grab encounters. The young men and women of Williamsburg in that time were hobbled by the prevailing morality which held that good girls might permit impassioned groping, but only bad girls would allow boys to "go all the way." Sexual frustrations were worked off at battered card tables which, together with moth-eaten sofas, were standard equipment in these dens of hotly desired but seldom achieved iniquity.

More serious gambling, usually high-stakes poker, took place at the Jefferson Street Democratic Party Club, when there were no political chores to be done, and in fancier social clubs. Most prestigious of these was the Bo Cab S.C., housed in a brownstone on Vernon Avenue and owned by a group of former street boys who had grown up to be successful businessmen, teachers, doctors, and lawyers. Their clubhouse facilities included a backyard handball court, an exercise room, Ping-Pong tables, a ballroom, and several smaller rooms for quiet card games. In a typical exercise of neighborhood philanthropy, when the club men moved to more spacious quarters, they deeded the building for one dollar to a group of younger men who hoped to move up in their time as their benefactors had done.

All of this gambling could be described as social, at least insofar as the players knew each other either as friends or neighbors. On an entirely different level was the floating crap game run by Yonkel Butch in garages and factory lofts. Well-heeled gamblers came from all over the city to play in these games because, like the women who dealt with him by day in his father's butcher shop, they knew they could expect fair weight from Yonkel Butch. Those of our elder brothers who worked as coffee gofers and lookouts reported that many thousands of dollars changed hands in these games, and young men of my age thought of Yonkel Butch's floating crap game as the highest experience to which a gambler could aspire.

For those who preferred something other than dice, cards, or the numbers game, there were two alternatives: betting on the horses or on baseball games (football, basketball, and hockey were not then big betting propositions). Bookmakers in two pool rooms on Broadway (our *Brooklyn* Broadway) took baseball bets. Everyone was a baseball fan so there was heavy action in those two pool rooms. Horse racing was another matter. Hardly anybody I knew had any interest in playing the horses, and it was a long time before I learned about betting on the races and discovered the whereabouts of the horse rooms. These were run under very tight security, as was Yonkel Butch's floating crap game, because of the double standard with which our parents and the police judged different kinds of gambling.

Police maintained a hands-off policy toward the "social" kinds of gambling, particularly the card games played in candy stores, homes, and social clubs. None of these were ever required to pay protection money so far as I know, and none was ever raided. The numbers game was in a different category. Here, too, there was no police interference. But, as Solly the runner told me when he thought I was old enough to know, police looked the other way because they were paid to do so. Similarly, pool-room baseball bookies operated more or less freely in return for appropriate payoffs. But the floating crap game and the horse rooms were under constant threat of police interference, even when payoffs were made—not to speak of the additional threat from stickup men attracted by the big money available in these operations.

Like the police, our elders adopted different attitudes toward different kinds of gambling. Card games at home or in candy stores and social clubs were acceptable, even to some grownups who didn't really approve of *any* kind of gambling games. The elders might sneer at no-goods who couldn't find any better use for their time and money, but seemed to look upon these games as a necessary evil and so offered no real opposition. On the other hand, they were intolerant of gambling which involved what they thought of as "real money"—the games run by Yonkel Butch and the betting on baseball and the horses. Only the lowest of low lifes would engage in "real money" gambling, and for such as these there was no tolerance.

However, as I learned early in the game, nothing is as respectable as success. Exceptions were made for certain gamblers. Although it was widely known that Yonkel Butch was the proprietor of a floating crap game, our elders preferred to think of him as that portly, soft-spoken, nice young man who worked in his father's butcher shop. Also, Cubsy Siskind, who drove a truck in the garment district and was said to have mob connections, was one of the most respected persons on Siegel Street, even though he was known to be a big gambler who frequently played in Yonkel Butch's games.

The distinctions drawn were confusing and could be painful. The parents of a girl who was forbidden to date me because they considered me a gambler were themselves poker addicts who played for stakes far beyond anything I could have managed. But they played as members of a club on a fashionable block of Bushwick Avenue near Highland Park, and such activity was viewed as a proper social pastime for fine folk.

The distinctions and warnings had no restraining effect on me and my friends. We had begun to gamble before we began to go to school in the ancient red brick schoolhouse, Public School 24. We played children's games at first—marbles and mumbly peg, mainly—then a card game we had learned from our older brothers, banker broker, in which a banker makes several piles of face-down cards and players bet on the piles they hope will contain bottom cards higher than the one left for the banker. We began with stakes of marbles, ten-a-penny picture cards of sports heroes and movie stars, and soda bottle caps.

As soon as we had money to play for we played for money. And when we did, our games took on a special social character. Our child's play had been preparation for the real thing—winning and losing money—and that certainly was involved in our new action. But my reading of gambling history persuaded me that there was something more valuable in the games we had begun to play— something my friends and I might have understood and appreciated if it had been called to our attention. It wasn't, so we did what we did without awareness of its significance and derived from our gambling social benefits we didn't try to understand.

3.

ARCHAEOLOGICAL evidence and anthropological explanations suggest that the first known gambling was organized for the social benefits it provided to the prehistoric peoples who engaged in it.

The earliest evidence consists of an artifact believed to be the first gambling device. Known by its Latin name, *astragalus,* it is a die-like object with two rounded ends and four flat sides that are variously inscribed. *Astragali* were made originally from the ankle bones of sheep or dogs and later from wood, stone, or metal. Large numbers have been dug up at sites in Asia, the Middle East, Europe, and the Americas, suggesting that the invention of the *astragalus* was a world-wide phenomenon. Archaeologists estimate that the oldest find was in use forty thousand years ago—which gives gambling a long history, indeed.

Astragali appear to have been the most common gambling device prior to the development of six-sided dice about five thousand years ago, probably in India or Iraq. The point system—marking each face of the cube from one to six so that opposite faces add up to seven—is believed to have been added to the six-sided dice about 1500 B.C. in Egypt. With minor modifications as to size and the material used in making dice, these are the cubes widely used today in such games as craps and backgammon. But the *astragalus* in its original form is still used by some Arabs and American Indians, perhaps in the same ways it was used forty thousand years ago.

Archaeologists have found other prehistoric objects which may have been used for gambling, or for the related activity of fortune telling. But, like dice, these seem to be more recent modifications of the *astragalus,* among them three inch "throwing sticks" made of wood or ivory.

Later evidence suggests that *astragali* and the other early objects were first used in lotteries: games or procedures in which winners are chosen or outcomes determined purely by chance. Perhaps the best known accounts of such lotteries are in the Bible, which is filled with stories (twenty-eight, by one count) of issues being resolved by drawing or casting lots—presumably by withdrawing one *astragalus* from among several held in a container, or throwing them in patterns of varying value. Joshua, in one instance, divided conquered Canaan into parcels and distributed the land among the twelve tribes of Israel by lot.

We can only speculate about the purposes served by gambling and gambling procedures in earliest times. But there are abundant clues in more recent legend and folk lore references, as well as additional evidence from artifacts unearthed by archaeologists.

This more substantial evidence suggests that prehistoric communities dating back to the last of the Neanderthal people may have used gambling procedures to settle questions which, as one historian has observed, "it would have been invidious to answer in any way except by chance." That may explain the continuing use of lotteries to decide who should be drafted for military service, or for jury duty, or for other tasks which individuals might hesitate to take on voluntarily.

Primitive peoples may have used *astragali* in lotteries to determine when and where to hunt, who should do the hunting, and how the catch should be apportioned. One scholar suggests that, in hard times, such lotteries may have been used to determine which member of the tribe should be sacrificed to feed the others. The guilt or innocence of accused persons also may have been decided through "ordeal by lot," as it was somewhat later in India. And leaders of prehistoric communities may have been chosen by lot, as Saul was, the first King of Israel. The Old Testament records that when the twelve Hebrew tribes expressed a desire to choose a king, God arranged through Samuel to conduct a series of three lotteries for that purpose: the first to select the tribe, Benjamin's, from which the king would come; the second to choose the family, Matri's, from which the king should be chosen; and a final lottery to select the member of that family, Saul, to serve as king. With respect for religious sensibilities, it might be said that God had rigged this game, since before the draws took place God revealed to Samuel that he had already chosen Saul.

Even the ultimate gamble, whether to go to war, may have been decided for prehistoric peoples by a throw of the *astragali,* as it was for later cultures, among them the early Germanic peoples. Possibly inspired by that precedent, Prussia's late-nineteenth-century leaders spoke of war as "throwing the iron dice"—a gamble they won on each of the occasions when they did go to war, against Denmark, Austria, and France.

Gambling for personal gain—or loss—also has been a prominent part of everyday life for more than five thousand years. Legends of peoples as geographically diverse as Mayan Indians, Germanic tribes, and the early inhabitants of China and India tell of gambling for high stakes and include bet-your-life examples of primitive compulsive gamblers who wagered their wives and children, and their own lives as well, on the throw of dice or *astragali.*

More substantial archaeological evidence is provided by paintings in Middle Eastern tombs and drawings on pottery, believed to be between five thousand and six thousand years old. These depict gamblers playing with *astragali* and accountants keeping tabs on the action. The finds include crooked dice buried with their owners, though there is no evidence to indicate whether cheating was the cause of death in these cases.

M Y friends and I didn't have to contend with life and death problems. Our needs were much more modest than those of the first gamblers. But they were important to us and, like the first bettors, we satisfied them by gambling. The basic problem for us, as for so many other people in that time, was an acute shortage of money. The issue caused a crisis each weekend over the question of how to achieve a more satisfactory distribution of scarce resources to finance our Saturday night entertainment. We resolved the issue on Saturday afternoons by letting cards or dice redistribute our wealth.

Two of the older fellows in our group had left high school at age sixteen to take working papers so they might work legally if they could find jobs. Others found occasional after-school jobs. Few of us arrived at the weekend with as much as a dollar in our pockets. Those who worked turned over most of their earnings to their parents, as they were expected to do. The rest had to manage on small allowances, as little as twenty-five cents a week.

I was in a separate category. After school and on holidays I relieved my mother behind the counter of her candy store on Siegel Street and, without her knowledge, helped myself to a dollar or two each week, in addition to cigarettes, which would have cost almost another dollar a week if I had been required to pay for them. I tried to tell myself that my embezzlements were simply compensation for work performed and that my mother would have given me as much if I had asked. But I knew that to take someone else's money without permission was theft. I burned for it, but continued to tap the till.

To rationalize my sin, I blamed it on my mother, assuring myself that I would not have had to do what I did if she had not barred me from the one opportunity I had to earn money, by working as a peddler's helper on Saturdays, and more often during summer vacations from school. The Sarter family owned a stable across the street from my mother's store and rented rigs—a horse and wagon—for two dollars and fifty cents a day to peddlers, who paid that much again to young men they chose as helpers. Wagons were loaded at six in the morning with crates of fruits and vegetables, and the workday continued until the last of the produce had been sold to shoppers in the streets along the route.

A good day could end by four or five o'clock. More often the last sale was not made until hours later, and I can recall returning to the stable as late as eleven. But two and a half dollars, plus eats, was good money, and the jobs were eagerly sought after. Nevertheless, I could have worked as often as I wished, if my mother had not forbidden me to take work from those who needed it more. I worked only when there was no one else available, and when I had no other income I tapped my mother's cash register. Meanwhile, to hide my crime from my friends, I concocted stories about part-time jobs I had been lucky enough to find and conducted myself as though my financial position was no less precarious than theirs.

On Saturday afternoons, dressed in going-out clothes, our group gathered at Prager's candy store on Bushwick Avenue to discuss the weekly dilemma: what to do about Saturday night. The issue was of great importance to those who felt they worked hard all week, in school or at jobs, and were entitled to the fun they expected to have on this night.

Occasionally, the problem was resolved by invitations to a party.

More often, the things we did or wanted to do cost more than we could have managed. A movie at the Echo Theater on Bushwick Avenue, posed no great financial problem, since the admission price was only fifteen cents. But the Echo usually showed low-grade B films, and ushers constantly sprayed the audience with foul scents in a vain attempt to overcome even more obnoxious odors. Most of us also could have managed single admissions to the better neighborhood movie houses—Gem, Commodore, Loew's Broadway—where a ticket cost twenty-five cents. But, to go out in real style, with a date, for dinner and a show at the movie-and-stage-presentation theaters in downtown Brooklyn or uptown Manhattan, where admission prices ranged up to ninety cents at the crème de la crème Radio City Music Hall, was another matter. That kind of Saturday night could cost three dollars or more, even if one dined modestly at a neighborhood Chinese restaurant, where a meal of soup, chow mein or chop suey, with jello, canned pineapple or almond cookie for dessert, plus tea, cost twenty five cents per person. That kind of money few of us could manage from our own resources.

In these circumstances gambling served us well as a medium of exchange and accomplished a satisfactory result more efficiently than any other manner we might have devised. If we were seven or fewer and an apartment was available, we played poker. If we were more than seven, which was usually the case, we shot craps in backyards or basements of tenement houses.

Within an hour or two, rarely longer, our several small sums would have been rearranged into one or two large accumulations of capital. The lucky winners were then in a position to do much more than they could have with their original holdings, while the losers were not much worse off than they had been.

Two other aspects of our weekly exercises continue to impress me. I cannot remember any sore losers or gloating winners. And I do remember that winners were generous. Quite often dateless winners treated losers to eats and a movie and, occasionally, loaned them more than they had brought into the game.

I suppose we could have managed our affairs without resorting to gambling. Other young men in our circumstances did. But I don't think any other procedure available to us could have produced such general satisfaction as we got from our Saturday afternoon fevers, which is what the first gamblers may have thought about their social gambling.

Eventually, new priorities combined to break our Saturday pattern and separate the true gamblers from the casuals. One by one, members of the group fell away. Leon, never much of a gambler anyway, got a Saturday job delivering I. Miller shoes. Charlie fell in love with the beautiful Julia, and decided to spend more of his Saturday time with her. Melvin decided to save his money so he could go into the garment business. More often now I also worked as a peddler's helper on Saturdays.

Those of the true gamblers who remained eventually went off in search of richer action. Some joined social clubs, where gambling was the dominant feature of the social scene. Others turned to betting on baseball, and in season spent Saturday afternoons at the poolroom watching inning-by-inning results as they were reported on ticker tape, or listened to play-by-play radio broadcasts.

My interest turned to playing poker with older fellows in the neighborhood who played for much higher stakes. When I was seventeen, I worked for a year as a floor boy in the composing room of the *New York Times* and was astonished to find there even more gambling than I had observed in Williamsburg. Round-the-clock poker games were available in rooms above a bar opposite the Times Building on Forty-third Street and in the Diplomat Hotel a block away. Bookies, who accepted bets on baseball and racing at nearby betting parlors, showed up frequently at the Times Building to collect on phone bets or to pay off winners who didn't want to be seen at the betting parlors. And members of the printers' union ran a weekly numbers game. My participation was confined to the poker games, which I recall as an example of gambling's dollar democracy, as high-ranking, well-paid editors mingled with and pitted their skills against low-ranking, low-paid clerks on equal terms, dollar for dollar.

By then gambling had taken on a special meaning for me, in addition to serving as a way of trying to win money. My playing was the kind of thing young people seize upon to pretend they are grown up. I had certainly moved above the level of the Saturday rites with my friends. Now I played to demonstrate to myself and my audience that I was one of the men, doing what adults did, and was entitled to be ranked in that company.

When I moved on to become a compulsive gambler I was, so far as I have been able to determine, the only one of the Saturday gang to do so. Some of my Williamsburg cronies became fairly active gamblers but none, as far as I know, went on to compulsion. Nor did either of my brothers. Why I became a compulsive gambler and the others did not was a question I tried to answer during my period of research and reflection.

ANSWERS available in literature on gambling reflect different research interests. Sociologists have concentrated on more or less active, but not necessarily compulsive, gamblers, mainly from lower economic ranks. They describe the process they have observed and analyze the function of gambling in the lives of those studied. Psychologists have worked with groups of compulsive gamblers to record their patterns of behavior and their conscious motivations for that gambling behavior. Psychoanalysts have probed deeper into the psyches of compulsive gamblers to seek the unconscious causes.

In general, according to the sociologists, gambling serves as a "safety valve" or "escape hatch" for persons who cannot, or believe they cannot, succeed in more conventional ways. Expressing the consensus, Robert D. Herman, editor of the anthology, *Gambling,* observes that gambling is "reactive to a context of deprivation" and "commercialized gambling offers to many people efficient means of enhanced self-esteem and gratification."

One researcher takes that line of reasoning a step further, with an explanation suggesting that gambling is an opiate of the people. Nechama Tec, who studied soccer pool bettors in Sweden, found that gambling offers hope to those "who are least capable of fulfilling their mobility aspirations through conventional avenues." As a result, Tec concluded, "instead of turning against the original sources of their deprivations and unfulfilled aspirations, bettors are relieved through gambling of some of their frustrations and, hence, are less likely to attack the existing class structure."

As to the behavior of compulsive gamblers, psychologists say compulsive gamblers are like gamblers in general, only more so. As the psychologists explain it, the need for self-esteem and gratification is much stronger among compulsive gamblers, and they seek to satisfy their needs aggressively. Jay Livingston, who studied a Gamblers Anonymous group in New England, found that the compulsive's "major problem is one of success or failure as defined in terms of money." In pursuit of the money to resolve that problem, the compulsive gambler engages in a drive for power which gets its energy from "an intense competitive urge" so strong that it carries over in the group therapy of Gamblers Anonymous. In *Compulsive Gamblers,* Livingston reports some in the group studied would "look down on the others for not being as compulsive as they."

Psychoanalysts consider the apparent drive for power merely a screen for an unconscious need to lose. Variations on that theme dominate psychoanalytic case history reports. Among the theories that have received somewhat less prominence is one I thought worthy of more attention than it has received. That is the suggestion that compulsive gambling may be the reaction of a narcissistic person who was "rejected by [his] father." That explanation did not seem terribly useful to me, but the phrase "rejected by [his] father" lingered as I explored the dominant psychoanalytic theory that compulsive gamblers play to lose, not win.

The concept of the need to lose was first put forth, hesitantly, by Sigmund Freud in what he called a "trivial essay" on the "bewildering complexity" of Feodor Dostoevsky's personality, which others have since referred to as "Freud's study of Dostoevsky." Writing in 1928, forty-seven years after the Russian author's death, Freud speculated that Dostoevsky hated his tyrannical father and repressed an unconscious desire to kill him, and as a result he was compelled by guilt to punish himself. Freud suggested that Dostoevsky's compulsive gambling may have been one of several self-punishments the troubled author devised.

Following Freud's lead, several psychoanalysts have since reported evidence that, for reasons similar to but mostly different from the one Freud thought he detected in Dostoevsky's case, compulsives gamble out of a need to lose. The most elaborate and most frequently cited variation on Freud's basic idea is one developed by an associate of Freud, Edmund Bergler, who, before he died in 1961, had dealt with sixty compulsive gamblers.

In Bergler's explanation, compulsive gambling begins with what he calls "a sort of megalomania." That is an exercise of the "pleasure principle" experienced by all children, a satisfying fantasy of omnipotence. Normal children eventually discard that fantasy in favor of the "reality principle," an understanding that the real world is not subject to their commands. Putting aside childish notions is the prerequisite for mature growth. But Bergler says that is unacceptable to some children, whom he calls "psychic masochists."

In this explanation, the psychic masochist refuses to accept reality and grow up. That kind of child prefers instead to hold onto infantile notions, in an act of rebellion described as "pseudoaggression." At the same time, the psychic masochist unconsciously understands that such behavior must be punished and is only too willing to seek out and accept punishment. According to Bergler, gambling provides an ideal opportunity. It encourages fantasies of winning while assuring the punishment of losing, since gamblers rarely win in the long run.

Some of these explanations may be valid, as far as they go. But, in every case, crucial questions are left unanswered. For example, as the sociologists explain, many unsuccessful men and women probably do find in gambling a way to hope for something better than they have. But the sociologists have almost nothing to say about the many other persons who would seem to have all that one could want of success, self-esteem, and gratification—yet gamble, some compulsively.

Psychological observations about the drive for power which inspires compulsive gamblers also seem right enough but somewhat inadequate as a total explanation. Many other intensely competitive men and women seeking power don't become compulsive gamblers. Why some and not others? And why gambling as the vehicle for the power drive?

As for psychic masochists who unconsciously need to punish themselves, why do they turn to gambling for that purpose? Freud believed that Dostoevsky's preferred means of self-punishment was "hystero-epilepsy," epileptic fits of "severe hysteria" which simulate death. Edmund Bergler acknowledges that there are "thousands of possibilities" for self-punishment and attempts to explain why some psychic masochists choose gambling, specifically. But his explanation is a restatement of what he has already said and so leaves the basic question unanswered.

Disappointed by the results of my exploration, I felt like the unsatisfied diner who complained that the food was poorly cooked and the portions too small. For more, I would have to look elsewhere. There being nowhere else to go, I turned my attention back to my own experience.

COMPARISON of my experience with explanations offered in the gambling literature reveals parallels between the way in which I reached my decision to become a horseplayer, and thereby a compulsive gambler, and the ways in which that process is described by various researchers. I became a horseplayer when I was nineteen years old because that seemed the only way in which I could hope to break what I had come to think of as a nine-year losing streak.

Nineteen is the age at which most of the compulsive gamblers studied by Jay Livingston began their heavy gambling. The hope of success not otherwise attainable is the motivation sociologists ascribe to the gambling of disadvantaged individuals. And the losing streak which led me to compulsive gambling was, as the psychoanalysts might say, the product of childhood influences, but not exactly the kind they have described.

The long run of bad luck began with the most traumatic event of my young life: the separation of my mother and father when I was ten. That circumstance was the key to my childhood experience, as

I have come to understand it. The breakup was an unwelcome turning point, separating a "before," which I recall as having been mainly a happy time, from an "after," which became increasingly disagreeable. Although speculation of this kind is beyond proof, I think it is reasonable to believe that I would not have become a compulsive gambler if my parents had continued as husband and wife in a home shared with their children.

Probably, my parents were mismatched and the odds against continuation of the marriage were too great. My father was a city boy from Warsaw. He was a tailor, the son of a peddler, and he enjoyed the pleasures of urban living. He was little concerned with the traditions of Jews who came from the *shtetls* and farms of eastern Europe, and he arrived in America at eighteen in 1910 eager for the opportunities the new land offered. My mother, on the other hand, was a peasant girl, content with country life. At seventeen, she reluctantly left the farm her father worked on lease in northwestern Russia and dutifully joined the family in migration to America so that her five brothers could escape being drafted into the czar's army and she and her three sisters might better be able to find proper husbands. By chance, her family had remained outside the sweep of anti-Semitic pogroms that ravaged Jews elsewhere in Russia. As the stories she told about her life on the farm made clear, she loved the place where she was born and, given a choice, would have preferred to remain there.

In America, she remained duty-bound to her family and, after they married, my father became part of her family circle, subject to her family's traditions and the disciplines these imposed. That must have made things difficult for them, as it did for me during my growing up, because of the contradictory traditions by which the family lived.

I think that the move to the new world may account for a sort of schizophrenia in the family's attitudes. The family was in one phase warm, caring, sharing, generous, and cooperative. In that tradition, as the family emigrated in twos and threes, earlier arrivals worked and saved money to pay the way for the others. Newcomers were housed and fed in the homes of the earlier arrivals until they could stand on their own two feet. Later, help of other kinds was given to those in need. During two periods of economic distress, the family assisted my parents with interest-free loans to finance unsuccessful ventures, a dry goods store and a butcher shop. Interest-free loans and gifts also were given by the more fortunate to those disadvantaged by unemployment. In that way the family overcame the deprivations of the Depression with less difficulty than most.

But by then another tradition was becoming more obvious, a pattern of competition and criticism. In that tradition, my elders played winners and losers constantly, and their respect went most enthusiastically to the winners. Losers were considered unfortunate or incompetent. And winners had a way of damning with faint praise that was particularly offensive. As an example, it might be said of a loser that he was making a living but said in such a way, with a grimace of distaste, as to make it seem that the breadwinner under discussion really was little more respectable than someone receiving home relief from the government.

Successful businessmen were most respected. Six of the nine brothers and brothers-in-law were successful in small business: three as grocery-store keepers, one as a wholesaler of paper products, another as an electrical contractor, and the sixth, at first as a partner in the electrical business and later as a supervisor of operations for his older brother, who took over the business in a reorganization. Only three were wage earners: my father, a tailor, and two uncles, Daniel and Willie, wiry little men, neither much more than five feet tall, who were iron workers. And they were out of it as, more and more, money became the prime topic of conversation at family gatherings, which in the past were best remembered for the great quantities of food and drink and the happy sounds of music or unaccompanied singing, another family tradition.

To my distress, as I grew up the sound of music was less often heard and more often there were angry discussions of money and property. Soon the talk turned into feuds, which fractured the family as quarreling parties stopped talking to one another and partisans chose sides. I was troubled by the atmosphere of conflict, and can recall longing for the harmonies of the earlier, easier tradition.

In spite of that atmosphere of conflict, my mother and father appear to have begun well as husband and wife. Intermittently, as the state of the economy permitted, my father earned wages substantial enough to provide an abundance of food and drink for the holiday guests who filled our cold-water flat on Bushwick Avenue. Then the exquisite skill of my mother, the finest Jewish cook at whose table I ever ate, magically transformed what in other hands would have been merely first-quality chicken, meat, fish, vegetables, and other odds and ends, into banquets of delicacies, one more delicious than the other.

My father was always at the center of events in that time: offering toasts to large gatherings at our table laden with my mother's wonders; discussing family matters or the problems of the world with other family elders; taking me often to the Folly on Graham Avenue to see a bill of vaudeville acts breaking in material with which they hoped to make it to the big time, then, after the show, going to the New Light cafeteria for my favorite snack, apple pie a-la-mode and milk; or, going along on shopping expeditions with uncles and cousins who wouldn't think of buying a suit or a coat without asking my father to serve as maven, his "golden hands" examining garments to determine the quality of the fabric, cut, workmanship, and value. And my mother in the circle of matriarchs, fondly feeding, tending, giving, sustaining. My two brothers and I thrived in that atmosphere. I was a happy child, a good student who loved school, and a cheerfully dutiful son.

Even now I find myself wishing it were possible to remember only the happy times. But my review has called to mind other, less agreeable events in which my father was also at the center. I have been reminded that the good things had stopped happening some time before the final separation, and that my parents had been separated and reunited twice before their final parting.

In my new awareness, I can recall that my father was absent, playing pinochle in Mr. Baron's candy store, when my mother gave birth to the last of their three sons, my brother Rube, in our flat above that store. That offense seemed somehow less terrible after I discovered in Shakespeare a line referring to Henry VIII (a degenerate compulsive, some might say, who is reported to have lost the bells of St. Paul's Cathedral in a dice game rigged by disgruntled courtiers) playing a card game, primero, on the night Anne Boleyn gave birth to the future Queen Elizabeth. I can also remember another night during an icy winter when my mother tried unsuccessfully to rouse my father just before dawn to open their butcher shop across the street to receive a delivery of meat and then had to go herself to perform the chore.

Apparently, I was aware of other tensions and discords which,

34   PART ONE

until I began this review, I had chosen to forget. The evidence is indirect: reactions suggesting a good deal of fear, anxiety, and insecurity inspired by the tumultuous separations and reunions of my parents during the years when I grew from seven to ten. I can now recall a recurring dream: my body rising from my bed and floating through a window, then falling, falling, with no one to catch me and save me.

My father would have saved me, I felt certain, and I would have excused any sins of my father, if that would have allowed us to continue as a family. I think that most of the family, like me, would have been willing to forgive and forget. But an effective minority, led by my mother's eldest sister, my Aunt Mary, acting as a family court, carried the issue to its unhappy conclusion. Aunt Mary had served as the matchmaker for my parents. Now she became the prime mover in tearing them asunder.

Aunt Mary pressed three charges against my father. One, when I learned of it in the course of my research, came as a distinctly unpleasant surprise. My father had resumed a youthful romance when his old love emigrated from Poland and settled with her husband and two children on a farm in New Jersey. Unfortunately for him, he had at approximately the same time become an economic liability through his inability to get and hold steady employment. And he was considered a gambler.

I loved my mother and father and was offended to learn that someone else could have come between them. The employment problem was another matter. I recall laughter among family elders discussing my father's complaints of water on his knees and elbows, but did not understand until much later that his complaints described symptoms of arthritis and the onset of complications from Parkinson's disease, which frequently incapacitated him. As for the charge of gambling, that seemed to me absurd, since my father played only for pennies and not as often as his critics let themselves believe.

Reexamining the facts with the help of the dimming memories of survivors and the search into my own mind, I have satisfied myself that the critical charge against my father was neither the affair with his first love nor his gambling. The gambling was clearly unimportant, and an affair could have been forgiven in other circumstances, as such things were for others in other circumstances. My father's lover returned to her husband and children and resumed her place in that household, her lapse forgiven. Within our own family circle, a ménage à trois involving one of my affluent relatives was accepted matter of factly, except for some snickering by those not involved. My father, I am convinced, also would have been welcomed back within our family circle if only he had remained a successful bread-winner, which, through bad luck, his physical deterioration never again allowed him to be. He died ten years after the final separation from the after-effects of Parkinson's disease aggravated by the rav-ages of arthritis, a combination which turned him into a shrunken corpse.

After the breakup, my father virtually disappeared from my life. I saw him seldom at first and not at all during the last nine years before he died at the age of forty-seven. The last time I saw him, when I was twelve years old, I was carrying out my part of a weekly ritual that had given me reason to hope my parents might be reunited yet again. My mother was by then the proprietor of a candy store, and my father, unable to work as a tailor because of arthritis, had found a job as night watchman at a large apartment construction project in the Sunnyside neighborhood of Queens. As his way of paying dues, I suppose, in hope of renewing his membership in the family circle, he gave my mother a portion of his earnings. Each Saturday for several months, in a labor of love and hope, I went by subway to Sunnyside to collect his payments.

There was a sadness to these visits—whether because my father had been forced to take such a menial job or because I sensed the hopelessness of my mission, I do not know. But I recall that the feeling seemed to overtake me after the visits, as a sort of hangover in payment for the pleasure of being with my father and the satis-factions I derived from the unvarying routine of our meetings.

We began always with a courtesy call at the tailor shop of Mr. Berkowitz, who rented a room in his nearby apartment to my father and treated him respectfully. Mr. Berkowitz always had something pleasant to say to me and received admiringly my responses to his questions about my work at school and my extracurricular activities. Once he gave me two passes to the Ringling Brothers Barnum and Bailey Circus he had received for allowing posters to be displayed in his store windows, and my mother permitted me to go to the big show with an older cousin.

At a certain point in our visits, my father would say to me, "You must be hungry." Mr. Berkowitz would say, "Of course he is." Then, my father would escort me across Queens Boulevard to a cafeteria to eat a fifty-cent special: steak with French fries and sliced tomatoes and, for dessert, apple pie with vanilla ice cream and milk.

Afterward, we would go for a walk or, in poor weather, sit in the watchman's shack where my father spent his nights, to talk about matters of interest to me until my father would say, "I'm afraid it is getting late. Your mother will be worried. You should be starting home." He would walk with me to the elevated train station on Queens Boulevard, then stand watching until I reached the top of the stairway, where I would turn and wave good-bye.

One Saturday afternoon I waved good-bye without knowing it was the last time. For reasons never explained to me, the visits ended, and gradually it became clear that there was no further reason to hope my father would ever rejoin our household. I do not recall being instructed to avoid my father. After the misleading, confusing Sunnyside episode, people simply stopped talking about him. He had become a non-person. In that hostile atmosphere I didn't have to be told it would be wrong for me to try to find him and be with him again.

The sense of loss was made larger by still another loss. My mother, who previously had been available whenever I needed her, was, after the final separation, gone for the greater part of most days, working to support her broken family: as cook in a vegetarian-dairy restaurant on Graham Avenue, as an ice-cream packer in the Dairy Maid plant on Maujer Street, then—before she was persuaded to accept a loan and buy the first of her two candy stores—as a chicken plucker, for which she was paid five cents apiece, in a poultry market on Lexington Avenue in Bedford-Stuyvesant.

In place of my parents stood my mother's eldest sister, my Aunt Mary, as self-appointed guardian and judge, a frightening presence who did great harm with the best of intentions. Whatever she may have had in mind, I remember only that she seemed determined to make my life miserable—through hostile comment on all my actions, most of which she considered sins, and through advice which, if followed, might have turned me into a very confused saint, since her perceptions of good and evil differed grossly from mine.

Aunt Mary rarely spoke to me about my behavior. She preferred to deal with me through my mother, as though my mother were her puppet repeating much, if not all, of what Aunt Mary wanted her to say to me. With great reluctance I have allowed myself to come to understand that, although she was never harsh with me—as Aunt Mary was on the rare occasions when she addressed me directly— my mother was, nevertheless, a mouthpiece for her sternly judgmental sister at a critical time in my growing up.

My mother never scolded or spanked me. But, under Aunt Mary's urgings, she did something with the best of intentions—to protect me from the abuse of critics—which may have been more painful than any physical penalty could have been. She urged me to "stay out of people's mouths"—to avoid doing those things which might lead others to speak ill of me. For a long time afterward, her well-meant advice made me acutely anxious about what others might think of anything I did. One long-running result was the secrecy in which I conducted my business as a compulsive horseplayer, hiding from everyone who mattered to me what Jay Livingston has called the "unsharable secret" of compulsion.

Until I was willing to share the secret with others, none of my friends and relatives whose opinion was important to me knew of my private life as a compulsive gambler. I can't imagine what Aunt Mary would have said if she had known. She died before I began to share my secret. But she could not have devised any more severe punishment than she imposed on me through my mother for sins she would have considered less terrible than my compulsion.

Aunt Mary, whose own four children were already grown by then, began to make her presence felt in my growing up during the earlier separations of my parents. With my mother at work during those times, I began to take liberties which might not have attracted me if she had been at home. I became a rover, exploring the streets of Williamsburg far and near, sometimes simply sight-seeing, at other times searching street litter with my friend Leon for discarded cigarette packages from which we could salvage foil. A junk man on Cook Street paid us five cents a pound for our gleanings, and we spent the proceeds on tempting delights purveyed by pushcart peddlers: baked sweet potatoes; hot knishes of white potatoes or groats; roasted nuts and beans; lovely fat, brown, salty pretzels; luscious boiled frankfurters and sauerkraut; freshly squeezed lemonade; and shaved ice "snowballs," flavored with any of a dozen syrups.

Occasionally, distracted by the wonders of the streets, I returned home later than my mother would have wished. When Aunt Mary learned of such incidents she warned my mother that I was falling in with bad friends, "little gangsters"—a description that probably no other grownup would have thought to apply to Leon or the others with whom I roamed the streets.

There were street gangs in Williamsburg at that time, but their inclinations to violence were satisfied by games: punch ball, hand ball, roller-skate hockey, and touch-tackle football. In an exceptional instance, while doing an errand for my mother, I was trapped by a rival street gang and, in a desperate attempt to escape my tormentors, tripped, fell, and broke my right arm. The cast I wore for weeks afterward made me a hero among my friends who believed, without correction from me, that I had been hurt while courageously fighting my way out of an ambush.

Aunt Mary's reaction was different. Speaking in Russian, she told my mother that I was running wild and that if I didn't stop I would grow up like you-know-who. My mother translated the first half of her warning. I surmised the rest. Aunt Mary repeated similar dire warnings when, against my mother's instructions, I was careless in crossing Bushwick Avenue to buy a bargain cup of lemon ice from the candy store opposite Baron's and was hit by an automobile. My wound, a break in my scalp which required several stitches, was less painful than Aunt Mary's stern warning that my behavior was causing my mother great distress, something which I would not have wanted to have on my conscience.

Soon after the final separation, while my mother was at work, I invited some of my friends to our flat after school on a raw, wintry day to play cowboys and Indians. At one point in the game, I poked one of the Indians who had been bound by my group of cowboys. He fell like a log, fracturing his jaw on the pedestal of a round mahogany table, my mother's most treasured piece of furniture, which stood in our front room.

The victim's parents knew from their son that his hurt had been the result of an accident. They assured me that they did not blame me. But our hysterical next-door neighbor, Mrs. Bean, screamed at me that I was a terrible boy who had hit my friend with a hammer. She carried on for two hours before her elder son, arriving home from work, led her away.

Paralyzed by guilt and fear, I refused to return to school for two days, certain that my schoolmates and teacher would believe I had hit a playmate with a hammer. When my mother persuaded me to return to school, I found, with only small relief, that things were much as they had been. I moved back into the classroom routine and took refuge in the work at hand.

That summer, after it had become clear to me that my father had been requested to leave our home without any possibility of reconciliation, there occurred an episode which almost certainly could not have taken place if my father, who opposed child labor, had been at home. My Uncle Louis, husband of my mother's youngest sister Molly, gave me a job in his grocery store and sandwich shop, which was located opposite a row of loft factories on Moore Street. The job required me each morning to cover four of the eight lofts in the two buildings served by Uncle Louis, taking lunch orders in a machine shop and three garment lofts. Back in the store, I helped Uncle Louis and Aunt Molly make sandwiches and fill containers with coffee, tea, and milk and rush them to the lofts in time for the lunch break. In the afternoon, I returned with a pail of iced soft drinks and a basket of snacks to sell and to collect for the lunch orders delivered earlier.

It was hard work for a ten-year-old, but it pleased me to know that I was helping my mother, who was given two and a half dollars a week for my services, almost enough to pay the rent of twelve dollars a month on the cold-water flat on Ellery Street where we had moved soon after the disastrous game of cowboys and Indians. My mother told me we had moved in order to save four dollars a month on rent. I believed we had made the move to escape from the scene of my scandals.

I had mixed feelings about the job. I didn't mind the hard work, though it kept me from the summer games of my friends. In lieu of that, I enjoyed mingling with the friendly grownups who worked in the lofts, and I enjoyed the sense of responsibility I felt in my role as a breadwinner—a word which I heard often enough in my childhood to know there was nothing more important than to be what that word meant: a winner in the struggle for a living.

I was proud to be a breadwinner for my mother, but I had also grown accustomed to having some spending money of my own; and my work for Uncle Louis left little time or energy for other income-producing activities. That condition was aggravated by the fact that my mother didn't offer, and I didn't ask her, for an allowance. She knew Uncle Louis permitted me to eat as much as I wanted of the luncheon leftovers, and probably felt that was enough. Certainly I had more cake, soda, and sandwiches than any of my friends would expect or get, but that wasn't the same as having money of my own to spend as I wished. There were other rationalizations. Grownups doing the work I was doing would have been paid much more than my mother received for my labor and would not have done more than I did. Also, other breadwinners got cash allowances from their parents. It required little urging to persuade myself that there would be nothing wrong in reserving for myself a coin or two from the piles of money I brought back to Uncle Louis each afternoon.

I began by hiding a nickel or a dime each day, using the ill-gotten gains to buy delicacies Uncle Louis didn't sell or to pay for tickets to local movies. My embezzlements went undetected and success encouraged me to think of more—enough, for example, to pay for street-car fare, admission to a movie in downtown Brooklyn, and a snack. Emboldened by my ability to make off with nickels and dimes, I stole two quarters one day. My crime was exposed when the coins fell through a hole in my pocket to the kitchen floor in the home of my Aunt Minnie, where my brothers and I often ate supper when my mother was working late, as she was that summer in the Dairy Maid ice-cream plant.

Some psychologists view petty theft of this sort as a cry for help from a troubled child. Whether because the concept is faulty, or because it was not understood by my elders, my cry went undetected and unanswered. Aunt Minnie, whom I had heretofore thought of as a kind and gentle woman, fell on me in a fury, demanding to know how I had come by so much wealth and suspecting the answer. Frightened by her wrath, and by the knowledge that something terrible had been discovered about me, I made several stammering attempts to explain. None of my answers satisfied her. Finally, though terrified, I insisted that I had simply overlooked the coins and would certainly turn them in to Uncle Louis the following day.

Still unsatisfied, she kept at me until her husband, my Uncle Daniel, hurried from the front room to quiet the hue and cry and comfort me. At last, my aunt and uncle pretended to accept my explanation, and we sat down quietly to supper. But I knew that we had not resolved matters.

Late that night Aunt Mary came to our flat. Unable to sleep, I was sitting with my mother at the kitchen table, receiving over and over again her assurances that I was believed and that nothing bad had happened. I knew that was a lie the moment Aunt Mary walked in and said in Yiddish, "Well, Gyp, what will become of you?"

The two sisters spoke for a while in Russian, which my mother did not translate. But I could understand from its tone that the conversation involved stern suggestions which Aunt Mary was making and my mother was resisting.

Aunt Mary departed unsatisfied but left me tormented by the thought that I had committed a wrong which surely would become known to everyone in the family and would cause them to look down upon me as they did my father. Again, my mother assured me that I was a good boy and that everything would be all right after I had returned to Uncle Louis the money I had forgotten to turn over to him that afternoon. But it was no use. I slept badly and dreamed that I was being shot to death in my bed by gangsters with machine guns.

The next day, Aunt Molly, who had only reluctantly consented to have me spend the summer working for her husband, made no reference to my crime. She continued to treat me, as always, with affection. Whether under urging from her or as a practical matter, since a replacement would have cost more than he paid for my services, Uncle Louis permitted me to continue on the job but thereafter took the precaution of reconciling my cash in and out, something he had not done before. Most of the rest of the family forgave me or at least said nothing about what had happened, though I was not sure for a long time afterward that they had forgotten. Aunt Mary was unrelenting. Like a hellfire preacher trying to save my damned soul, she kept after me, no longer relying on my mother to convey her messages, talking to me directly now, hammering into my mind a cathechism:

I am bad.

I must be a good boy, and never again take what is not mine.

I must earn the trust and respect of good people.

I must keep out of trouble.

I must no longer add to my mother's burden of woe.

I must remember all my mother is doing for me.

I must grow up and take care of my mother.

I must not grow up to be like my father.

Her instructions and their Oedipal implications troubled me less than the understanding she had impressed on me that, much as I wanted to, I was incapable of performing as she instructed. Nor was Aunt Mary alone. I can remember echoes of Aunt Mary's words sounded by other voices. Recalling all this now, I am appalled by the gratuitous cruelty of those who felt it was their duty to teach me that there was something abhorrent about my father and that I had inherited from him only that.

FREQUENTLY, perhaps too often, my mother took pains to assure me I was a good boy and that others thought so, too. But her efforts provided small comfort, not enough to erase from my mind the belief that others "had me in their mouths," saying things I would not wish to have been said, telling each other that I was a worthless and incorrigible misfit.

To make matters worse, the guilt, anxiety, fear, and hopelessness generated by the attitudes of my teachers were compounded by a new confusion over right and wrong. I had begun to recognize that grownups did not always practice what they preached. But I had been unconcerned about that until, just weeks after my sin against Uncle Louis, there occurred an exercise of the double standard which became a depressingly influential part of my education.

I had been taught and believed that one of the most terrible sins anyone could commit was to violate Yom Kippur, the Day of Atonement, most sacred of our High Holy Days. I had been taught also, and believed, that to question one's elders was an offense almost as serious as failure to observe the strictures of Yom Kippur. So I didn't know what to make of what was clearly a sin involving Aunt Mary, my mother, and Aunt Mary's elder son Harry, a real go-getter who eventually became a millionaire.

Harry had already earned the respect of most family elders as someone on the way up, but I knew him as a malicious person who enjoyed calling me Gyp when we met. He had recently started doing business as a purveyor of frankfurters and rolls to fast food establishments in Harlem and was worried that a day away from his route might permit competitors to cut in on his trade. To avoid that, his parents, who were highly regarded in the Williamsburg community for their piety, granted permission for him to work on Yom Kippur— a sin as great as eating on this day of fasting when Orthodox Jews are required to abstain from every activity other than prayer. With a helper and an early start, Harry could cover his route in time to get to the family synagogue on Beaver Street before his absence could cause critical comment.

I was chosen to be his helper.

At a time when I was thinking about becoming a rabbi as a way of giving truth, I was appalled that my mother should have been persuaded to press me into service for this sinful business. But, deeply hurt and angry, I complied with my mother's request to do this dirty work.

We drove off in my cousin's truck at three that morning, our holiday clothes covered by overalls. Working swiftly, we completed deliveries in time to race back to Brooklyn, park the truck several blocks away, and arrive at the synagogue shortly before nine o'clock. When someone remarked on our tardy arrival, my cousin said we had been visiting another synagogue, adding a lie in the house of God to his other sin.

For months, I burned with my guilty knowledge, barely able to contain it, bewildered by the terrible thing that had been done and by my mother's complicity. I remember wishing my father were present. Eventually, I concluded that my mother had acted under the duress of Aunt Mary's pressure and was, therefore, guiltless. I dismissed the others as hypocrites. I also decided that, henceforth, I would not consider myself a religious person. But that rebellion inspired more guilt than satisfaction.

I recognized the holiday sin as a symbol of the greed, hypocrisy, and malevolence which followed as the family's early tradition of generous cooperation was eclipsed by the commitment to free-fire competition. I was distressed by the exercise of a double standard of morality that permitted and approved sin without penalty in certain cases and by the evidence that elder authority was fallible and not always to be trusted. Then, during my reexamination of this and other disagreeable events in my young life, I uncovered a long-hidden impression that cast this episode in a new light and enabled me to understand that this incident may have helped give me a head start toward life as a compulsive gambler.

My understanding of the connection between childhood experience and the gambling life has been assisted by a Freudian insight which receives no attention in the gambling literature but seems pertinent and significant to me. Writing in a broader context, Freud observed: "I cannot think of any need in childhood as strong as the need for a father's protection." Theorists who have drawn heavily on other Freudian concepts to explain compulsive gambling make no reference to this one, the implications of which seem obvious to me in each of the dispiriting events which followed the departure of my father. That is particularly true for the Yom Kippur violations, though the full effect of my unfilled need went beyond the hurt of any single incident.

On that long-ago holiday, any of several of my cousins could have handled the sinful work as well as I, or better, but none of them was called upon. Their fathers would have been outraged by the suggestion that they should do what I was commanded to do. And Aunt Mary, for all her disregard of other people's values and sensibilities, would not have dared to ask, much less command, them.

Even then I understood that the same would have been true for me if my father had been present; though, as will be shown, a father's presence is not at all the same as a father's protection. In this situation, my father's presence would have held me safe. He would have reacted as my uncles would have done. Ironically, although my father was not devout, he was holiday-religious, out of respect for the family's professed orthodoxy; and he would not have tolerated involvement in the holiday sin committed by members of the family who were highly regarded in our Williamsburg community as defenders of the faith.

Only the absence of his protection made my humiliation possible. That much I understood then. I had been made aware often in other ways that a fatherless child cannot expect the respectful treatment accorded to others. What I came to understand upon reflection is something else I must have known then without recognizing—that only someone of no standing, a worthless loser, would have been chosen to do what I was forced to do. My selection confirmed that status and reinforced my perception of the low esteem in which I was held and which increasingly I shared.

Reflecting upon why trusted influential elders should demean children and why the protection of a father is vital for healthy growth, I hesitated for a long time before accepting the answer, which now seems obvious to me. It is that people in every circumstance act in accordance with their competitive needs. Vulnerable children, without a father's protection, are ill-equipped to defend themselves against the superior force of competitive adults—whose needs can turn them into emotional cannibals, feeding their egos on the tender psyches of their unprotected young.

The unwelcome reality of competition as the central motivating force in an acquisitive life and of the parental-child exploitation that it involves is obscured with the aid of at least two rationalizations. One is the image of influential adults as sympathetic protectors serving the best interests of children—an image which is true for most adults, but not for all. The other is a tendency to think of competition as something only others engage in: athletes, politicians, business people. In fact, no one is immune from the basic facts of life—that society is a competitive arena and that to get what one needs and wants one must respond to competitive challenges.

Competition is moderated and the reality of ever-present competitive challenges is softened by rules of fair play, laws to protect weaker competitors from unrestrained exploitation, compassionate social customs, cooperation in behalf of common objectives, and the inherent decency of most human beings, even in the most intensely competitive situations. However, none of this changes the controlling fact that to live in a competitive-acquisitive society is to compete.

That is an unattractive prospect for many, and it is least attractive for those who fear that "Winning isn't everything, it's the only thing," as the challenge of competition was defined by Vince Lombardi, the late, great coach of the Green Bay Packers, who won more National Football League championships than any other team before their luck ran out. The consequence of the need to compete and try to win, as Thoreau observed during his withdrawal from competitive life at Walden Pond, is that "The mass of men lead lives of quiet desperation"—coping with the challenges of competition while trying to hide from the reality.

The chances of winning are obviously better for some than for others. For instance, past performances would lead a handicapper to conclude that the odds favor men over women, whites over blacks, the better-educated over the unschooled, and perhaps most surely, those who have been properly nurtured over those who have been emotionally damaged by childhood traumas that destroy confidence and weaken competitive resolve. Yet everyone feels the pressure of competitive challenges—the vulnerable child perhaps more keenly and more fearfully than others.

Anyone, regardless of childhood background or experience, could become a compulsive gambler given appropriate inspiration. In his short novel, *The Gambler,* Dostoevsky builds the climax around an exceptional character, Grandma. Dostoevsky tells readers nothing about the seventy-five-year-old lady's childhood, but it is clear that she was brought up to be the straight-laced matriarch of a landed Russian family who had never even thought of gambling. Then, in an outburst provoked by her displeasure with her feckless middle-aged heir, who is squandering his substance on the roulette wheel and on a French woman the old lady considers an adventuress, Grandma goes wild and in a few days loses the family's fortune at the roulette table in Roulettenburg.

However, personal experience along with the case-history evidence in the gambling literature have led me to understand that, in real life, the people most likely to become compulsive gamblers—whether for many years or for the duration of just one passionate splurge (which can cost as much as a lifetime of gambling)—are those who have been prepared for it by childhood lessons in losing. Dostoevsky, himself, is just such a case. The son of a brutish father, Feodor grew up to be a compulsive gambler as well as great writer.

As I have come to understand the connection between the absence of a father's protection and the formation of compulsive gamblers, the vulnerable child, denied reasonable competitive opportunities and rewards, is drawn to the special attractions gambling holds for those who have been programmed to think of themselves as losers. In gambling, they find efficient means to fulfill their expectations.

I found, and I believe other uneasy competitors find, three powerful attractions in gambling. First, no special skill or competence is required, just good luck, which could happen to anyone. Second, there is no responsibility for the outcome—it is all up to the horse, the dice, the cards, or whatever surrogate force the gambler has chosen to depend upon. Finally, by the logic of compulsives, who do not always assign appropriate weights to the different probabilities, it doesn't matter how often you lose. One big winning can make you well, as a gambler would say—as though losing, not gambling, is the sickness. Which is, of course, how competitive society views the proposition.

I do not mean to suggest that all defeated children lacking the proper emotional nutrition provided by a father's protection grow up to be compulsive gamblers. There are far too many other self-damaging, punishment-perpetuating options available to emotionally deficient children for any single method to hold a monopoly.

Also, the absence of a father's protection is not in every case destructive to healthy growth. Many unprotected children manage to grow up whole and make stable lives for themselves, either because they are lucky enough to find helpful father substitutes or because they have the ego strength to defy destructive elders and maintain a healthy sense of self, though I am not sure how emotionally battered children ever manage that.

However, such exceptions do not alter what appears to be the basic pattern. Reflection upon my experience and the case-history evidence has led me to conclude that a history of early defeats in unequal competitions made possible by the lack of a father's protection is powerfully influential in the childhood formation of compulsive gamblers.

As I have observed it, the process moves through two stages. Frequent defeats at the hands of competitive elders predispose vulnerable children toward gambling. Adolescent frustrations compound the demoralization, reinforce the inclination, and intensify the need for a way out of an intolerable situation in which there appears to be no more hopeful way to win and thereby prove one's worth.

In these circumstances, a father's protection is vital to assure failsafe security by providing two vital safeguards against defeat. I think the more obvious one—serving as a shield against unwarranted hurt—may be the less important. Growing pains are unavoidable in the best of circumstances. More critical is a father's assistance in defending against defeat by providing the guidance, respect, encouragement, and support which give the child the nourishment for healthy growth and the confidence to cope effectively with the competitive challenges each must meet.

Freud spoke of a father's protection but might more accurately have said father-figure or equivalent thereof. What matters is not the source but the availability of the emotional sustenance which nurtures self-esteem. A good sense of self developed early makes more likely the ability to stand off unfair competitors and eventually to choose realistic goals, make consistent efforts, and enjoy reasonable satisfactions without recourse to gambling or some other self-damaging activity.

Whatever the source of the essential contributions, good intentions alone cannot guarantee desirable results. With the best of intentions, the responsibility for protection can be corrupted by elders who demand too much for, or from, their children. Having myself erred occasionally by being over-protective of or too demanding of my children, I am aware that it can be difficult to strike an effective balance—doing but not overdoing what is necessary for secure, stable growth. It seems to me therefore altogether remarkable that so many fathers and other influential adults, without special instruction or incentive, do manage to provide the balanced environment within which confident growth can take place.

Without that kind of protection, childhood can become preparation for defeat. As I have come to understand my experience, unending harassment and humiliation and the removal of my father resulted in depletion of my competitive resources. That left me susceptible to the peculiar attractions of gambling as a way to achieve the success I wanted but did not believe I deserved or could accomplish.

My brothers were not affected as I was because they did not share my experience. Rube, three and a half years younger, was not quite four when the turmoil brought about by the sequence of separation began and not yet eight by the time the process of my indoctrination by Aunt Mary came to a climax in her Yom Kippur caper. Harry, four years older, was shielded from much of the fallout because, fortunately, he was occupied elsewhere. Early in the family crisis he became a member of the choir in a large synagogue. Thereafter, most of his time, when he wasn't in school, was spent rehearsing, performing, or socializing with friends in the choir. As long as his voice remained strong, he had encouragement from father substitutes—the choir master and the fathers of other boys—and from family elders who were proud of his fine voice. When his voice changed, Harry found after-school jobs which further limited his contact with the sources of my difficulties.

In my struggle to find steady footing, I, too, was not without resources. To the contrary, I had allies who could have been much more valuable than they were if I could have allowed myself to accept them at face value.

I knew my mother loved me, but felt she was too much under the influence of her eldest sister, my chief enemy. I felt safe also with my mother's youngest sibling, my Aunt Molly, and visited her as often as possible, knowing I could always count on a cheerful, affectionate, encouraging welcome, no matter how busy she might be or how heavily burdened with her own concerns. Aunt Molly was young enough to have been my older sister, and I treasured her. Others also were attentive, in particular three uncles who might have served as substitutes for my absent father if I had been prepared to accept substitutes.

Other palliatives also were available to me, most satisfying of these, food, though no longer only at my mother's table. As a wage worker and then as a storekeeper working long hours every day of the week, she had to limit her kitchen activity to quick, simple meals. Tasty and nourishing as these were, they could not fully satisfy my hunger, for food and something more. I balanced my diet by eating out as often as earnings from after-school occupations and occasional pilferings allowed. I avoided provoking questions by also eating my share of what my mother served without adding any more flesh to my skinny frame than could be accounted for by normal growth.

No matter how unhappy or demoralized I might be, a good meal invariably cheered me: fish-cake sandwiches at an Italian seafood store on Knickerbocker Avenue, frankfurters and beans with cole slaw at a luncheonette down the street from the Loew's Broadway, delicate pork chops with spectacular home fries and surprisingly delicious, freshly cooked spinach at a Horn and Hardart cafeteria on Forty-second Street, or the ingeniously contrived triple-decker sandwiches and hearty home-cut-and-cooked French fries, followed by the best coconut-custard pie I have ever eaten, at a sandwich shop operated by Filipinos on Graham Avenue. I am reminded of the custom of allowing a condemned prisoner an anything-you-want last meal before the execution. There may have been something of the same rationale behind my frequent last meals, none of which was satisfying enough to make me forget the fix I was in.

The placebo effect of good and kind attentions was not enough to overcome the sense of loss which burdened me. Like Sisyphus condemned by Zeus forever to push a stone up an impossibly steep hill, I carried before me wherever I went the awareness that I lacked the thing I wanted most: the presence of my father and the protection and comfort he could have provided. For a longer time than I have been able to measure, there was not a day when I did not wish my father could be at home.

It was not his absence alone that hurt. I might have been able to accept that pain if the family had behaved with some regard for my father as a person and with greater concern for the effect of their attitudes on his wife and children. Instead, with their little-disguised denigrations they dehumanized him and made me wonder whether I, too, was like that evil man who had been disembodied by authority of the powerful elders of my family.

I can understand that I could have hated him—and my mother, too—for placing me, unarmed, in an exposed position of danger and discomfort, a situation in which my mother sometimes appeared to be an ally of my attackers. Also, I suppose it would not have been unnatural in the circumstances for me to worry that I might have been in some way responsible for the separation of my parents in the first place.

I spent a terrible lot of time wrestling with my conscience, trying to determine when I might be guilty, and when not; what was right and wrong, good and bad, and whether, good or bad, I was entitled to a place within the family circle or must consider myself an outcast. I was entirely willing to accept punishment for wrongdoing—stealing money from Uncle Louis, for example—though to be called Gyp seemed an unfair humiliation. But I couldn't understand why I should be accused of wrongdoing for acts that were accidents. Nor did it seem reasonable to be badgered endlessly about activities which seemed to me entirely harmless, such as roaming the streets, whether for sightseeing or to find a way to scrape together a few pennies, so long as I did not come home too late from my rovings.

Despite my best efforts to resolve these issues and still the turmoil, my ruminations appear to have led mainly to guilt, self-hatred, melancholy, and confusion. Uncertain reactions and mixed emotions combined to produce, on the scale of one to ten, a misery index near ten and readings for self-esteem and confidence close to zero. Yet all of this seems to have left me still with some desire to make something of myself and find some peace as a respectable member of the family.

To atone for my larceny against Uncle Louis, I sought new ways to earn honest money: collecting free sawdust from a lumber mill to sell to storekeepers as floor cover for a nickel a sack, four or five sacks on a good day; running errands, most often for Amelia, a heavyset Lutheran spinster who kept house for an aging father and two bachelor brothers and who, because of her weight problem, found it burdensome to do daily food shopping at several stores in the neighborhood, a chore I was happy to perform in return for a nickel plus a crumb bun and a glass of milk; and, on too-rare snow days, earning a dollar or more clearing sidewalks for storekeepers and householders.

At about the same time, unhappy about being called Shrimp, Shorty, or Runt by some of my peers whom I did not consider friends, I persuaded my mother to buy enough Lifebuoy soap so we could get as a premium a height and weight chart on which I recorded my progress in a program to increase my height and weight. For weeks, I ate more than ever before and religiously performed chinning, stretching, and weight-lifting exercises, then abandoned the program as too much trouble, and left it to nature to solve my problem and enable me to grow to normal proportions.

These efforts drew the appreciative attention of my mother and Aunt Molly, and their's was praise enough. However, reflection upon that time has made me aware that on another matter of greater importance—being skipped a grade in elementary school for the second time—I was deeply disappointed when only these two shared my pride of accomplishment. Apparently, I accepted the silence of others as still another indicator of how far I had yet to go before I had proven that I could make something of myself that would merit the approval of my critics.

I wanted to make of myself a rich man, so I could take care of my mother. I knew that rich men didn't have to deliver frankfurters and rolls on Yom Kippur. I knew that money was valued by my elders above everything else—more than fineness, intelligence, and piety, to all of which they gave lip service, while their deepest respect went to those with the most money. My Uncle Sam, the electrical contractor, had intelligence and was admired as a founder of the Young Israel of Williamsburg synagogue, but he was spoken of much more often as a rich man than as a wise or pious man. I wanted very much to be like that. But I believed that if such success should ever come to me, it could be only because I was getting away with something to which I was not entitled. Caught in that trap—very much wanting to work at making a success of myself in a way that would be recognized, but lacking the confidence in my ability to do so—I would have been in a proper frame of mind to find gambling attractive, though I was still years away from making the decision to gamble seriously.

One other factor, I think, directed my progress. That is my understanding that children tend to try to be what they believe their guiding elders expect them to be—not what adults say they expect, but what they reveal of their true expectations through their attitudes toward their children. Young people are too intelligent to be persuaded by words when every action belies what is being said. And children who have come to understand that their parents expect them to be losers are likely to try to live up to those expectations, possibly even thinking that they are doing the right thing: If that's what they think I am, that's what I am and will be.

Whatever the unconscious motivations, I remain bound by the facts to the understanding that whatever route one may take to compulsive gambling the journey begins with a confused response to competitive challenges. And for most, if not all, the starting point is childhood defeat in adult-child competitions made possible by the absence of a father's protection.

I am encouraged in my understanding by the uniformity of case-history evidence in the gambling literature. In all the case histories I have read in which the facts of childhood experience are reported, the evidence, as in my experience, shows a pairing of childhood defeat in adult vs. child competitions and the absence of a father's protection as motivating factors. However, as though to emphasize that a father's presence does not automatically assure protection, in all but one of the cases I examined, fathers are present not as protectors but as aggressors or as accomplices in the process of defeat.

One theorist offers a collection of case histories of gamblers identified alphabetically. "Mr. B," deprived of protection by a father who was "a nonentity," was ignored by his mother, the family breadwinner, who concentrated her attentions and affections upon her young children. "Mrs. C." was an only child whose father "begged for love" from an unresponsive wife who not only rejected her husband but joined him in rejecting their daughter. The mother of "Mrs. D." was a "willful" woman who separated herself from her family behind a wall of hypochondria and was indulged by her husband, who joined her in ignoring their son. In the case of "Mrs. E.," the parents loved each other but excluded their only child from their affections.

Other childhood experiences reported in the literature more closely parallel my own. Two in particular attracted my interest. "Mr. A." had insensitive parents, a "puritanical mother" and "moralistic father," who, like my Aunt Mary, were "always preaching and teaching." The second, described by another analyst, was a Polish immigrant who was virtually orphaned by the separation of his parents when he was seven years old, which was my age when my parents began the process of separation. After the separation of his parents, the boy was sent off to serve as apprentice to a shoemaker. He was not again part of a family until he emigrated to America and became a successful businessman, husband, and father. The analyst reporting this case history says this patient did not seek treatment because of his compulsive gambling but rather because of a "sense of depersonalization," a sort of orphan feeling of apartness or alienation— a kind of nothingness which attended me for a very long time after the separation of my mother and father.

A more detailed illustration of destructive emotional abuse in the absence, not of a father, but of a father's protection, is drawn in a biography, *Mank,* by Richard Merryman. This is the story of Herman Mankiewicz, who collaborated with Orson Welles on the screenplay for *Citizen Kane* and wrote or collaborated on other popular films.

Mank, who died in 1953 at the age of fifty-five, was a gifted child whose father, a professor of languages, envied him and resented his talents. The father, a stereotypical old-school Prussian autocrat, bullied, degraded, and demoralized the boy with verbal abuse and was assisted in this by other family elders who joined in tormenting the vulnerable, impressionable youngster.

Young Mankiewicz grew up believing he was an incompetent who could never amount to anything. That understanding remained unaffected by his success as a drama critic in New York, as one of the highly regarded wits of the Algonquin round table, and throughout his long and productive career in Hollywood. In despair, Mank became an alcoholic and a compulsive gambler—a painful pairing of compulsions that imposes burdens heavier than most neurotics might be able to carry.

To the published record, I can add my knowledge of another compulsive gambler with whom I shared childhood. Harold, to give him a name, was neglected by his hard-working father and shielded by an over-protective mother from the rigors of growing up. The mother exaggerated his frailty, kept him at home when his schoolmates were at their rough games, reinforced his diet with daily doses of cod liver oil, and, as he grew up, provided him with an endless supply of excuses and rationalizations to explain his inadequacies and failures. Then, finally, she persuaded him to enter into what became a miserably unhappy marriage in order to avoid the military draft.

The father, who died of overwork at the age of fifty-two, seemed not to have liked his son very much. He left the boy's upbringing to his wife, while he hid behind a screen of cynical, mocking humor directed at those he considered his betters. His hostile humor served as a bitter commentary on his inability to achieve the heights to which his wife aspired, while also providing a loser's philosophy for his son.

Looking back over the record, it seems to me curious that, despite the weight of evidence, the psychoanalytic commentators have ignored what the record shows regarding the childhood formation of compulsive gamblers. They have given no attention to what appears to me to be the dominant features of the early "reality experience," the things that actually happened to their compulsive gamblers in childhood. While exploring parent-child problems, they say nothing about the central force of competition in life for parents and children.

They speak of conflict, rebellion, aggression, but not of competition, as though that word is taboo. And none of them makes any reference to Freud's evaluation of the need for a father's protection. Concentrating instead on their probes for unconscious motivations— what one describes as the gambler's "masochistic elaboration" of reality experience—they have produced a variety of different explanations. Since each explanation has found some support by other experts, any or all of them could be correct though different.

Possibly "a sort of megolomania" practiced by "psychic masochists" in childhood is the cause, as Edmund Bergler argued. Perhaps compulsive gambling is, more simply, as Iago Galdston has suggested, an unending plea to Lady Luck to say whether an abandoned child was loved by parents who renounced responsibility for the child. Or, it may be, as Ralph Greenson has analyzed it, that "a revival of Oedipal fantasies" and "unconscious homosexual, anal-sadistic, oral-receptive drives" are among the root causes of compulsive gambling.

However, I have found little or no persuasive support for those ideas in my experience or in my reading of the evidence presented for them. Nor have the theorists persuaded one another. One of the more prominent analysts dismissed all explanations other than his own as "not too enlightening." I have little to add to that—other than the suggestion that it might have been more enlightening to have looked more closely at the way people live in our competitive-acquisitive society and how they cope with the competitive challenges all face, too often without benefit of a father's protection in childhood.

SOMEHOW, despite childhood defeats, my desire to compete and make good remained intact. I wanted to earn a lot of money, take care of my mother, and be respected by people like Aunt Mary.

Two months after my unhappy experience as the dishonest helper of Uncle Louis, I got my first big chance. My mother, who abhorred borrowing, was persuaded to accept a loan of four hundred dollars from her elder brother Benny to buy the lease for a candy store on Grattan Street, in the Bushwick section of Brooklyn.

It was a bleak, mixed neighborhood of working-class flats and an industrial complex that was centered on a Long Island Railroad freight depot across the street from the store. We lived in a two bedroom apartment behind the store. Our living quarters were warmed by a box-shaped coal stove which was also used for cooking when my mother had time for that. The place, first seen on a gray autumn day, was depressing and the move stirred melancholy, as each of our moves did. But Grattan Street proved to be a garden of opportunity.

I remember it as the place where I spent the most satisfying part of my adolescence.

Within weeks, in response to customer demand, I had established a business of my own—home delivery of newspapers before and after school. Then, at the suggestion of workers in factories facing the railroad freight yards, I added another after-school enterprise; selling candy, cigarettes, and, in warm weather, soda, to men and women who worked ten hours a day or more, until six or seven in the evening.

Inspired by what I had learned of the catering business from Uncle Louis, during the following summer I organized a lunch business serving workers in the area for whom there were too few eating places nearby. I built a pushcart from junk parts and made my way through the streets selling sandwiches and soft drinks.

For almost three years, all my ventures prospered. For two summers the sandwich business was especially profitable, allowing me to earn more in ten weeks than many grownups in our neighborhood could earn in a year as the Depression deepened.

Best of all, my performance earned me my first compliment from Aunt Mary. She told my mother that I was a "hustler," a word which then meant an enterprising, productive person who knows how to turn an honest dollar. Aunt Mary had no higher praise. I do not recall any greater reward or any surer feeling of accomplishment in my life until then.

And the money was good. I earned tips each week from customers on my newspaper routes, which my mother instructed me to keep; and during the summer, I held out a portion of my earnings from the sandwich business before turning over the bulk of my profits to her. Like a gambler counting his money between deals, from time to time I contemplated what I was doing and was greatly pleased with what the record showed. I hoped that it could go on forever, so I could always be thought of as a well-heeled hustler.

Unhappily, that bubble burst when, for reasons having nothing to do with economics, my mother sold her store on Grattan Street. We were one of two Jewish families on the street. The others were mainly of Italian or Irish descent, and Aunt Mary had persuaded my mother that if we continued to live there my older brother Harry, approaching marriageable age at seventeen, might become involved with a gentile girl, a *shikse*. That was something my mother would have wanted to avoid no less than Aunt Mary, but she yielded reluctantly and on her own terms.

Customers buying on credit had piled up tabs which came to some four thousand dollars for rolls at a dime a dozen, milk for six or seven cents a quart, cigarettes at two packs for a quarter (ten cents a pack for Wings and Twenty Grand), newspapers for two or three cents, candies at prices ranging from a penny to a nickel, and ice-cream cones for three and five cents.

When Aunt Mary asked what she was doing to collect, my mother replied, "Nothing. They haven't got with what to pay me."

Aunt Mary persisted. "You can't give away all that money."

"I'm not giving anything away," my mother replied. "They gave me a good living and they would pay if they could." She had long since repaid Uncle Benny from her first earnings, deposited more than two thousand dollars in a savings account, and was being paid twelve hundred dollars by a man who wanted to buy the store. "It's enough," she said.

"You are a fool," Aunt Mary said.

"Let it be," my mother replied, and that was that. Those who could pay anything paid what they could. For the others, my mother threw away the book, closing an incident which reminds me how much I loved my mother. If I also hated her, it must have been for setting a standard of conduct too far beyond my reach.

Whatever it may have accomplished for my mother's debtors, the move left me high and dry. Sale of the store wiped out my newspaper routes and my afternoon snack run. People in Siegel Street, where my mother bought her second candy store after trying unsuccessfully for months to find a job, didn't require home delivery of newspapers. And there were enough stores nearby to service workers in the loft factories which were situated opposite tenement houses on Siegel, Moore, and McKibben Streets.

I hoped, however, to salvage the summer sandwich business with the help of Nino, a friend from Grattan Street, whom I invited to join me as an equal partner. But that move also proved to be a total loss, except for the instructional value of lessons in greed and competition.

Nino, who had been excessively grateful for my offer of a partnership, tried to force me out and take over the business himself the day before we were to start our seasonal rounds. I thwarted that move by complaining to his mother and father, a man highly esteemed on Grattan Street as a former school teacher in Italy. But it was to no avail. As we moved into the territory the next day, we found to our dismay that more businesses had closed and, in what remained of the route, a man operating a mobile canteen from a remodelled truck had usurped our market. A few former customers remained faithful, but they were not enough. After two weeks of heavy losses from unsold goods, we yielded the ground to our better-equipped competitor.

Although I could not be altogether pleased with my mother's move and the loss of my enterprises, I was not entirely disappointed. Examining now the state of my mind then, I detect an ambivalence, similar to my mother's perhaps, about profiting from people less fortunate than I. While I felt urgently the effect of the family's competitive drives and wanted to be successful, and thus honored, I seem to have been drawn more strongly to the tradition of compassionate generosity. I wanted to make a better life for my mother and myself, but felt also a need to help make the unfair world a better place for everyone to live in.

My social consciousness had begun taking shape by the time I was ten, in 1928, a year marked for me by the final separation of my parents and by Herbert Hoover's victory over Alfred E. Smith for the presidency. Late on election night, as I heard newsboys shouting extras reporting Smith's defeat, I cried. I was disappointed that "Our Al," a former liberal governor of New York whom people in my neighborhood spoke of as "a man of the people," had lost. I was also frightened that Hoover had won with the help of the Ku Klux Klan—barbarians who hated blacks, Jews, Catholics, and immigrants, and sometimes killed people they hated when they weren't just voting against them. I recall vaguely feeling that someone must do something to end such terrible unfairness.

Early emergence of social consciousness was not unusual in the Williamsburg slums. Only the obtuse or unfeeling could fail to see and respond to the variety of life in our streets. Most of my neighbors who were eligible to vote expressed their feelings by regularly giving margins of four to one and more to candidates of the Democratic Party. Others took part in meetings, rallies, and petition drives organized by various political groups. My mother, who could not pass the literacy test and was therefore ineligible to vote, adored FDR and kept a rotogravure picture of him clipped from a newspaper in the top drawer of her dresser until she died.

I was early aware of injustice and deeply disturbed to learn that things could be bad for some people, even when the winners in the family insisted times were good for everyone. I remember, in 1928, when things were, indeed, supposed to be good for everyone, seeing families evicted from cheap flats, their belongings piled on the sidewalk because they couldn't pay their rent. The sight provoked a good deal of anxiety. I remember hoping we would never have to be evicted. I knew also that even in good times not everyone worked and that not everyone who worked earned enough. During an early separation, my mother worked in the Dairy Maid ice-cream factory and had to take in two boarders in order to make ends meet. Clearly, even in good times things were not good for everyone—not even for some who were smart and strong and wanted to work hard.

I could not understand why this should be so when, as family elders said so often, "Anyone can make a dollar." I simply knew that not everyone could make a dollar and that some were rich while others were poor. Some day, I let myself think, I would learn the reasons and find a way to improve things and make the world what it should be: a nice place for everyone to live in.

Ignorance was the problem, I thought. If people knew the truth, they could put things right. My job, as I began to think of it, was to find and teach truth. By my thirteenth birthday, I had considered whether to be a giver of truth as a rabbi or as a teacher and rejected both—the former because of my Yom Kippur disillusionment and the role of teacher because it seemed too limited.

Then, one afternoon in the library of Boys High School during my junior year, I knew suddenly what I must do. I am skeptical of those who claim to have received a call, so I hesitate to record just such a revelation—though it is true.

Each day for a week, I had used study periods to read a book about the exploits of a young newspaper reporter. I don't remember the story or the title and am uncertain about the author's name. But I remember clearly that, when I had finished reading the book, I knew I must be a journalist.

A complete plan shaped itself in my mind. First, I would get a formal education and a degree certifying that achievement. Then I would go to work, preferably as a foreign correspondent in dangerous areas of the world, filing timely dispatches on significant developments. Later, with more time to reflect on my experience, and enough experience to reflect upon, I would write more fully in a book, or books. As my decision and that plan took shape in my mind, I felt some of the exaltation that born-again Christians say they feel upon learning they have been saved.

Soon, however, it became clear that being a giver of truth as a journalist was easier said than done. Much of what I read contained different facts on the same subject or interpreted the same facts in different ways. Obviously, only an educated person could hope to know how to find and evaluate truth. A college education was essential, and that presented a difficult problem. My performance as a student had deteriorated steadily, a circumstance not unusual among children of broken homes. After sailing easily through elementary school, I ran into serious trouble at Isaac Remsen Junior High School; and high school became a disaster.

Memory of that time is brightened by two triumphs over excellence-oriented teachers at Boys High School who had little time or patience with students who did not seem strong enough to make Arista, the honor society. In one instance, despite the forecast of failure by a particularly insensitive math teacher who was coach of the school's championship math team, I scored the highest grade in my class, ninety-eight, for an unusually difficult Regents examination in trigonometry. In the other, a faculty advisor who refused to accept me as a regular member of the prestigious Boys High Weekly newspaper staff nevertheless permitted me, as a freelance outsider, to interview and write reports of my encounters with show business personalities—among them Fannie Brice, Gypsy Rose Lee, and George M. Cohan. These proved to be popular with readers and encouraged me to believe that I could become a journalist, despite the faculty advisor's unwillingness to recognize my potential.

However, in class, things went from bad to worse until finally I stopped trying. I cut classes frequently and, in what was to have been my final term, flunked two subjects. As a consequence, it became necessary to return for an extra term in order to graduate. I tried to persuade myself that it was the fault of my teachers and that I didn't really care and wouldn't return, like a dumbbell, to repeat the courses I had failed. Under urging from my mother, I changed my mind and did return, embarrassed but resigned to the extra term as punishment for my sins.

When, in recalling that time, self-pity intrudes on the memory of what should have been a positive growing time and was not, I remind myself how lucky I was compared to others who have followed. Boys High today is no longer an elite school. Now called Boys and Girls High School, the student body consists mainly of black students, many ill-equipped to break through the walls that separate them from the best and the whitest. Any problems that I or my schoolmates encountered pale when compared to what the students of Boys and Girls High today must overcome, in school and out. I hope there are at least some teachers who understand and care enough to be able to teach students who have not yet learned how to compete successfully.

I was young and white and, despite my defeats, still hopeful when I graduated from Boys High three months before my seventeenth birthday. Like gamblers who speak only of the bets they won, I left Boys High feeling like a winner.

10.

THERE was no reason for my good feeling, other than the satisfaction of having earned my high school diploma, finally. Beyond that there were only problems. I very much wanted to go to college as the next step in my progress toward a career in journalism, but there seemed no way in which I could.

The city colleges of New York were open, free of tuition, for students who had maintained honor-roll grades through high school. Those who, like me, fell short of that standard could go to night school on payment of modest tuition fees. That alternative was unappealing. Night school, for those who worked by day, meant lighter course loads and a much longer time to graduation. Besides, I had already decided that if my grades didn't bar me and if I could raise the money—about six hundred dollars a year for tuition, room, and board—I would go to the school of journalism at the University of Missouri, an excellent school where students actually worked on their own daily newspaper.

Optimism was encouraged when, soon after graduating from Boys High, my Uncle Sam, the middle one of my mother's five brothers, an electrical contractor who was then the most affluent member of the family, offered to pick up part of the financial burden. He told me that, if I could find a job to support myself in Missouri, he would pay my tuition. That left the problem of how to get to Missouri and support myself until I could find a job.

While I tried to find a solution, I worked at occasional part-time jobs as a counter man at drugstore soda fountains. These jobs paid poorly and could not be expected to yield a grubstake, at least for a while—particularly since I invested a portion of my earnings in poker games, some of which I organized to help an unemployed cousin and his wife pay their rent by cutting the pots.

Meanwhile, I became the beneficiary of the kind of help that my neighbors so often gave to one another. My benefactor was Mr. Rose, who worked in the mail room of the *New York Times* and moonlighted as a club-date tenor. Occasionally, on returning from a booking, he would favor the audience in my mother's candy store with his rendition of a favorite song, usually "Roses of Picardy" or "Laugh, Clown, Laugh."

Upon learning that I hoped for a career in journalism, he suggested that I might start in one of the mechanical departments. He knew the superintendent of the composing room at the *Times,* Mr. Penney, and offered to arrange an interview. As a hedge against the possibility that I might not make it to school in Missouri, or anywhere else, I went to see Mr. Penney, a tough-talking, whiskey-nosed, kindly man. He said there were no openings at the time, but assured me he would write my name high on the waiting list for a job as floor boy, assisting journeymen printers who set type and made up the page forms. That seemed promising, but not enough to bank on.

Then, through a series of decisions I still find impossible to explain, I decided my best hope of getting to Missouri would be to find a backer more affluent or generous than my Uncle Sam. I may have been under the influence of the inspirational novels of Horatio Alger, in which ambitious young men—like the hero of *Pluck and Luck*—make their way to success aided by wealthy benefactors with an eye out for plucky young fellows needing just a bit of luck to make it. In any case, for reasons that elude me, I chose as my hoped-for benefactor Colonel Jake Ruppert, owner of the New York Yankees baseball club and the Ruppert Brewery on Third Avenue in Manhattan.

I don't know why I should have tried to get help from the patron of Babe Ruth and Lou Gehrig, except that it didn't seem to involve any great risk. I had nothing to lose. A rejection would leave me no worse off. And there was the chance that Colonel Ruppert might say yes. My reading of the sports pages suggested the colonel was a generous, approachable sportsman. I sent him a letter saying that I had just graduated from Boys High, had something unspecified to discuss that might interest him, and would appreciate an appointment. The colonel replied that he would be pleased to see me.

His reply took me by surprise. I had been certain I would know how to present myself if the opportunity arose. But as the appointed day approached, I was much less sure about that and sorely troubled by bad conscience. It seemed wrong to ask help of this kind from a stranger. I thought of it as begging and debated whether I had or should have the right to impose myself as planned.

Finally, I persuaded myself that I was simply making a request, which Colonel Ruppert could turn down if he chose. It wasn't a matter of right or wrong, I argued. It was only a question of whether he would say yes or no. Then I began to worry that he would say no and probably throw me out of his office as an opportunist. So torn, I steeled myself for the meeting and appeared at the old-fashioned office, solid with heavy wood furniture, to be greeted by a heavy-set, smiling, gray-haired man who said:

"You're the young man who wanted to talk with me. Well, what have you got to say?"

I could say nothing. Having come this far, I had run out of confidence. As I stood there, I was paralyzed by the thought that I was an impostor and had no right to impose on this important man. I stared at Colonel Ruppert. My face burned with embarrassment, and I choked up. I managed to squeak something to the effect that what I had come to talk about was not important after all, and I was sorry to have troubled him. I think I wished him good luck with the Yankees that season and retreated from his office in a panic that was unrelieved until I had escaped into Third Avenue, still needing some way to get to Missouri.

Another gamble, a small miracle in the form of a winning bet on the numbers game, solved my problem. I had rarely bet on the numbers, looking upon it as a sucker's game in which a thousand-to-one shot paid off at five hundred to one, after an obligatory twenty per cent tip to the runner. However, on a day in June, five months after my graduation from Boys High, I bet ten cents on number 492. And that night Solly the numbers runner brought me my winnings, fifty dollars.

I received it as a sign from God. I knew I must use this money to go to Missouri and find a job which, together with Uncle Sam's tuition money, would enable me to get the education I needed. I spent a dollar and twenty-five cents for an imitation leather suitcase, cleverly made of black cardboard, to hold my few belongings, including three newly purchased pairs of underwear. About ten dollars went for a bus ticket from the Greyhound terminal on West Thirty-fourth Street. The remainder of my stake was to pay for room and board until I could find a job in Columbia, Missouri.

That search proved futile, despite one apparent break. During my second week in Columbia, I was hired as a stock clerk in a men's haberdashery shop. But the next morning, when I reported for work, after having already written to my mother to tell her of my good luck, my erstwhile employer informed me sadly that I could not have the job after all. A young man from Missouri had applied, and the shopkeeper informed me, "We have to take care of our own, first."

For five weeks I canvassed every job possibility, but my luck had run out. After a final morning of job hunting, I spent the last of my funds, fifteen cents, for a roast-beef sandwich with mashed potatoes and gravy and a cup of coffee, and, with my belongings wrapped in newspaper—my suitcase having been left behind to mask my departure from the rooming house where I still owed last week's rent—I left Columbia, Missouri.

Rather than return home as a loser, I hitchhiked to Cincinnati, hoping there to find a job with the help of Dinny, my friend Larry's older brother. Dinny had been forced to leave medical school because of his father's Depression losses but had found an important position as director of advertising and publicity for RKO theaters in Cincinnati, Louisville, and Dayton, Ohio. Dinny was as kind as I could have wished him to be. He fed and housed me and urged me to stay on in Cincinnati in the hope that something would turn up. But nothing turned up and the outlook was unpromising.

After three weeks I moved on to Detroit, where my mother's cousins had assured me things were picking up and there would soon be jobs in the auto industry. There, too, I was made welcome and enjoyed, not without guilt, overwhelming hospitality.

When it became apparent that jobs were no easier to find in Detroit than Cincinnati, I wrote to Mr. Penney at the *New York Times* to inquire whether there might now be a job for me. He replied with an offer of a position as substitute floor boy, filling in for others who failed to show up for work. He said I could expect to work three or four nights a week. I thereupon raced home to accept the best job opportunity I had ever had.

As it turned out, in addition to the great good luck of the job at the *Times,* my travels in the west led me to a valuable fringe benefit: a declaration of independence from the judgments and prejudices of Aunt Mary. During my stay with Dinny in Cincinnati, I responded to several help-wanted ads offering jobs as dishwasher, shipping clerk, and other unskilled, low-pay positions. I had been surprised by the turnouts, crowds as large as a hundred or more showing up as early as five in the morning, sometimes in heavy rain, each applicant hoping to be the lucky one who would get the advertised job. One evening after my return home, as my mother and Aunt Mary were discussing the fine job I had gotten at the *Times,* Aunt Mary remarked that only laziness kept people from working. She said anyone who wanted a job could get one.

With the memory of my job-hunting in Cincinnati still fresh, I said, "Aunt Mary, you don't know what you are talking about."

Aunt Mary withdrew in a huff. My mother also was silent, but I was sure I detected a smile on her lips. I took that smile and her silence as my release from any further obligation to pay attention to Aunt Mary's judgments and turned to make the most of my new opportunity.

11.

IT would be difficult to exaggerate the importance I attached to my job at the *Times*. I thought of it as a triumph that made up for all the frustrations and defeats I had thus far endured. Now I needed only to make one more move, to the editorial department. I hoped to make a good showing in the composing room. Then, having demonstrated my ability there, I would apply for a job as a copy boy, en route to my real work as a full-fledged journalist.

Meanwhile, I kept myself occupied and content. I played poker with the men at the *Times* and my neighbors at home but spent more time on more satisfying pursuits. I read a great deal and was reinforced in my determination to become a journalist by the inspiration derived from the memoirs of two outstanding journalists, *I Write As I Please* by Walter Duranty and Vincent Sheehan's *Personal History*. I also saw four or five movies a week and, working in the Times Square district, became a theatre-goer.

Girls also interested me very much, but I suffered from what used to be called an inferiority complex and from a smothering ambivalence inspired by terrible confusions about sexuality. When tensions were aroused by thoughts of boys and girls together, I had the choice of relieving myself by masturbating—taking the chance that it might stunt my growth or cause hair to grow on my palms, as some of my peers believed—or going to Myrtle Avenue, where for fifty cents black prostitutes accommodated white customers in an atmosphere of mutual hostility that was unrelieved by orgasm. I found some satisfaction in a new design for living with the help of a new friend, Murray, whom I had met during my last year at Boys High.

As a schoolboy, Murray had helped his parents, who were pushcart peddlers in the open-air market along Moore Street. After graduating from high school, he established a profitable cart of his own. We shared the same tastes, interests, and frustrations and felt more secure in the sharing. Briefly, we also shared the services of a white prostitute whom we met at a luncheonette on lower Madison Avenue to which we were directed by a cab driver. She told us she had become a prostitute in order to support her parents and a sister after losing her job as a secretary in a failed garment business. We contributed by booking her once or twice a week, taking turns with her in the bedroom of an apartment borrowed from an older friend. While we enjoyed our triangle, we also talked about how it might be to fall in love with a "nice" girl, the marrying kind.

That happened for me with Gladys, a ripely beautiful young woman with long black hair. We had lived in the same tenement for five years and I had thought of her often with longing, but believed she was beyond my reach. She was an outstanding student, already in her first year at Brooklyn College. She was also a talented singer, a strong-voiced belter in the Judy Garland style. Gladys was popular on the club-date circuit and had made filmed vaudeville short subjects for Warner Brothers, while I was, as yet, a nobody.

We had from time to time exchanged neighborly greetings in passing. Then, through the friendly offices of her aunt, we met formally and became sweethearts. Unaccustomed to such good luck, I found it difficult to believe that I was entitled to the affections of someone so grand, but I enjoyed them immensely. I was also inspired to accelerate my movement toward a job in journalism, in order to make me worthy of the woman I loved.

At what seemed an appropriate moment, I approached an assistant managing editor, an older man who sometimes talked with me about the values of a career in journalism, for whom I had often pulled galley proofs on late-breaking stories. When I told him of my ambition to become a copy boy, he replied, not unkindly, "Not a chance. We don't have any openings, and, if we did, you'd need a B.A. to get in. Hell, we've got a guy from Harvard with a graduate degree working as a copy boy."

That response, though greatly disappointing, should not have led to the discouragement it provoked. By objective standards, even without the possibility of the career I had chosen, I still enjoyed a choice of alternatives that most others would have found richly attractive at a time when, despite six years of slow improvement in the economy, unemployment was still at about fifteen percent of the work force. I could stay where I was and become a journeyman printer. Or, I could accept another offer from my Uncle Sam, who wanted to subsidize my training for what he promised would be a rewarding job in the new field of air conditioning. Also, as Gladys and I became steadies, her father, a small but profitable manufacturer of thermometers and other glass instruments, asked me to go to work in his shop.

One way or another, I was assured of the opportunity to earn a good living. But these prospects were unacceptable. I refused to consider them seriously. Instead, I began to think more and more of what had been for some time a comforting dream, the idea of owning my own newspaper, a weekly for the students of the many colleges and universities in the metropolitan area.

I was not unaware that I lacked the two critical ingredients for entrepreneurial success: adequate financing and experience. To support my dreaming, I minimized their importance. My mother had saved almost three hundred dollars for me from that portion of my pay I handed over to her almost every week, and I persuaded myself that this would be enough to begin raising additional capital from investors and revenue from advertisers. As for experience, which concerned me more, I alternated ambivalently between assuring myself that my experience was sufficient and trying to hide from myself the fact that it was not.

If I could have admitted the truth, I should have known that I was reluctant to proceed with the dream of a journalistic empire, but felt compelled to get on with it because to give up might reveal that I hadn't known what I was talking about in the first place. My mother or Gladys could have stopped me if either had asked me to put aside my plan, but both were encouraging, though my mother gave her approval with some apparent reluctance. A respected father, if he had been present, also might have persuaded me it would be better to wait until I had more experience and capital.

In the absence of my father, one other person could have prevailed upon me to put aside my venture. I think that Gladys's father, proceeding with respect for my ego, need only have said that my idea had merit but would have a better chance of success later, when I had more experience and money; and I would have accepted his counsel. But his reaction, when I outlined my plan, was hostile. He dismissed the idea as damn-fool kid stuff, unworthy of someone who wanted to marry his daughter. Better, he insisted, I should take the job he had offered me with his company. When I said again that I could not, he offered me a curious alternative.

"Go ahead with that kid stuff, if you want to," he said. "But if you fail, and you damn well are going to fail, then you and my daughter are finished."

Unaware then, I have since come to admire the clever way in which he framed his ultimatum. If he had given me a choice of surrendering my dream or giving up Gladys, I might have chosen her. But he had carefully hedged his bet. I could proceed, but not fail. If I failed, he was rid of a loser as a prospective son-in-law. On the other hand, if, miracle of miracles, I succeeded, he had a winner as candidate for a place in his family circle. He had "dutched the book," arranging his bets so that he could only win regardless of the outcome.

For me, there was no easy way out. I felt compelled to take the bet because to do otherwise would have branded me a quitter, in my mind if not in his. I took the bet and lost. My planned newspaper never advanced beyond the dummy, sample stage.

Worse, after struggling for five months to find backers or advertisers, while at the same time working on the editorial design and trying to recruit staff members, I found that my losses included my job at the *Times*. I had been granted a three-months leave of absence in order to concentrate all my energies on my project and had neglected to ask for an extension before the deadline. When I did go back to request reinstatement, I was informed that I would be put at the bottom of the waiting list, a gentle way of saying my services were no longer required.

The father of the woman I loved was not gentle. He forbade her to see me. After several unsatisfactory surreptitious attempts to defy his edict, we stopped meeting. Within six months Gladys had married someone else, and, for the first time in my life, I felt completely hopeless.

Hopelessness was nothing new. I had felt it often since the separation of my mother and father. But this was something more, a sense of utter defeat, as though I had been left for dead by an invisible enemy. I felt like a burned-out failure who could never hope to do anything right. Still I wanted to find a way to compete and succeed.

I could see no acceptable options, and the logic of hopelessness persuaded me that, as things stood, I was not likely to find any.

By the same logic, I felt that I had nothing more to lose, no matter what I did. I began to think of gambling as the only way to end the losing.

I had found a full-time job as counterman at the Village Pharmacy in Greenwich Village and had registered for two courses in the evening session at Brooklyn College. But these were stopgaps: a way of earning money, which I needed in any case, and a way of filling time. I worked, went to school, and took part in social activity with friends. And I thought constantly about becoming a serious gambler.

One issue that caused me some difficulty was the knowledge that it was extremely difficult to win as a gambler. As proof that I was sound of mind, I conceded that reality. But I also argued that there was at least the possibility of winning and of winning big, and that this was more hopeful than anything else I could see on my horizon.

I was encouraged also by a naively wrong-headed understanding of the laws of probability. In my understanding, what people spoke of as "the law of averages" was a kind of savings bank into which one deposited losses until, eventually, accounts were balanced by winnings, and deposits could be withdrawn with substantial interest.

In fact, certain events occur with a guaranteed frequency—ten-to-one shots win once in eleven times, for example—but only after an infinite number of plays are made. Meanwhile, each time a ten-to-one bet is made, the bettor has only a nine percent chance of winning and a ninety-one percent chance of losing. Gambling operators with much smaller percentages in their favor against bettors are the only assured winners.

This is only half the problem facing gamblers. Even if the laws of probability could be overcome, there would be still another obstacle to make winning all but impossible: the policy of discounted payoffs which prevails in commercial gambling. That is the practice of short-changing winners by paying them less than the true odds would entitle them to.

Discounted payoffs are handled differently in different forms of gambling, but the effect is the same: to pay the gambler less than the true payoff. As an example, in parimutuel horse racing, the true odds are set by the amount of money bet on each horse in a race. If eleven hundred dollars is bet in the win pool and one hundred of that is bet on one of the entries, the odds on that horse are ten to one or ten hundred to one hundred. Thus, a winning two-dollar ticket should be worth twenty-two dollars.

However, before any bettor collects any winnings, a portion of the betting pool is taken for state and local taxes and operating income for the track. The average "take" at American tracks has been approximately fifteen per cent. When fifteen percent is taken from the eleven hundred dollars, only nine hundred and thirty-five dollars remain to be distributed to winning bettors. The discounted payoff becomes only eight dollars and thirty-five cents to one or eighteen dollars and seventy cents for a two-dollar ticket rather than the twenty-two dollars to which the true odds would have entitled the bettor.

The effect of discounted payoffs may be more clearly seen in so-called sports betting on football, basketball, and other sports. In that kind of betting, it is possible to lose by breaking even, as many gamblers often do. In this form of betting, favored teams are penalized a number of points, theoretically to make a game an even-up proposition. However, to bet on either of two teams in a game, the bettor must pay the bookmaker a "vigorish" of ten percent, putting up eleven dollars in the hope of winning ten on the even-up proposition.

A bettor who risks equal amounts—eleven dollars, for example—on each of two games must win both games to come out ahead. That bettor will have put up a total of twenty-two dollars on both games. If one team wins and the other loses, the bettor will receive ten for the eleven bet on the winning game, twenty-one dollars, leaving the bettor a loser by one dollar after an even split.

In casino games—except slot machines, for which the take may be twenty-five percent or more—the discount of payoffs is smaller and generally invisible. But it can be seen clearly in roulette, where the true odds against hitting any of the thirty-six numbers other than zero on a wheel with two zeroes is thirty-seven to one, but the payoff is only thirty-five to one, a discount of five-and-a-quarter percent against the bettor. On some European wheels, there is only one zero, which reduces the discount without altering its long-term effect.

Whether the take is as little as one-and-a-quarter percent on craps or as much as fifty-five percent on lotteries (making state governments the most avaricious of gambling operators), discounted payoffs guarantee that gambling operators, without risk to themselves, are the only certain winners. In most forms of legal commercial gambling, such as horse racing, the operator's winnings come "off the top," before the discounted remainder is distributed to short-changed winners. In every form of legal commercial gambling, no operator ever has reported losing more to gamblers than was taken by the operator in any accounting period.

Knowledge of the realities is not likely to have stopped me—any more than it stops the uncounted millions of gamblers who every day in increasing numbers attempt to achieve the impossible. If the facts had been pointed out to me, I believe I would have understood the negative long-term effect of losing one hundred percent every time I lost, while collecting something less than one hundred cents on my dollar any time I won. But I don't think that understanding could have kept me from my decision.

Undeterred by a real understanding of the probabilities and without consulting Murray or Leon or anyone else whose advice might have turned me from my mission, I decided to become a gambler, a horseplayer. It could be said my decision was made by choice but not by preference.

It seems to me reasonable to speculate that if I had been able to make it at Boys High and then go on to college to prepare properly for a career in journalism, or if I had been given a chance to learn the kind of job I wanted at the *Times* or another newspaper, or if I had been successful in my publishing venture, I would not have become a gambler. I know that I would much rather have been any of those. I wanted to be successful at an occupation of my choosing. I became a gambler because I seemed unable to become anything else I wanted to be.

I did not decide to become a *compulsive* gambler. I don't think anyone begins with that in mind. My decision simply was to make serious gambling a part of my life, something I would do to try to make big money in addition to whatever else I might do about making a career and earning a living in an approved way. I had seen that luck is a powerful factor in life, and I hoped to turn it to my advantage as a gambler.

Unpleasant truth may be difficult to accept—in this case because talk about luck in life sounds like the alibi of a loser. But testimony about the influence of luck upon human affairs comes from respected winners.

Even a psychoanalyst, talking about the reliance of compulsive gamblers on luck, observes, "Without luck success is impossible," though he goes on to caution that "luck alone is not enough; only the combination of luck-plus-personal-initiative spells success." Much the same note was sounded by philosopher Sidney Hook in a statement following his retirement as Emeritus Professor at New York University. As though to confirm that some things take a long time to learn, Hook wrote: "The older I grow, the more impressed I am with the role of luck or chance in life. The distribution of wealth in the world depends almost as much on luck as on energy, foresight, and skill."

One of the more sensitive observations on the subject is credited to Robert F. Wagner, a poor boy from the Yorkville neighborhood of Manhattan who achieved success as a lawyer and as a compassionate congressional leader of the New Deal and author of the bill enacting the National Labor Relation Board in 1935. When a friend complimented him on his success, Senator Wagner, whose mother supported him as a domestic day worker, is reported to have replied, "Yes, I made it. That was luck. But think of all the others."

The most poignant witness on the subject of luck in life that I encountered in my readings is Thomas Jefferson. In 1826, six months before his death at the age of eighty-three, Jefferson observed that "every pursuit of human industry" is a matter of luck for "there is not a single one that is not subject to chance, not one wherein you do not risk a loss for the chance of some gain." Jefferson's remarks were contained in a petition to the Virginia legislature asking that body for permission to become a gambling operator. His request was for a license to conduct a lottery that would enable him to remove a burden of debt from his estate.

Jefferson had piled up the debt in his role as generous family elder and lavish host to a great number of guests at Monticello during the seventeen years after his two-term presidency. A winner in all his pursuits, he had hoped to repay the debt by selling land around Monticello, but hard times had cut land values to a level at which he could not raise enough from the planned sale. Instead, he was persuaded to offer the land as prizes in a lottery, which was expected to yield more than he could have raised by selling the land. License was granted, but Jefferson died before the lottery venture could be carried out, and his debt was liquidated after his death by other means, including land sales.

Historian John Samuel Ezell has described Jefferson's petition as a "sad obituary on that great life," and there was for Jefferson's admirers an unfortunate spectacle in one of the founding fathers of the nation being reduced to pleading for the right to run a gambling operation to free his estate of debt. But, as might be expected from the Sage of Monticello, Jefferson's petition also produced something of value: a contribution to understanding the role of gambling in competitive-acquisitive society.

In the past, Jefferson had been hostile to lotteries of the kind he was now asking permission to operate for his own purpose. Apparently anticipating criticism about the morality of his proposal, he addressed himself to that issue, drawing distinctions between three kinds of gambling. Indisputably moral, he argued, are those gambles—farming, industry, commerce—"which produce something useful to society." Wholly immoral, he said, are the "games which produce nothing and endanger the well-being of the individuals engaged in them or of others depending on them." Among these he listed "cards, dice, billiards, etc.," all of which Jefferson had played as social pastimes. In a third category between these extremes, Jefferson said, "There are some games of chance, useful on certain occasions and injurious only when carried beyond their useful bounds." Such, he argued in the self-serving declaration, are lotteries of the kind he hoped to find useful in resolving his problem.

Considerations of morality aside and with respect for the great man's need to rationalize, I think it is more accurate to recognize Jefferson's three categories of gambling as two, which I have come to think of as competitive gambling (farming, industry, etc.) and dependent gambling (cards, dice, billiards, etc.). In my understanding, gambling is, as Jefferson suggested, the essence of competitive-acquisitive life. To live one must compete for whatever one needs or wants to acquire, and to compete is to take chances—to gamble.

In competitive gambling, men and women take chances on themselves and bet on their own ability to compete successfully in jobs, professions, or business enterprises. Dependent gambling—the kind usually meant when people speak of gambling—means betting on someone or something other than one's self—a horse, a team, a deck of cards, a pair of dice, a roulette wheel—to do in games of chance what dependent gamblers cannot do or believe they cannot do for themselves.

During the course of a lifetime, everyone necessarily makes a number of competitive bets in the form of decisions about how to compete in the workaday world. Most individuals also place some reliance on dependent gambles. Surveys indicate that four out of five adult Americans depend upon games of chance often enough to say they participate at least occasionally in dependent gambling. The issue, as the statistics indicate, is not which of the two kinds of gambling to choose but, since most people engage in both competitive and dependent gambling, how to strike an acceptable balance between the two.

Hedging of a similar kind is practiced by unwise horseplayers who, despite the disadvantages, may place a main bet on a preferred horse and a "saver" bet in the same race on a second horse they fear as a potential spoiler. At the races, at least one bet is all but certain to lose. Both bets can win only if the two horses finish in a dead heat, a rare occurence. In real life, it is more possible, theoretically at least, to win both competitive and dependent bets.

That is the kind of straddle I chose for myself. Like jockeys in ancient Rome who rode standing astride two horses, I made approximately equal bets on my competitive career choice and hedged that with dependence on my avocation as a horseplayer. I believed that, even if I couldn't manage a winning two-bet parlay, I would have a better chance to succeed in either or both ways by balancing each bet with the other and dividing my efforts between the two.

12.

As I experienced the mechanics of decision in choosing to gamble seriously, the process was accompanied by a good deal of careful thought which seemed sensible at the time. My objective was to find what literary critic Christopher Lehman-Haupt says he found and rejected: a way to win as a horseplayer. In the course of reviewing a book about how to win at the races, Lehman-Haupt revealed that he had been a winning horseplayer but had given it up because playing the horses was "too much like the rest of life."

The problem for Lehman-Haupt was that playing the horses was drudgery, requiring long hours of work with the "little numbers" of the past performance records—a process made even less attractive by the fact that his efforts paid off at an average rate of only one dollar and twenty-five cents an hour. I can understand why he would have been dissatisfied, but his decision to quit wouldn't have made sense to me.

Given a system with a guaranteed winning margin, which is every gambler's impossible dream, I would have begged, borrowed, or stolen enough betting capital to multiply the winning rate of one dollar and twenty-five cents an hour by a thousand, or more. Then, with winnings from that guaranteed system, I could have bought the *New York Times* and hired any former horseplayer who might find reviewing books less like the rest of life.

My goal was more modest and, I finally persuaded myself, more practical. Having decided to become a gambler, I had to select the appropriate medium. Since my objective was to win a great deal of money, the game I chose had to offer the possibility of big winnings. It could not be a game of direct competition with friends or acquaintances who might hurt me or be hurt by me. And it had to be something I could do in secrecy, since I still believed ambivalently that gambling—at least gambling of my kind—was not respectable.

Cards and dice failed on each count. Yonkel Butch's floating crap game did offer the prospect of big winnings, but counter-balancing that was the fact that I would have no privacy and, more important, couldn't for a long time at least put together the required minimum entry stake of one hundred dollars. Games like roulette were not available to me. And betting on baseball would have violated my love of the national pastime as a purely athletic competition which should not be soiled by gambling (except perhaps to support one's home team, though the Brooklyn Dodgers lost too often to inspire my consistent betting support).

Only horse playing met every requirement. It was a pure betting proposition, as private as any gambling could be. The competition was anonymous, whether through the parimutuel machines at the track or with a faceless bookie represented by his sheet man in a horse room. And, most attractive of all, starting with very small wagers one could win great amounts of money. For these reasons I chose to become a horseplayer.

Previously, I had understood my rejection of head-to-head games only as a reluctance to win from or lose to friends and neighbors. Jay Livingston suggests another reason. He points out that in games like poker a player is under the scrutiny of those whose respect he desires and risks being diminished in their esteem by losing. I suppose that was a factor in my thinking. Livingston also reports that two out of three of the gamblers he studied made horseplaying their first gambling choice for reasons similar to mine; and he says that, when novices were ready to move on to serious gambling, they received "technical assistance" from friends, peers, and "immediate age superiors."

An age superior, Jackie, provided the technical assistance I needed. Jackie, about as old as my brother Harry, was a failed welterweight boxer who had become a money lender. He didn't play the horses but financed several horseplayers and other borrowers at an interest rate of twenty percent per week. He made me promise that I would never borrow from lenders such as he, and that became one of the few promises I kept as a horseplayer. After several days of studying past performance data under his tutelage, I was ready for action, and Jackie escorted me on my first visit to a horse room.

It was in a building on Broadway which I had passed often without suspecting what was inside. A green baize curtain with the words "Bushwick Benevolent and Protective Association" in gilt-edged lettering hung on a brass pole and covered most of a store-front window. I had assumed that it was a clubhouse, like that of the Elks—the Benevolent Protective Order of Elks—or the Knights of Columbus and was surprised to find that it was a blind for a betting office, protected by a burly guard who opened the door without a word when he spied Jackie.

"He's laying chickie for cops. Crooks, too," Jackie explained.

His words enhanced the sense of the forbidden, enriched my thoughts of the money to be made in this place, and sharpened the anticipation with which I approached the first act in my career as a horseplayer. We passed into a room filled with battered tables and chairs and a shabby lunch counter behind which an unshaven man in a soiled apron slouched under a sign advertising sandwiches, egg dishes, and coffee. Beyond was another room crowded by a billiard table, and in the far corner a door opened to a stairway which led to the horse room on the floor above.

There, the bookie's agent sat with his sheet at his desk, a wooden table under a loudspeaker that broadcast the details of each race. The results were entered on a ledger sheet on which all bets had also been recorded. The sheet man, a runty fellow who, like the counterman downstairs, had not shaved on this day, greeted Jackie with a grimace which I took to be a smile. The room itself was tired-looking. Its wooden floor was bare, the walls needed paint, and the furniture consisted of two wooden tables, each with three or four rickety chairs at which three players pored over racing records oblivious to everything else. Yet it was bright with sun which streamed in through two windows overlooking a yard green with sumac trees and weed growth. No one seemed alive in this dingy hideaway, and the sun seemed out of place. Only my commitment to a career as a horseplayer kept me from leaving in disgust.

While Jackie talked business with the sheet man, whom he introduced to me as Henny, I studied the entries for the next race at Jamaica. My analysis indicated that a horse called Toniana was the probable winner. Jackie seemed to agree.

"Could be," he said.

Toniana had opened at eight-to-one and now, four minutes before post time, stood at five-to-one, indicating increasing support among bettors at the track. The sheet man solemnly recorded my bet on his ledger form: one dollar, to win—in accordance with Jackie's instruction that straight was the only way to bet. Jackie explained that only suckers bet place or show. The odds for second and third place are disproportionately lower than for first place, and the percentage is therefore much greater against the bettor.

During the moments before post time, the telephone on the sheet man's table rang several times and he engaged in quiet conversations. I could hear only some of his remarks: the time the bet was being recorded and his ritualistic declaration, "You got it," or, "You got it, kid."

"Credit players," Jackie explained.

Credit players were the elite. I was sure the time would come when my credit would be good enough to permit me to do my business by telephone without wasting time in such a dreary place. Meanwhile, I waited for the loudspeaker to broadcast the result of my first bet. The mechanical voice of an announcer broke in to report the position of each horse at various points in the race: the start, quarter mile, half, three-quarters, stretch, and finish.

Toniana broke well and was third, two lengths behind the leader at the quarter.

"Good position," Jackie said.

Positions were unchanged at the half.

"He's holding," Jackie said, though Toniana was a filly.

Toniana had moved up to second position, half a length behind the leader, at the three-quarter mark.

"He's moving," Jackie said, again ignoring the gender of the beast.

Toniana fell back to fourth position in the stretch. Jackie said nothing.

Seconds later the announcer called the order of finish. Toniana was out of the money.

"Died," Jackie said.

It didn't matter. I had wanted to win and would have preferred to win, but it had gone against me. I accepted things as they were and, in the manner of losers everywhere, comforted myself with a superstitious assurance. A poor beginning meant a rich end, I told myself. For reasons even less comprehensible, I persuaded myself that I should favor horses with the highest proportion of i's and a's in their names. (Toniana's i-a rating, for three i's and a's out of seven letters, was a .43—well above average.)

As I examined the entries for the next race, there was a commotion. "Raid," the sheet man announced, scooping up his papers. That was a word with a 0.50 i-a rating, higher than Toniana's. It was also a word which sent the sheet man and the other three players clambering over a window sill and onto a fire escape that led down to the yard. Jackie took my arm and led me down the fire escape. We raced through half a dozen back yards and hurdled the intervening fences until finally we found ourselves safely on the street, around the corner from the Bushwick Benevolent and Protective Association.

While Jackie and I stood struggling for breath, I tried to sort out my emotions and concluded that, all things considered, I was satisfied with my baptism by fire as a horseplayer, although things had not gone as I would have wished. I didn't like the tone of the place or the look of the people in the horse room, and despite my superstitious consolation to the contrary, I knew it was always better to win. Also, I could not hide from myself the fact that I had been badly frightened by the prospect of being arrested. Such a scandal would have caused great pain for my mother and for me. This was the least agreeable aspect of my debut. But Jackie reassured me on that score.

"Arrest almost never happens," he said. "If it does, the bookie goes your bail right away, and they send a John Doe to stand trial if necessary."

"Then why pull raids?" I asked.

"There's a new captain at the precinct," Jackie explained. "The new guy's gotta make connections, work things out. They'll be back in action tomorrow," he said. And it was as Jackie forecast, for them and for me.

13.

In my mind's eye, I can see myself diligently pursuing my chosen trade with a great deal of hope and with equally great concern for secrecy. For, while I tried to persuade myself that my gambling was right for me, I knew that my mother and others who mattered to me would have considered it terribly wrong and would have thought less of me for being engaged in such an activity.

Maintaining my cover was a constant problem because of the work that goes into betting on the horses and the need for time and a place to do that work. No other form of gambling requires so much preparation. A card player need only pick up his hand and play it. A crap shooter has only to watch the dice roll. The bettor on sports events, such as basketball or football, learns all he needs to know before betting simply by perusing the sports sections of newspapers and by talking with other interested parties.

From the horseplayer, much more is required. A horseplayer who wishes to take informed risks must study and evaluate page upon page of past performance data, the "little numbers" which report in great detail the history of each horse in each race and provide the basis for evaluating the probable performance of each entry. It is possible, of course, to bet on horses without knowing anything about them and many do so, allowing themselves to be guided by other handicappers, by touts and tipsters, or by betting on jockeys, post positions, or some other standard of selection that has nothing to do with the relative capabilities of the horses in any given race. Blind betting of that sort increases the already-high odds against horse-players.

Since I meant to bet intelligently, I needed time to study the past performance records and a private place in which to do this work. Betting at the track would have resolved both problems. None of the people from whom I needed to hide my secret was likely to be found at a track, and the half hour intervals between races allowed ample time for handicapping each race. But that freedom was unavailable to me. Like most horseplayers who do not live near race tracks, it was a long time before I saw a horse race while it was being run. I did business with horse-room bookies for more than three years before I made my first bet at a track.

It would have been convenient to do my work at home, studying the *Morning Telegraph* or the *Racing Form* at my leisure, but I couldn't risk discovery. In the circumstances, the horse room became my office. There, I needed only to take the precaution of scanning the street before entering and leaving my sanctuary. I quickly became a regular at Henny's. I worked a split shift at the Village Pharmacy, from ten in the morning until two in the afternoon and then from five until closing at ten. On my days off I spent the entire afternoon at Henny's. On working days, I raced between Greenwich Village and the horse room, half an hour each way by subway, and crammed as much study and betting as I could into the time available. It was a hectic process, but I seem not to have minded. On the contrary, there was an air of busyness about it that I found attractive.

Robert D. Herman, in a study entitled "Gambling As Work," reports that horseplayers in action "emulate traditional, entrepreneu-rial roles." That seems to have been the case with me. I found something very businesslike, and appealing, in what I was doing; and I am led to think that the requirement for hard work of this kind may be especially appealing for gamblers who, like me, were brought up in an entrepreneurial work-oriented atmosphere. Like a businessman studying market research reports before launching a new product or opening a new sales territory, I analyzed the probabilities for each race, made my decisions, then placed my bets and awaited the outcomes, writing off losses as they occurred or going to the accounts-receivable department to collect when I won.

After hours, for those lucky enough to have come away from the day's racing with money in their pockets, Henny provided still more action. He moved downstairs to the billiard table, on which he banked card games: blackjack or banker broker. At the billiard table, Henny's personality was transformed. Perhaps because he enjoyed this more than writing bets, the dour, laconic little man became cheerfully voluble.

"Get a hunch and bet a bunch," he chanted. "Nothing grows in your hand but your dick," he advised hesitant players. Should one win and depart, Henny, still cheerful, called after him, "Tell them where you got it, but don't tell them how."

Neither his more agreeable after-hours personality nor the games attracted me on those occasions when the end of the day found me with cash on hand. I came to Henny's to bet on the horses, not on card games. Except for an infrequent flyer, I did not play cards at Henny's.

Away from the horse room, I would have appeared little different from my friends and the other young men of Williamsburg. A psychoanalytic researcher in an attitudinal profile on the compulsive gambler lists as point two of six, using capital letters to emphasize this point: "THE GAME PRECLUDES ALL OTHER INTERESTS." That is not at all what I experienced nor does it resemble the behavioral reality of other compulsive gamblers I have encountered. All have had other active interests and in some cases interests of higher priority than gambling. In the circumstances, it could be said that either the researcher was wrong on this issue or that I, and at least some other compulsives, were exceptions to his rule.

Whatever the case, I had and used time and energies for activities other than gambling. I continued to read a great deal—most particularly the newspaper reports of the deteriorating situation of the Loyalists in Spain, Hitler's continued depredations against the Jews, and his incredibly successful maneuverings toward what became the Munich Pact, which gave him Czechoslovakia. I also worked hard at my job and submitted employment applications to New York newspaper editors.

When my work schedule permitted, I dated girls or went to the movies with Leon or Murray, with whom I discussed career plans, sports, and politics. I also greatly enjoyed and made time for frequent visits to talk with Uncle Daniel or to let Aunt Molly feed me and boost my morale with optimistic forecasts of my future. Weather permitting, I played soft ball, punch ball, handball, or roller-skate hockey. All in all, I was fully occupied and comfortable, if not entirely content.

Probably, I could have lived for a long time with this pattern. Many of my friends and neighbors did live similarly humdrum lives, richer in hope than in material rewards, for years until World War II brought changes. As luck would have it, change came earlier for me.

14.

FOR some time, my brothers and I had urged our mother to retire from the candy-store business. We argued that, even with the occasional relief help she allowed us to provide, she worked at least ten hours a day, seven days a week, and, at the age of forty-six, was obviously being worn out by this routine. She never complained. But, sometimes, when the burden grew too heavy, she would smile and say, "Life is a dream"—things will be better in the next world.

We hoped to make things better for her in this world and thought that her withdrawal from the fishbowl existence of a candy-store keeper would be a step in that direction. Rube, who had allowed himself to be persuaded by Mom to switch his career interest from music to accounting because accounting promised a better chance to make a living, calculated that we earned less than twenty cents an hour for all the hours we worked in the store. We argued that we could do as well without the store and my mother could have more time to spend with her family, which she greatly enjoyed doing.

As things worked out, in the years after leaving the candy store, my mother did spend a good deal of her free time visiting with her sisters. An image from that time remains fondly secured in my memory: I am standing at a window of our first-floor apartment, looking out on Bushwick Avenue. Below, my mother is returning from one of those visits, her smooth-skinned, flat-cheeked, Tartarian face aglow, her shoulders squared, her chin up, pausing to greet a neighbor, then marching on, her face lit up with an enigmatic smile which I understand to mean that she is saying to herself—life is a dream.

Usually my mother discussed important decisions with Rube, Harry, who by then had married and moved to Flatbush, and me. But she had said nothing to indicate she was responding to our urging until, a few months after I began my career as a horseplayer, she gave the store to a nephew who had recently married and then lost his job. "He needs a living," she explained. She said nothing more about why she had given away rather than sold the store.

Her decision, although I had encouraged it, caught me off guard and caused mixed emotions. The giveaway removed the one source of emergency financing available to me—her cash register, which I could tap for a dollar or two whenever my earnings at the Village Pharmacy proved insufficient to sustain me until the next payday. My unauthorized expropriations had troubled me deeply, calling into question my professions of a desire for an honest life of truth, so I was pleased to have this source of temptation and tension eliminated forever. But I was also greatly concerned about how I would manage without that source of emergency financing. I told myself that I was prepared to sacrifice my career as a horseplayer, so that my earnings might be used for the family's sustenance. But, while I thought of the satisfactions that might accrue from being a family breadwinner, I also schemed to reserve at least a few dollars a week with which to continue in action, while my mother enjoyed life at home.

Fortunately, it never came to that. When she announced her plan to dispose of the store, my mother made it clear that she was not ending her working life. She soon found a job in a paper-box factory which paid enough to have sustained the household on a minimum level without any contributions from my brother or me, though Rube continued to turn over to her most of his earnings. For several weeks,

I also turned over to my mother the greater portion of my earnings. Then, without complaint or comment from her, I began reducing my contribution until, often, it came to nothing.

That caused another crisis of conscience, which was resolved in my mind by the understanding that when I became a big winner I would easily make up for all I had taken or had not given. Still, it continued to trouble me that at nineteen I was being supported by my mother, who was paying the rent and buying food for the family from her wages and from the after-school earnings which Rube dependably brought home each week, to my shame.

Happily for my peace of mind, I had already developed an ability of some magnitude to rationalize unpleasant truths and thereby reduce or, for periods of time, remove from my mind altogether any knowledge of this sort which could only disturb me without, as I told myself, helping anyone. It was cheering also to know that my mother found her work in the paper-box factory congenial. She worked half as many hours as before, sat at an assembly-line table rather than standing all day behind a counter, and brought home amusing stories which suggested that she enjoyed working with the other women, old and young, mainly of Italian origin, who were employed in the factory. In these ways and others, I comforted my conscience so I could concentrate upon trying to find the way to become a winner.

During this period I also began to pray, something I had never before done knowingly. For years I had gone to the synagogue and spoken prayers in Hebrew without understanding what the words meant. Now I prayed in English, silently, before going to sleep, and tried to strike a bargain with God. If He would make it possible for me to become a winner, as a horseplayer or as a journalist, I would be His servant forever. As a fall-back position, I proposed that if He would only destroy Hitler, Mussolini, and the fascist Japanese (who had recently shelled an American gunboat in Chinese waters, creating the Panay Incident), I would consider that reason enough to become His servant forever. But, after a while, I stopped my prayers because I began to feel self-conscious about what I was doing. As an atheist, it seemed to me a gross violation of principle to hope to be able to call upon God under the pressure of my unfulfilled needs.

Then, as if to answer my prayers, though I had not asked for this specific beneficence, I received an offer from Dinny to come to work in Cincinnati. Except for greetings exchanged through his brother

Larry, we had not been in touch for three years, not since my brief exposure to Dinny's hospitality on my way home from Missouri. Now I read and reread a letter from him asking me to come to work as assistant in the advertising and publicity department of RKO Midwest Theaters for a salary of nineteen dollars a week. That, except for my earnings as a sandwich man, was more money than I had ever before earned—and for a job more promising than any other I had yet held.

It seemed a small miracle—a lucky, happy accident of friendship that had opened up a fine, new opportunity. I responded immediately; and three days later I was on my way west again, to seek a new life but without surrendering the dominant feature of the old. Bright as the promise of the future had become, I saw no reason to give up one thing for another. Until there was a more substantial reason to do so, I did not intend to end my dependence on the horses. More accurately, I didn't even think about it.

PART TWO

COMMITMENT

15.

CINCINNATI in the summer of 1938 presented two contrasting faces. It was a serene, comfortable, middle-class town which, stabilized by the presence of two large corporate headquarters—Procter and Gamble and the Kroger grocery store chain—seemed to have weathered the worst of the Depression with less strain than most cities. It was also a river town that had carried forward the tradition of offering to residents and visitors every commercial pleasure, especially gambling.

In both aspects, as residential community and gambling center, the stratification that was imposed or inspired by money or its lack was more obvious in Cincinnati than at home. Back home, in Williamsburg, the very poor, the merely poor, those better off, and some quite affluent often lived side by side, sometimes in the same tenements, and—at least in candy stores—mingled socially. In Cincinnati, the poor lived mainly in the slums around the edges of the downtown business and entertainment center. The more affluent lived in leafy residential neighborhoods on the hills surrounding the downtown area, in communities named Walnut Hills, Clifton, College Point, Avondale. The most affluent went farther out, to a roomier, posh enclave, Indian Hill.

People at all economic levels gambled, and the stratification was apparent also in their gambling. Gamblers with little to risk tended to patronize the horse rooms in town or to play poker in games run after racing hours in pool rooms. More affluent gamblers did their work in race track clubhouses or by telephone with bookmakers or went across the Ohio River to Newport and Covington, Kentucky, to shoot craps and play roulette or blackjack in luxurious casinos—Beverly Hills and the Lookout House—which were illegal but operated openly. However, most of the gambling took place in horse rooms, one of which seemed to be in the back of virtually every bar, cigar store, and pool room—nine, to my knowledge, within one block of the RKO Palace Theater Building where I worked. That led me to think of Cincinnati as the most active horse-racing town in the history of the world—until I learned that in Rome during the first century A.D., bettors could choose from among one hundred races a day.

Everything I saw confirmed that money made a difference. By a happy coincidence, my personal financial position improved even before I went to work. Upon my arrival, Dinny informed me that my salary had been increased from nineteen to twenty-two dollars a week, because two jobs had been combined into the one I was to fill.

That information was communicated to me at dinner in Dinny's house on the night of my arrival. He and his wife and infant daughter lived on the Kentucky side of the Ohio River in a huge stone ranch house, which featured a picture window that ran the length of the living room and looked out across the river to Cincinnati.

Dinny said he was renting the house, because he couldn't afford to buy it. I wondered how many more raises I would need before I could afford to rent or buy such a magnificent house. I didn't stop to think that my good fortune, a three-dollar raise, meant bad luck for the superfluous other person whose job had been eliminated. I simply accepted the pot-sweetener as an omen of good luck still to come.

Any qualms I might have felt were dissipated by my discovery that there wasn't really work enough for one person. My job was to provide support services for Dinny, his chief assistant, Whit, who wrote most of the advertising and publicity copy, and three artists who designed the ads for ten RKO theaters in Cincinnati, including all but one of the first-run houses and three other theaters in Dayton, Ohio, and Louisville, Kentucky. My duties consisted of several undemanding chores, such as monitoring ad production schedules for the three cities and delivering publicity materials to the drama editors of the Cincinnati newspapers. Only two of the several simple tasks held any interest for me, daily visits to "film row" and regular but less frequent visits to the drama editors.

Film row, about a mile from our office, was a group of factory-loft buildings in which Hollywood producers maintained "exchanges" to store prints of their films and "exploitation" materials—press books, still photos, posters—for distribution to exhibitors in the area. I went to the exchanges most afternoons to select from among hundreds of still photos those that were best suited for use in ads and newspaper photo layouts for the new films opening at RKO theaters.

This was one of two tasks I performed without direct supervision—though my superiors retained a seldom-exercised veto power over my selections. This task also involved the great responsibility of handling company money—cash advanced to me by the manager of the Palace Theater in our building, usually five or ten dollars to pay for the stills. The money inspired mixed feelings: pride over the trust represented by the advances and fear that I might somehow lose the money, the unspent balance of which, together with receipts for expenditures, was to be returned to the box office the morning after a shopping expedition.

No such concerns spoiled the pleasure of my other preferred duty: to visit the drama editors once or twice a week for what I thought of as editorial conferences. On these visits, I delivered schedules of theater bookings for two weeks in advance, together with stills, press releases, and information for use in advance publicity, and discussed with the editors the relative values and prospects for each of the movies and vaudeville shows on the schedule.

Unlike the editors and reporters with whom I had experienced only passing contact at the *New York Times,* these were the first newspaper people with whom I had a true working relationship: E.B.

"Rad" Radcliffe of the *Enquirer,* lean, laconic, a former general-assignment reporter who had become a conscientious student of films and theater; Groverman Blake of the *Star-Times,* a Cincinnati blue blood who looked a little like Errol Flynn and, like that swashbuckling film star, had created something of a legend as a heavy-drinking free spirit; and Ed Carberry, like Rad, a student of drama, a roly-poly, rumpled man who was considered a bohemian only because, as far as I could determine, he was unconcerned about his personal appearance and sometimes wore untidy sweaters to work.

Usually, all my work was done before lunch and it soon became a problem how to use my free time. The logical solution, it seemed to me, was to persuade Dinny and Whit to let me do something more responsible: some writing, for example. They were agreeable and assigned me to compose brief press releases for B movies and captions for the photo spreads I delivered to the editors. I cannot recall which paper first published one of my press releases or captions, but I do remember that I soon came to feel I was ready for a career in journalism if I could find an opening.

The added duties left me with still a good deal of free time, which I used to see movies, in our screening room or at one of the theaters (I saw more than one thousand movies during two years in Cincinnati and unsuccessfully tried to believe, as a respected trade-magazine editor insisted, that there was no such thing as a bad movie). More often than required, I also made excuses to visit the drama editors. Each of them generously gave me time he could have put to better use and listened with apparent respect to what I had to say about his reviews and about movies in general.

Working on a morning paper schedule that frequently kept him late at the office, Rad was more easily accessible than the others. I spent a good deal of time with him, at dinner or over drinks after his work was done or simply sitting unobtrusively in his office watching him work, and thinking of the time when I, like Rad, would be a newspaperman.

When we became friends, Rad was one of the two people in whom I confided my ambition to be a newspaperman. Whit was my other confidant. I thought he wrote too well to be just a copywriter for RKO, and, as we became friends, I told him so. We talked about writing and other matters during comfortable sessions at his house, a cottage in College Point, to which I went often for weekends. Whit and his wife Vee were childless and treated me like a son, though neither was much more than ten years older than I.

It pleases me still to remember that I knew them before the television epoch. Without TV to watch, we were able to devise our own entertainment, which involved good food, a great deal of beer, unlimited conversation, and much cigarette making. Even well-paid white collar workers like Whit, who earned almost three times as much as my salary, found it convenient and economical to roll their own cigarettes. If Whit and Vee had drunk less beer, they would have had more money to buy factory-made cigarettes. Their budget priorities led them to choose instead to buy Bull Durham cigarette tobacco at five cents a sack, cigarette papers for another penny or two, and a Target cigarette-making machine—which was more sanitary than hand-rolled cigarettes because it used water rather than saliva to seal the paper wrapper. The process enabled production at a cost of about six cents for a pack of twenty cigarettes. Since we all three smoked, the machine was in constant production during my visits.

Whit was fond of Ernie Pyle's writings, as were many people who would later be called "Middle Americans." In those years, before he became the idol of G.I. Joe in World War II, Ernie Pyle drove around the country with his wife and wrote unpretentious, warm, personal columns about the people they encountered—the same sort of writing he later did during the war, until he was killed at his work. He was syndicated by Scripps-Howard, but, although I read the *New York World-Telegram,* a Scripps-Howard paper, I didn't become familiar with Ernie Pyle until I began reading the *Cincinnati Post.* When I did, I found it easy to share Whit's enthusiasm for Pyle's so-human style.

Whit and I agreed also on many other things—good movies, among them *The Ox Bow Incident, The Grapes of Wrath,* and *The Wizard of Oz* (which I saw eight times during the weeks it showed in Cincinnati); good movie criticism, of which we thought there was too little; and good writing (Whit introduced me to John O'Hara and William Faulkner, in whose disparate writings we shared pleasure). We were not, however, of like minds on other matters: Whit was critical of FDR and of the New Deal, both of which I ardently supported. But disagreement did not foster disharmony and may, in fact, have served to make me think harder about issues which concerned me.

That was true also of another friendship which sustained me in Cincinnati, one of several relationships from which I seem to have needed something more than companionship. Rad and Whit were close enough to my age for me to think of them as wise and respected older brothers. Jules, an insurance broker who had written an annuity program for Dinny and visited the office frequently to transact business with Dinny and other clients, was old enough to be my father, and I may have thought of him as a stand-in for the parent I had not seen for eight years when I left home for Cincinnati.

We met on one of his visits to the office, and when I had come to know him well enough to wish to impress him—as I soon did—I declared my intention of purchasing an insurance policy, with my mother as beneficiary. Jules, a slender, grey-haired man who dressed like an executive but could as easily have been taken for a rabbi, put me off. If my objective was to give my mother greater security, he said, that might better be done by sending her the fifty cents a week my policy would cost. But I remained insistent, out of a need to impress myself as much as him, and Jules proposed a compromise, a policy that cost half as much. That began a relationship from which I might have benefited much more than I did if I had been able to act upon his sage counsel.

Within weeks of my arrival in Cincinnati, I had reason to feel like a settled burgher. I had made good friends and my social calendar was full: beer, conversation, and cigarette making with Whit and Vee; dates on Saturday nights with one of several girls to whom Jules and his wife Sylvia or others introduced me; potluck dinners on Sunday at Jules and Sylvia's lovely colonial house in Avondale; and, during the week, get-togethers with Rad, and classes two nights a week at Cincinnati University, where I had enrolled as a sign of my good faith in pursuing every possible route to realize my ambition of becoming a journalistic giver of truth.

Why I should have wanted to endanger this richly satisfying situation by continuing my dependent gambling is a question to which my search has produced only clues. Two in particular may be meaningful.

Although I would not have found it possible to believe then, I think now that, despite my acceptance by people whose respect was important to me, I felt at a distance from Jules and Sylvia, and Whit and Vee, and Rad and the others with whom I shared my time but not myself. I think I felt like an undeserving poor relation. To understand this sense of alienation, it seems reasonable to explain that, with all the affection I felt for my friends, I felt also a "differentness"—a feeling that I was not like them, did not deserve to be, and could never be, no matter how much I wanted to emulate the way they were: respectable, responsible, comfortable, established. I must have felt also, as a by-product of my competitive spirit, envy for the things they had and—although I hesitate to recognize it even now— hostility, or, at least, competitiveness, which was masked effectively by the warmth of our good feelings for one another.

I was very much aware of great differences between us in the material circumstances of our lives and can understand that my envy could have run deeper than I would then have allowed myself to think. Until I was thirteen, my mother, my brothers, and I, had lived in cold water flats with uncovered wooden floors. We didn't have central heating, which was then referred to as "steam heat," before we moved to Siegel Street. Until just prior to my move to Cincinnati, we had lived with the cast-off furniture of others, except for some goose-down bedding from "home" that my mother treasured. Only recently, after giving her store to my cousin, my mother had spent a large portion of her remaining small capital to equip our new centrally-heated tenement apartment with new furniture and with inexpensive floor coverings. I was impressed that all my friends in Cincinnati lived in homes of their own, one family to a house, with attractive upholstered furniture, real wool carpets, and at least one car in each garage.

I had never before spent time in such splendid surroundings. Whatever else I may have experienced below the level of awareness, I hoped eventually to be able to support such comfort for my family, and the sooner the better.

What seems clear now was not clear then. I could not have recognized that I was a highly competitive, deeply troubled young man. I saw myself as I believed others saw me: as a sober, conscientious fellow doing everything an upstanding young man should do. My work at the office was well-regarded. I attended classes at the university as scheduled and did the homework as assigned. I enjoyed my social time with the attractive people I had come to know and wrote letters home every week. When there was nothing more compelling to do, I read, and sometimes played small-stakes poker with my neighbors at the YMCA, where I had taken a room for five dollars a week. My life was an open book, except for the unsharable secret that within a week of my arrival in Cincinnati I had established a working relationship with a bookmaker.

16.

ODDLY, I was ambivalent about the gambling scene in Cincinnati, as I was about gambling in general. I thought of my gambling as not nice but necessary, so I was both pleased to find that my need could be served so conveniently and shocked that it should be. Back home, lines were clearly drawn and respected. In Brooklyn, playing cards in a candy store or at someone's home, or betting on the numbers game, were considered pastimes rather than gambling and, as such, were conducted openly, as part of the regular daily routine. Betting on horses or playing in Yonkel Butch's floating crap game was something else. That was real gambling. It was considered wrong by respectable people and was conducted furtively, behind guarded doors (as it should be, I would have said).

In Cincinnati, there were no distinctions and no barriers. Anyone could make a bet as easily as buy a pack of cigarettes, and often one conducted both transactions in the same establishment. It was all very discreet, and seemingly conducted with approval of the police. Still, although I intended to continue my betting, it didn't seem proper that something regarded as terribly wrong in New York should be accepted as quite all right in Cincinnati.

Often, in the years when I felt guilty about my gambling, it comforted me to believe that the ease of access in Cincinnati was at least partly to blame for my increasingly active involvement. But I knew in my heart that I would have gambled as much back home in Brooklyn, or anywhere else.

Gambling activity increases—more people gamble more often—as the availability of gambling opportunities expands, at least up to a saturation point. But it does not follow that to prohibit the practice would put an end to it. Legal and social prohibitions have nowhere succeeded in doing anything more than making it more inconvenient to gamble.

My own experience and observation demonstrate that those who want to gamble usually find a way to do so, even in conditions of great difficulty. During World War II, when I was briefly a prisoner of war in Romania, many of my fellow POWs, flight crews from the U.S. 15th Air Force and R.A.F., fabricated playing cards from bits and pieces of cardboard and played, mainly hearts and blackjack, for I.O.U.'s redeemable after liberation. Those who participated experienced a remarkable exhibition of generosity. On the day we were liberated, the winners declared a general forgiveness and tore up the promissory notes of all debtors, some whom had signed chits for thousands of dollars. It is the only instance I can remember in which losers were winners and winners lost for winning.

In Cincinnati, ease of access simply made it more convenient for me to continue gambling, and I saw nothing better to do with that time. I can only speculate about how I might have reacted to different circumstances. My guess is that if I had been presented with a more attractive alternative or if I had been forced to choose between devoting myself to my job or continuing with my gambling, I would have chosen my job or the more attractive alternative. However, there was no more attractive alternative and, since I could manage both, there was no need to chose between the job and the horseplaying on which I depended for my big break.

Each morning I hurried to clean up my desk work before noon, so I could go to the horse room for a sandwich lunch and an hour of studying past performances and placing bets. At mid-afternoon, I returned to the horse room, en route to the exchanges or to visit the drama editors. If my early bets had won or if I had other disposable cash, I made a few bets. At five, when it was only two o'clock in California and there was ample time for bets at Santa Anita or Tanforan, I returned for a final effort, funds permitting.

The horse room in which I did my work was, like all the horse rooms I visited during my years as a horseplayer, a shabby place, unfit for anything better than the use to which it was put. I found the place attractive only because it was on an off-the-beaten-track side street four blocks from the office, close enough to be convenient yet safe from detection by those from whom I needed to hide my activity.

Entry was through a seldom-patronized, untidy bar. Beyond that was an unilluminated foyer with filthy bathrooms on either side and beyond that the betting office—a windowless room, dimly lit except for one bright bulb under a green glass shade which hung like a spotlight over the sheet man, Morris, who sat at one of two battered wooden tables in a corner. The only other furniture consisted of several wooden chairs and three or four copies of the *Racing Form*. In the gloom of the room, bettors moved like silent ghosts, revealing themselves only when they appeared before Morris to place a bet or collect on a hit, the term borrowed from baseball to describe a winning bet on a horse.

Morris sat in the spotlight constantly feeding himself, pausing only to remove a sandwich, a bag of peanuts, a candy bar, or a soda pop from his hands when there was business to attend to. He was an unusually friendly fellow for a sheet man. Most of those I knew were close-mouthed, business-like types. Morris made small talk with his clients and seemed really pleased to pay occasional winners.

One day, as I munched a ham and Swiss sandwich and concentrated on the entries for an upcoming race, Morris spoke to me. We were alone in the room, and for once he wasn't eating.

"What do you need this for?" he asked. "A bright kid like you, you got better things to do with your time and money."

"What do you mean?" I replied, seeking time to compose a more suitable response.

"Why don't you quit?" he asked. "You can't win, you know."

"I know what I'm doing," I said defiantly, annoyed to have a bookmaker's agent, of all people, recite the cliché everyone relied on to discourage gambling—as though I had not carefully considered that warning before embarking on my course. To end our little talk, I placed a bet and left sooner than I would have done if he had not spoken as he had.

My displeasure passed quickly, and I forgave Morris for his misplaced good intentions. But Morris behaved as though I had wronged him. After our brief discussion he was not again as friendly as he had been, and we conducted our business in a formally correct fashion.

I had begun my betting with a strategy which, although I didn't realize it then, was the most sensible way to bet: one race at a time, one horse at a time, and straight—to win, as Jackie had taught me. Unless I was working with earlier winnings, my bets were seldom for more than a dollar; until one day, for reasons I have been unable to bring under review, I bet on and won with a hundred-to-one shot. In New York, bookies generally limited payoffs to twenty-to-one; but in Cincinnati they paid full track odds, so I collected a bit more than one hundred dollars—my biggest hit up to that time.

With substantial new capital in hand, I pressed my bets, putting as much as ten dollars into a single bet. But my luck didn't hold, and in a few days I had bet away my big winnings.

Frustrated over my failure with the big bets and reduced once again to bets of a dollar or two, I changed strategy and began betting on parlays of two horses or more; round-robin parlays pairing each horse with each other from among three or four; if-bets, which specified that a certain amount from the winnings of one horse was to be bet on another; and if-reverse bets, which provided for a portion of winnings, if any, to be exchanged between two horses.

That worked no better than the more sensible one-horse bets, and I found myself constantly in need of short-term financing. I had not before borrowed to gamble. Now it became necessary to do so. I established a network of lenders among my neighbors at the Y from whom I could usually raise needed funds, five dollars or less, until the next payday or the next winner, whichever came first.

More and more often I also substituted a suitable portion of guilt for the five-dollar remittances I had promised myself to send home without fail. My food expenditures were lessened by frequent free meals, a blessing since I liked food too well to contemplate cutting very much from that portion of my budget. Except for shirts, I did my own laundry in the bathroom at the Y and spent on clothing only what was absolutely essential to maintain a neat appearance. My dating expenses were minimal, since dates invariably consisted of a movie, for which I had passes, and coffee or soda afterward and, quite often, dinner at the homes of my dates. Through such economies, I have calculated that I was able to reserve ten or eleven dollars per week for gambling, about half of what I earned.

Despite the constant pressure under which I functioned, I did not falter. It never occurred to me to quit. I continued to think of what I was doing as the long prelude to the big hit which would put everything right.

Some observers have argued that it is an appetite for action which keeps a compulsive gambler going in the face of persistent losses. It is said cynically that, for a compulsive gambler, losing is the next best thing to winning. That attitude seems to me to miss the point of action. I don't think many gamblers could be said to desire action for the sake of action itself. What they are after, and what I sought, is the possibility and the hope of winning, which is the essence of the action.

In a scientific vein, a psychoanalytic researcher has argued that the major attraction for a compulsive gambler is the "strange thrill" gambling provides, a "logically inexplicable condition" which one of his patients described as "pleasurable-painful tension." Something like that is present in gambling, but I don't think it is either strange or inexplicable or peculiar to gambling alone. As I experienced it later in life, that tension is present for an aviator in combat hoping to make it safely back to base, for an advertising executive wondering whether his presentation will convert a prospect to client, for a marketing planner awaiting the decision from the market place on a new product, for a writer hanging on an editor's decision, and for anyone hoping for some reward which may be granted or denied.

As I experienced it during my years as a gambler, there was the pleasurable-painful anxiety of anticipation when placing a bet—the pleasure of hope and the pain of uncertainty—followed by the pleasurable elation of winning or the painful disappointment of losing and the continuing hope that next time it would be the former rather than the latter.

Looking back upon my activity of that time, I am strongly impressed by the routine, even humdrum, quality of the gambling life. The pleasurable-painful thrill is present for all gamblers, but it is probably felt more strongly by the occasional gamblers than by the regulars, except when a regular is riding a winning streak. It doesn't seem possible to sustain a constant high of excitement while making a dozen or more bets each day, day in and day out. Living at such a high, I should think, would, sooner or later—and probably sooner—lead to an emotional breakdown. Putting a rein on the up and down process by treating it as routine apparently enables the regular gambler to keep going at a more or less even pace.

More important for me, I think, was something else: my social involvements, which provided a foundation of stability. I don't think I could have tolerated a life of only work and gambling, or of gambling alone. I never lost my taste or my need for the support and comfort derived from contact with my friends, with acquaintances at work, with teachers and fellow students at school, and with young women I dated. Throughout, I seem to have been aware that through being and doing with other people I kept myself whole.

None of this altered the situation in which my dependence on gambling had placed me. But, strengthened by the comfort I found in my life away from the horse room, I was able to continue to believe that eventually I would overcome the odds and become a winner. I should have preferred to achieve that state sooner rather than later. Except for that, I was reasonably content with the pattern of my life in Cincinnati.

My sense of well-being was disturbed only by the state of the world, which grew more perilous day by day. During my first year in Cincinnati, the appeasement of Hitler by France and England, with the silent consent of the United States, allowed him to take Austria by *Anschluss* before occupying Czechoslovakia as a consequence of the Munich Pact. In Germany, Nazi legislation and political violence against Jews came to a climax in The Night of Crystal, actually several nights and days in November of 1938 during which mobs were encouraged to break into and loot Jewish homes and shops. A refugee cousin of my mother told us that the mob which broke into his house in Berlin included former friends, respectable people, who helped themselves to the family silver, cameras, and some crystal glassware which had been part of his mother's dowry. I reacted to each of these events as a personal loss.

Back home, I could have taken part in the discussion about the meaning of all these terrible things. In Williamsburg people talked about such things in their homes, at work, in candy stores, wherever two or more gathered. Even my mother and Aunt Mary, who had formerly considered politics men's business, had become involved in the political talk as the menace of Hitler grew.

In Cincinnati, people also were concerned but I remember very little conversation about the world, as though it had been decided by unspoken agreement that it was rude to bring up such disagreeable matters. Anyway, it was indisputably more fun to talk about the Cincinnati Reds marching toward National League pennants in 1939 and 1940.

Like the other "good burghers"—as sports writers sometimes referred to the residents of Cincinnati, which had been settled by German immigrants—I talked about agreeable matters, paid closer attention to my own affairs, and for the most part kept my own counsel as the leaders of the world prepared to roll the iron dice, a situation that I viewed with growing dismay.

17.

REEXAMINATION of that time of my life has led me to an understanding that I did not then enjoy and an attitude of which I would not have thought myself capable. I have thought of my reactions to the world's sufferings during the Hitler era as the response of a passionate democrat protesting unfairness and injustice, but can see now that the pain of constant defeats suffered by those opposed to Hitler had a more discouraging and depressing effect.

There seems to have been a deep-seated feeling of malaise to which my response appears to have been the belief that only more terrible things lay ahead, that the world was going to hell in a handbasket, and that therefore nothing I did mattered.

Nevertheless, inspired, I suppose, by nothing so much as ambivalence, my go-for-broke activity in the horse room continued to be balanced by my struggle for respectable success. I continued to play the horses and to live the routine life of a serious young man on the make, giving the necessary attention to work, school, and social activities.

During this time, I became familiar with sex between men and women which did not involve an exchange of money and wished afterward that this could have been accomplished with less shame, anxiety, and guilt. Through the kiss-and-tell network I came to know a young woman who, according to the fellow who told me about her, went all the way with men she liked. After weeks of hesitation, I called and made a blind date with her for a Saturday night, having first reserved a room at the Gibson Hotel for three and a half dollars in the expectation that things would work out as my informant had assured me. The girl was an attractive brunette of my age, a gentle young woman who seemed to me as uncertain as I felt.

We went to a movie, and when we came out I suggested nervously that we might go to my room. She nervously agreed. In bed, we sweated and strained, grappled awkwardly, and, I think, were both relieved to have it over with when we were done. By the code of my elders, I was supposed to think less of her because of what she had let me do, and I tried but achieved nothing more than confusion and regret for what happened. As I saw her home, she invited me to return the next day for dinner with her family, and I accepted— I think only to show that I harbored no ill feelings over the not-nice thing in which she had involved me, as though I had been only an innocent bystander.

Her mother was a fine cook and dinner was delicious. But, as I talked with her mother, father, two younger brothers, and younger sister, I kept thinking of my guilty secret and wondering how these hospitable people might feel and act if they knew what had happened the night before. I knew before I left that I could not bear to live a double life with her and her family. I never saw her again.

With less of my time and energy given to gambling I might have found the opportunity to work toward what could have been a more sensible relationship. As it was, my social relationships were carried out entirely on the surface, and I felt no inclination to become involved in a distracting emotional commitment.

More important, I was approaching the end of my first year in Cincinnati and my first vacation visit home and was, as usual, short of funds. I continued to lose more than I won, and short-term deficit financing, making small loans from neighbors at the Y, became part of my weekly routine, though my needs had by now grown beyond the capacity of this system to satisfy. I had not sent any money to my mother for more weeks that I cared to count; and, to make matters worse, I had not paid my rent at the Y for a long time. The management was sympathetic about such things, slow to dun tenants until the arrears had grown excessive, so it was not until ten weeks had passed that I found a note in my mailbox suggesting I try not to let my outstanding balance grow any larger. Next would come a request to liquidate the balance.

As I wrestled with the problem, it seemed to me that the only way out was to float a bank loan. I had seen advertisements in the newspapers inviting people to come in and get money in the form of personal loans. I had previously understood that only business people, or others with solid collateral, could hope to borrow from a bank; yet the banks seemed willing to give money to anyone simply on the strength of a signature. Still, I hesitated.

Among the rationalizations I had devised to support my gambling was the notion that, as long as I stayed within the financial frame of my weekly salary, I could not be badly hurt. Now it appeared to be necessary to break out of that restriction, and I was reluctant to move. Finally, as always, need overcame hesitation and I borrowed two hundred dollars. I had been informed that, based on my salary, I was qualified to borrow two hundred and fifty dollars for two years. I chose the smaller figure as adequate to my needs and as a demonstration of what seemed to me commendable restraint. I was comforted by the thought that I could easily repay the loan in the two years allowed to me if my luck didn't change and much sooner if it did, as I hoped and believed it would.

With that burden off my mind, I paid off my arrears at the Y, put aside fifty dollars for my mother, and returned to action vowing to do a more careful job of handicapping. The hundred dollars left from the loan lasted five weeks, despite increases in my wagers to five and even ten times as much as I had risked previously. I was pleased to have gotten such a long run out of the money. I was more pleased that my mother's mite remained untouched, and that contributed to the intense enjoyment of being home again, though to enjoy my vacation I first had to overcome a painfully disagreeable development.

Upon my arrival my older brother Harry informed me that my father had died two months earlier, after a long illness, from the effects of Parkinson's disease. He said he and my mother had decided to withhold that information until my arrival, because they had not wanted to upset me, and because it would have been difficult and expensive for me to come home in time for the funeral.

I was outraged. It was the only time in my life when I can remember having been angry with my mother for valid cause. I said I wished they had let me know my father was ill and had given me an opportunity to decide whether to be present at his funeral. I said nothing more but cannot be sure whether I didn't know what else to say or do or whether I was silenced by guilt over my failure for nine years to have been with that troubled man who had been so important to me and could have been more so. Even now, I am not certain whether I was moved by guilt or grief. I remember only my sadness over his absence.

The need to attend to present matters left little time to brood. Jules and Sylvia and their son Stanley had come east to visit the World's Fair of 1939, and my mother spread a grand feast for them. Throughout my visit, I was inundated with dinner invitations, while my mother and brothers fussed over me as if I were a person of consequence. I also dated girls, including one who had been unfriendly before, went to parties, and spent time with Leon and Murray. As though ravenous, I devoured all the good feeling I found, yet seemed to need something more.

For weeks I had planned a special sentimental journey, the reasons for which are not yet clear in my mind. Early on the morning after my arrival, I took the subway to Bowling Green and, starting from The Battery, walked up Broadway, making detours along side streets well remembered from other times. With a junior high school friend, Maurice, I had made Saturday expeditions to explore the city. With other friends, later, I had gone to the restaurants of Chinatown and Little Italy and to Yonah Shimmel's for knishes. Alone, I had explored the fur and garment districts while job hunting and Times Square and Greenwich Village while working for the *New York Times* and the Village Pharmacy. Now, I retraced those steps—whether to try to walk back into the past and thus eliminate what had happened in Cincinnati, I do not know.

It was simply good to feel the security that walking gave me. I stopped for a huge breakfast at Ratner's Dairy restaurant on Second Avenue; I had lunch at a bar and grill on Forty-ninth Street where a steak with onions and french fries and all the bread and pickles anyone could eat still cost only forty-five cents and beer, a nickel; and I accepted an egg cream from my former boss at the Village Pharmacy. It was curiously reassuring to find that everything was as I had remembered, that it was still all there, and that it was, for me, mine.

I remember clearly still the feeling of belonging as I trudged the streets, wanting to be everywhere at once, wanting to experience it fully, as though these places and buildings and people in the streets, like my family and friends, knew me and welcomed me and made me feel that I belonged. No matter what had gone before, I felt stronger for being able to believe that I was not alone here, at home.

18.

SOON after my return from New York I was reminded that, although Cincinnati could not be for me what my hometown was, I had strong ties there, too. I awoke one Sunday morning in my room at the Y with unbearable chest pains. The desk clerk tried to reach a doctor; and when he couldn't I called the RKO office, where a switchboard operator was on duty during weekends, to ask for the house doctor. He wasn't available, but I was put through to the physician covering for him and, as instructed, took a bus to meet him at his office. After a brief examination, the doctor suggested I might be having a heart attack, though apparently not a severe one, since he gave me a bottle of pinkish medicine and instructed me to go back to my room and stay in bed.

I took the medicine as prescribed, but the pain did not let up. The next morning I called Dinny to tell him that I was too sick to work. Luckily for me, his end of our conversation was overheard by Ike Libson, the man who had owned all the Cincinnati theaters which

RKO now owned through purchase from him. Mr. Libson remained interested in the operation as an overseer, pending full payment of the money due him for the property. This morning he was making one of his periodic visits; and, as he often did, he exercised a paternal interest in the people who worked for him.

Mr. Libson instructed Dinny to inform me that he was sending his personal physician to see me. Within minutes, the doctor appeared, examined me, and declared that I was probably suffering from a spontaneous pneumothorax, a collapsed lung for which there was no discernible cause. Rather than wait for an ambulance, the doctor drove me to the hospital in his car. There, his tentative diagnosis was confirmed and treatment proceeded. Within five days I was released from the hospital. My bills for the hospital and the doctor's services were paid by Mr. Libson in an act of generosity that was often needed, but less often forthcoming, in those years before group health insurance became a standard feature of employee compensation.

Mr. Libson was in the tradition of the European immigrants who became movie pioneers after first proving their mettle as small businessmen in other fields. But he was different from the noisier, flamboyant moguls; though, like some of them, he had been a peddler and then the operator of a nickelodeon before becoming the proprietor of the dozen movie theaters he had sold to RKO.

He could have been typecast as a grey-haired big business executive. He was short, a little man who, like my steelworker uncles Daniel and Willy, carried himself in a way that suggested greater size. He wore clothes of British styling, walked, head high, with measured step—like a king, as I remember—and spoke softly in a midwestern accent. I never heard him raise his voice, though he must have done so on occasion. And I never heard anyone speak of Mr. Libson without respect—not merely for his position, but for him as a person. He was, in fact, held in awe by everyone, Dinny as well as the elevator operators, and by no one more than I, who would have been pleased to emulate him.

Upon being discharged from the hospital, I went to Mr. Libson's office to thank him for his generosity. It was the first time I had talked with him, except to say hello when I saw him on his visits to the RKO office. He was solicitous about my recovery, and fatherly in his concern about my well-being, and he took the occasion also to express satisfaction over reports he had received about my work.

The next time we talked, about three months after our first conversation, it was under quite different circumstances. By then, World War II had begun with Hitler's invasion of Poland. By then, also, my life had resumed its familiar pattern. I had moved back into the gambling routine from which I had taken leave during my illness. I felt guilty to be indulging myself in that way while Europe burned, but I also felt compelled to concentrate on my own problems. Once again, I had fallen behind in my rent payments at the Y and had managed only twice to send remittances to my mother despite her urgent need.

During my vacation visit, I had learned that my mother had been laid off at the paper-box factory and worked only now and then as a practical nurse for a disabled elderly woman and as housekeeper for a young widower and his two little daughters. It obviously pained Rube as much to tell me as it hurt me to hear that for six weeks during the past year he and my mother had lived almost entirely on potatoes, at a penny a pound, and milk for a nickel a quart.

My mother had refused to let Rube quit school and go to work full time. She had also declined to ask assistance from my older brother and his wife or from her own brothers and sisters because, I now understand, to do so she would have had to explain why she was in such tight circumstances when I was supposed to be sending her five dollars every week. It is impossible to measure accurately the great shame I felt or the ease with which I dismissed the matter with a promise to myself to make up for my delinquencies as soon as winnings should make that possible.

It was in that frame of mind that I next had an opportunity to talk with Mr. Libson privately. We met in the lobby of the RKO Palace building one evening as I was on my way home after having worked late on a picture layout. He was arriving for a conference with some people from the RKO head office in New York. Protocol in such a situation would have required nothing more than a perfunctory exchange of greetings, and I was prepared for a passing hello as we continued on our separate ways. But Mr. Libson detained me.

"You look well," he said. "How do you feel?"

"I'm all better and I would like to thank you again for all you did for me," I replied.

"I'm glad you are better," he said. "I'm also glad to hear that you are doing a good job in the exploitation department." I replied that I was happy in my work and looking forward to the future.

"Keep up the good work and you'll have a very good future," Mr. Libson said, in what I thought was a parting remark but was not. "How do you like Cincinnati by now?" he asked.

Suddenly our conversation had taken a turn that I could not have expected. "I like Cincinnati very much," I said. "But,"—and this seemed to me later a stroke of genius, since given a moment of rational thought I could not have permitted myself to speak the lie— "I would like it better if my mother and brother were with me."

"Why don't they come?" Mr. Libson asked.

Until then I had not borrowed more than ten dollars from anyone except the bank and was inexperienced in the kind of borrowing about which Damon Runyon said, "a story goes with it." But intuitively now I recognized that such an opportunity had arisen. Presumably without intending to do so, Mr. Libson had presented me with an opening for a big touch.

"It would cost too much to move my family here, and we don't have the money," I replied, in what I hoped was a dignified and perhaps vaguely pathetic tone.

"How much would it cost?" I was delighted to hear Mr. Libson ask. I had no idea, but the figure of two hundred and fifty dollars spontaneously took shape in my mind, probably because that was the loan limit for which I had been qualified at the bank.

"Well, with the cost of moving furniture, the rental deposit for an apartment, and other expenses, I think it would take about two hundred and fifty dollars," I said.

"Would you do it if you had the money?" he asked.

"It would take a little time to make all the arrangements," I said, laying the foundation for a later lie to explain the delay and then the failure of the move to take place if Mr. Libson should inquire in the future. "But," I assured him, "nothing would make me happier than to have my family with me in Cincinnati."

"All right," he said. "If you got a loan of two hundred and fifty dollars, how long do you think it would take you to pay back?"

"I could pay five dollars a week," I said.

"No, no," he said. "That's too much. You will pay two dollars and fifty cents a week. See my secretary at lunch time tomorrow.

She will make the arrangements." And with that he walked into the elevator to go up to his conference.

The immediacy and ease of my success pleased me almost as much as the fact of the success itself. I had not expected so much, so quickly and so effortlessly. I felt I had revealed to myself an unknown and important talent.

AT noon the next day I received a check for two hundred and fifty dollars from Mr. Libson's secretary and signed a note promising to repay that sum, without interest, at the rate of two dollars and fifty cents a week for one hundred weeks. That number, one hundred, suggested longevity in my job and Mr. Libson's confidence in my ability to sustain my obligation into a distant future. In appreciation of that trust, I resolved to make prudent use of my new funds. I had budgeted one hundred and fifty dollars to clear the balance due on my bank loan, twenty dollars to pay my overdue rent, and twenty-five dollars to be sent home—leaving me fifty-five dollars in fresh capital to finance a new effort at big-ticket betting.

However, by the time I got to the bank, my resolve had begun to weaken. I paid only one hundred dollars of the balance, leaving myself with a more substantial reserve for betting. I made it a point of honor to send my mother a money order for twenty-five dollars while I was at the bank and went to the Y to clear my account. All that, I assured myself, showed good faith and good sense on my part.

On the way back to the office, I stopped in at Morris's and placed bets in the amount of thirty dollars, secure in the knowledge that even if these bets lost I still had seventy-five dollars in reserve. That fact inspired the feeling which, next to winning, gave me the greatest satisfaction as a gambler: the knowledge that, even if I lost, I was still "alive" and could try again another time.

Later that afternoon, before going to film row, I stopped in at the horse room and learned I had won ninety dollars. I placed fifty dollars worth of bets. On my way back to the office, I stopped at the horse room again and found I had won another hundred and twenty-five dollars. That raised my cash on hand to three hundred and twenty dollars, more of my own money than I had held before.

I thought, briefly, of repaying Mr. Libson's loan and explaining that a sudden change of heart would keep my mother from Cincinnati. I restrained that impulse, deciding instead to wait for one more winning day. I thought also about clearing the outstanding balance on my bank loan, but the bank was closed. However, the post office was still open, and I sent my mother another money order for twenty-five dollars with a note explaining that I had just been given an unexpected bonus at the office. Then I raced back to the horse room to get the results of some end-of-the-day bets I had left with Morris. I emerged with another hundred dollars in winnings, three hundred and fifteen dollars in all, more by far than I had ever won before in a single day.

That evening I treated myself to an expensive dinner and drinks. Afterward, I was restless, impatient for action, unwilling to wait for the start of another day in the horse room. A fever was on me, much stronger than ever before. I roamed the streets seeking relief, knowing that there was only one cure. I could have gone across the river to the fancy casinos, but lacked the energy to make my way there. I could have played poker for nickels and dimes at the Y, as I sometimes did, but was unwilling to risk what I had for the paltry potential winnings available in that game. I started toward Rad's office, thinking that if he were in we could have a drink. On the way I passed a pool room where, I had been told, a big-money poker game was in action around the clock.

The pool room was on one of the busiest streets in town; and, for that reason, I refrained from doing business there—except when I was short of time and could save the few minutes that would be required to get to and from my regular betting establishment. On such occasions I had observed the poker game and, emboldened by modest successes in small-change poker games, had thought I was good enough to beat the pool-room players if I had a mind to and could put together enough money to get into the game.

On this night both conditions were present. But, in still another exercise of prudence, before going in I returned to the Y and left three hundred dollars in the safekeeping of the night clerk, retaining something more than one hundred dollars for the game. There was a seat open for a table-stakes, pot-limit game, in which a player can bet as much money as there is in the pot at any time, and can bet or be responsible for calling bets in an amount limited to as much money as he has on the table before a new hand is dealt. I placed on the table all the money I had except for coins. That proved to be enough for only half a dozen hands.

Within thirty minutes I had lost all that I had brought with me. Disappointed but not dismayed, I returned wearily to the Y, retrieved my reserve from the clerk, and went to my room to rest for my return to my proper business the next day.

Though I would have preferred to win, I accepted my defeat as a learning experience. I had done something I had thought about for a long time and, at reasonable cost as I counted it, had learned it was something I should not do again. I could have returned to the game with my reserves, but the fever had passed. I seem to have understood that my previous successes at small-stakes poker had not prepared me for this quite different game in which I could not hope to compete successfully against far more competent players. Although I later had many opportunities to play high-stakes poker, I never again tried to make that my game.

REFLECTION on this time of my life has brought to mind a thought that underlies the ambivalence with which I pursued my course as a horseplayer. If I had known another person like me at that time, I would have been disapproving and, given an opportunity, would have strongly urged that person to abandon folly. But I knew no one else like me. As for myself, the curtain drawn around my unsharable secret effectively masked the reality of what I was doing and the need to think about it.

Apart from my willingness to accept the poker debacle as a lesson learned, I expended little or no mental energy on the possible philosophical or psychological meanings of my behavior. I simply went ahead as anyone might—as a painter, a merchant, a scientist, or a shoemaker, regardless of success or the lack of it, might continue painting, buying and selling, experimenting, or making shoes.

The next day at lunchtime I was back where I believed I belonged, in the horse room, eating a sandwich, selecting, betting, hoping. Within a month, I had lost my reserves and was reduced to a more heavily burdened position than before, with the loan from Mr. Libson and a balance remaining on the bank loan.

It was the most difficult time I had yet experienced as a gambler. Each week now my pay was reduced by more than ten percent as I made the required payments to Mr. Libson's secretary and tried to put something aside for monthly payments to the bank. Once again, remittances to my mother became intermittent and then non-existent. And I fell into arrears frequently at the Y, encouraged by the supportive management.

For the first time in my gambling life, I felt uneasy about what I was doing. I continued to hope, and to believe that there was reason to hope, that I would yet become a winner. But I worried about what might happen before that came to pass. It did not occur to me that perhaps I should quit. I thought only about how I might bring closer the great time of the big winning and how to keep going until then.

My most anxious concern was, as it had always been, to maintain the cash flow required to stay in action, and that problem was compounded by a new social development. Jules and Sylvia introduced me to Cherie, a pretty, blonde young woman whose family they knew, and I fell in love with her.

The difficulty arose from the coolness of Cherie's parents toward me. They, I later learned, preferred another suitor; a man three years older than I who was a successful salesman of children's clothing. He drove a Packard, dressed fashionably, and clearly was already in a position to be a good provider.

In an effort to impress Cherie's parents with my own stature, I brought gifts of flowers or candy or took her to dinner, alternating the two procedures to limit the drain on my resources. My extravagances had no apparent effect on Cherie's parents, and I began to worry about how to maintain this burden and a longer-than-usual losing streak through which I was then passing.

That dilemma was resolved for me through a disagreeable coincidence in Morris's horse room. I walked into the place early one Saturday afternoon with two dollars, hoping to win enough to finance a big date with Cherie that night, and was astonished to find Cherie's father there, talking to Morris.

Normally, I would have appeared at Morris's an hour later. But I had completed my Saturday morning chores, doing my laundry and getting a haircut, much earlier than usual, and with nothing better to do had, by a stroke of bad luck, gone on to the horse room early. As I walked from the bright sunlight through the dark foyer into the gloomy room, I was temporarily blinded. When my eyes could focus clearly, I saw Morris in cheerful conversation with another older man who, even with his back toward me, seemed somehow familiar. Bewildered, I recognized Cherie's father.

A quick retreat might have averted a confrontation. But I paused long enough to wonder what he might be doing in a place like this. Surely, he wasn't a bettor. If he were, why should he have come all the way downtown from his apartment in Avondale to place a bet? Unable to answer these questions, I turned to beat a hasty retreat. He turned at the same time and saw me.

I felt as I had when Aunt Minnie trapped me with Uncle Louis's quarters. I knew there was nothing I could say which would make any difference, so I smiled weakly, nodded in greeting, and left— hoping that he might think anything but the truth. I realized that there was no chance of an agreeable outcome, but I still had some bets to make. I went to the pool room on Vine Street and placed my bets there.

Later that afternoon, Cherie called me. She could not meet me that night, she said. She would not meet me ever again. I was not surprised by that news, having assumed that, whatever the relationship between Morris and her father, her father would have inquired about me and Morris would have told him all there was to tell. Once that sordid story became known to her father, I understood that I could not hope to see Cherie ever again.

I accepted that as socially correct, but was surprised to learn that Morris was Cherie's uncle, brother of her mother. When I found time to think about it, it seemed to me unfair that as sheet man for a bookmaker Morris was regarded as a big shot by his family, who considered horseplayers like me unworthy of respectful attention.

The break with Cherie hurt, particularly since the circumstances were uncomfortably similar to those which had led to the break with Gladys less than three years earlier. I wondered whether I could ever hope to manage a proper relationship with a woman. But I was more concerned with an immediate question, the fear that this exposure might shatter the shield of secrecy behind which I had thus far managed to hide my nefarious dealings with bookmakers.

As far as I could determine, none of my family, friends, acquaintances, or colleagues had any knowledge of my gambling. Now it seemed possible that everyone might find out. It seemed reasonable to expect that what her parents had learned they might report to their friends, Jules and Sylvia. If that happened, Jules might pass on such information to Dinny, who was his friend as well as an important client. And if he did, I couldn't know what might happen to me.

For days I sought anxiously for signs, but found none. Jules and Sylvia, in fact, seemed unaware that my romance with Cherie was over. Except for the end of the affair, nothing seemed to have changed. One day I saw Cherie and her older sister downtown. They looked at me blankly, as at a stranger. Uncertain, I made no effort to greet them. Otherwise, things went on as before.

21.

UNTHINKING and, to a degree, unaware, I moved through repeated cycles of betting—winning some, losing more, then raising money to bet again. More and more often toward the end of losing days, I had to race back to the Y to scrounge short-term loans for last-minute bets, ashamed of what I was doing but comforted by the knowledge that, as promised, I repaid these debts on schedule. I had also converted a business friendship into a small-loan source in the person of Dave, a fellow of my age who managed the exploitation department at the Paramount exchange.

Dave planned to make a career on the business side of the film industry and was clearly on his way. He did his job efficiently, was well-regarded by his superiors and customers, and conducted himself with a pleasant self-confidence I envied. Dave looked as though type-cast for the role of a success. He wore good clothes, always pressed, which made a slight paunch less noticeable. His shoes were shined every day, and he told me he had his hair cut every week. That seemed extravagant, though it made me wonder whether I should have my hair cut more frequently than once in two or three weeks. What impressed me most was that he had his finger nails manicured. Of all the other men I knew, only Dinny had his nails manicured. That put Dave in Dinny's class—a high class to be in, I thought.

More important, Dave was forthcoming. Toward the end of a losing day, while there was still time for late bets, I told him I needed financing for a hot date that night, and he had loaned me five dollars. Thereafter, I counted on him as part of my short-term financing network. Dave must have wondered why I couldn't manage my funds more efficiently, but said nothing, no matter how often I tapped him.

Despite the growing number of willing creditors, the availabilities grew inadequate to my needs. My loans from the bank and Mr. Libson had exhausted my long-term borrowing possibilities, and my quick-loan syndicate already included everyone from whom I would have permitted myself to borrow. I wouldn't have allowed myself to borrow from anyone at the RKO office, because that was too close to home. And I think I would rather have died than try to borrow from Whit or Rad or Jules. Their regard for me as a sober, honest, responsible young man was too important to be put to the risk of exposure a loan request would have entailed.

Other sources were needed, and there was only one other I had never before allowed myself to contemplate using—the money advanced to me at the Palace Theater for trips to film row. Now, to think was to act. I cannot recall the first time I misused company funds, but it soon became a habit. On days when my lunch-time and midafternoon bets failed, or during periods of empty pockets, I used the film-row money to make late bets. When I won, there was no problem. I returned the advance funds to the Palace Theater manager before going up to my office in the morning. When I lost, as more often I did, I had to scurry about, trying to borrow the money needed to make good the company advance.

The new system reduced the number of times I would otherwise have had to canvas my neighbors at the Y for loans, since my company-funded bets did win occasionally. I considered that a significant advantage, because I felt demeaned whenever I asked anyone for a loan, no matter the story that went with such requests. Still, the process of misusing company money and then searching out short-term rescuers when that money was lost caused a great deal of tension. I came to wonder why I did it, why I couldn't forego the dangerous procedure and restrict myself to betting only when I had cash of my own safely in hand. As I wondered, I continued on the perilous path.

Almost every day now, I announced trips to film row but went instead with the cash advances to the horse room. I am surprised to recall that no one questioned the frequency of those trips, though probably I could have managed satisfactory explanations. Nor were questions raised about the fact that so often I returned in full the money advanced to me, having bought nothing. I can only suppose that, since I was trusted, there was no cause for suspicion.

Still, that was unusual. Usually, the greatest care was taken with theater money. Every penny was carefully accounted for, money counting being the most important function performed by the bonded managers and assistant managers of the theaters. In such an atmosphere, it is difficult for me to understand why what seems to have been clearly questionable behavior was not challenged.

On my part, it could be argued that I was asking to be caught, and that may be so. I was tired, witless, and wanted nothing so much as to find a way out of an increasingly intolerable predicament.

Many years later, during a discussion of the war in Vietnam, I heard a woman express the fervent wish that America would end its involvement. "We ought to drop the bomb and wipe them out or just get out and forget about the whole thing," she said. I could understand her irrational equation between unilateral withdrawal and nuclear destruction of Vietnam as an expression of a somewhat similar ambivalence I think I felt during this crisis time in Cincinnati. I wanted the pressure removed, preferably through winnings which could put everything right. But I suspect that I may have been willing to accept, if not welcome, any resolution, no matter how painful, that would allow me to put this terrible problem behind me.

Encouraged by the ease with which I could manipulate the funds, I continued using the advance purchase money for bets, then borrowing at the Y to correct and hide these repeated petty larcenies. Twice, I encountered serious difficulties in raising overnight loans to make good the misused money—once struggling down to the wire and getting the last dollar I needed from a neighbor during breakfast at the Y, less than an hour before the deadline for turning in my cash and receipts.

On another occasion, I was not so lucky. I had signed a voucher for a ten-dollar advance at the Palace box office and by half past five had lost all the money at the horse room. As usual in the circumstances, I headed toward the Y to find someone who could lend me the funds to recover the petty-cash voucher with my signature that was being held at the theater.

My quest opened with a quick, but small, victory. The first person I asked, a young man who had a room on my floor, loaned me two dollars. Frequently in the past, when I had generally limited the advances to five dollars and spent only two or three on film row, two dollars would have been enough or almost enough to solve my problem. But, tonight, two dollars left me needing eight more, and I could find no one at the Y who could or would make them available to me. I asked everyone I had borrowed from in the past and added to those several residents I barely knew and would never have touched before. No one was able or willing to help.

By nine that night, I was forced to realize that I faced a serious problem. I called Dave at the Paramount exchange, hoping that he might be working late, but no one answered. I would have gone to his home in Walnut Hills, but I didn't know the exact address. I thought of taking a bus to Walnut Hills to roam the streets in hope of running into him, but dismissed that as a probable waste of time and bus fare.

Faced with the possibility of what would be the ultimate horror—disgrace and discharge—I tried to ease my anxiety by calling to mind the contingency plan for such a situation, fashioned when I had first started playing this dangerous game. The plan was simply to explain that I had lost the money by accident before I could spend any of it. That approach had seemed sure-fire to me at first. Mulling it over now, it seemed to have no more persuasive force than the explanations I had made to Aunt Minnie about the two quarters that belonged to Uncle Louis. I had little faith that this story could save me from the fate that awaited me, unless I could raise eight dollars more.

In that condition, on the brink of doom, I made a decision that still puzzles me. I refused to ask help from Whit, Rad, Jules, or Dinny, though any one of them could have provided the funds I needed to save myself. I reasoned that in order to ask help from one of them I would have to describe my predicament and the reasons for it and thus exposed, whether or not I received the money, I would have destroyed my relationship with the lender. I continued to hope that I could find salvation elsewhere.

I didn't think about Leon or Murray at home, from either of whom I would surely have received the required funds by telegraphic money order. But my friends at home didn't figure in my calculations.

At ten o'clock, I was no nearer a solution than I had been after receiving the two-dollar loan at the very start of my quest. I was desperate and also hungry, having eaten nothing since lunch. Since the cost of the repast, thirty-five cents including tip, could not greatly affect my financial situation, I went to the Coney Island Chili House on Vine Street and consumed a platter of chili on spaghetti and a Coke.

As I was eating, it occurred to me that there was a lender from whom I might be able to borrow the eight dollars and thirty-five cents I now needed: my bookmaker—not Morris the sheet man, who went home to his family in Avondale each evening immediately after the last payoff, but Chubby, the tall, fleshy man who owned the book where I did business and was rumored to have two or three other stands as well. I saw him often at the horse room, where he came several times each day to check the action. Occasionally, I had also observed him at a bar behind the Palace building that was frequented by the higher-paid members of the RKO staff.

Chubby seemed the perfect solution. I was a very good customer, having lost more than a thousand dollars—half my pay—during the past two years. That seemed sufficient reason for him to help me in my time of need—if I could find him.

I found Chubby at the first stop in my search. He was sitting with a man I didn't know at a table in the bar behind the Palace. He smiled in cordial greeting, and I restrained myself from the impulse to blurt my story, as I might have done if the stranger had not been present. Calmly, I asked if I might speak to him alone.

Chubby's demeanor changed. As though anticipating something disagreeable, he withdrew his smile and said, "Yeah," without enthusiasm. Still, he rose from the table and walked out to the street with me. There, under a street light, Chubby stood with his shoulders back, paunch forward, as though braced for an anticipated assault.

He listened stolidly as I told him my story. It was the first time

I had ever told anyone the truth about any aspect of my gambling. Chubby was unmoved. I don't know whether any story in support of a loan request could have evoked a sympathetic response from Chubby. The truth did not. Having asked Chubby to lend me ten dollars, to include meal money for the next day or two, I was appalled to hear him say:

"Sorry, no dice."

"What do you mean?" I asked.

"I mean I'm not lending you any money," he said.

"Why?" I argued. "I'm a good customer. Ask Morris."

"I know that," he said. "That's business. This is not my business."

"But I'm not asking for a lot . . . make it only eight dollars and thirty-five cents. That's how much I really need. I've got to have it," I pleaded.

"Not from me," he replied.

"Why not?" I wanted to know.

"Because if you get out of this deal, you're only going to get into more trouble; and you better face it now," he explained.

"But I won't," I assured him. "I'll never do anything like this again."

"Bullshit. You'll do it again and again and again. This way, maybe you'll have to stop."

I bristled. He had benefited from the evil deeds he seemed to be criticizing and now was unctuously declining to help me put things right. However, this was no time to debate rights and wrongs. He held all the cards. I groveled.

"Please, Chubby. I've always paid my tabs on time. I'll pay this one, too. If you don't lend me the money, I'm dead. They'll fire me. My life will be destroyed."

"Maybe they'll fire you, maybe they won't. Whatever happens, you won't be dead. Your life won't be destroyed. Take it from me," he said smugly. "This could be the best thing that ever happened to you."

"Chubby, Chubby," I pleaded. "I can't take it. Please lend me the money. I promise you'll never have any reason to regret helping me."

"That's the first true thing you said," he said. "I won't have any reason for regret, because I'm not lending you the money in the first place."

"Please."

"No." He turned and walked back into the bar. I slunk away into the shadows, sick at heart yet still concerned whether anyone might have seen me talking with Chubby.

Chubby's rejection cut my last tie to hope. My depression was not so deep, apparently, as to provoke thoughts of suicide. Rather, I was resigned to my fate. I had done everything I could think to do. Now, I could only try to convince my superiors that I had lost the money accidently. If they believed me, all would be well. If they did not, there was nothing more I could do to save myself. I went to my room and spent a fitful night in bed.

22.

In the morning I shaved, showered, and dressed meticulously—as later, during World War II, I did before going out on bombing missions. So prepared, I went forward to meet my fate, pausing en route for a full breakfast of sausages and eggs, which reduced my dollar and sixty-five cents to a dollar and thirty cents. When I arrived at the manager's office in the Palace, the manager, Mr. Bock, greeted me with a smile which did not survive my first words.

"I have a big problem," I confided. "I lost the ten dollars I took for an advance yesterday. I don't know how it got lost, but I didn't have it when I got home from film row last night."

"Oh," he said. "Do you have any purchase receipts?"

"No, there was nothing to buy. I lost the ten dollars," I explained.

"Oh," he said. "Okay. I'll be in touch with you later."

With the fat in the fire, I assumed that Mr. Bock would call Dinny and perhaps the general manager, Colonel Frudenfeld, or Mr. Libson. I was frightened but tried to assure myself that there was no way they could prove I was lying and hadn't lost the money accidentally.

I tried to believe that the worst they could do would be to dock me for the amount lost.

Back at my desk in the small office across the corridor from Dinny's, I tried to appear busy and unconcerned. Phones rang everywhere. Dinny walked from his office to the Colonel's office, returned to his office and talked on the telephone, then went back to the general manager's office, closing the door behind him—something that was done only when serious matters were being discussed in Colonel Frudenfeld's office.

Finally, Dinny emerged stone-faced from Colonel Frudenfeld's sanctum, came to my desk, and informed me that the colonel wished to see me. As I walked into the general manager's office I was no longer hopeful. The colonel, a tall, balding, distinguished-looking man, was sitting behind his desk. Usually smiling and benign, he looked now like a vengeful god preparing to wreak his wrath upon a miserable sinner.

"Sit down," he said, motioning me to a chair in front of his desk while he leaned back, as though readying himself to loose a bolt of lightning.

Seeking whatever advantage the first words might give me, I said, "I'm sorry about losing the money. I don't know how it happened. I'll be glad to make it good, of course."

He sat silent for a moment then said, "That won't be necessary. You know, in business, company money is a sacred trust. If we can't trust people, we can't have them working for us."

"But I couldn't help losing the ten dollars," I protested.

"I'm afraid that isn't so," he replied, speaking slowly and, I thought, with some effort now to appear sympathetic. "I'm afraid we have reason to believe that you lost it not by accident but by gambling.

"And," he concluded, "I'm afraid there is no longer a place for you in this organization."

Waves of shame and guilt and fear swept over me, threatening to drown me before I could leave his office. Visions of a career destroyed, of valued friendships lost, of painful disappointment for my mother when she learned what had happened, assailed me.

"I'm terribly sorry," I said, without further trying to dispute him.

"I am, too," he said.

When I returned to my desk, near tears, Dinny came into my

office. He seemed to be trying to be sympathetic, but I sensed that he was greatly disappointed and angry with me, as I knew he had every reason to be. He had sponsored me, taken the responsibility for me, and I had repaid him in this shabby way. I wanted to apologize, but didn't know what to say.

He said, "It's too bad. But at least you're not being left high and dry. You're getting two weeks salary instead of notice. Also, Mr. Libson told me to tell you that he is tearing up your note, so you don't have to worry about what you owe him. The ten dollars, too. You can clean out your desk and leave when you're ready."

Whit came by to ask what was going on. I told him. "Christ, kid, why the hell didn't you call me last night? You could have had the money, and this wouldn't have happened. Good Christ," he repeated. "Come on out to the house tonight," he suggested. For the first time I declined an invitation from him. I said I would call him that evening.

Then, suddenly, I couldn't bear to remain in the office any longer, knowing that all the clerks, secretaries, and bookkeepers were talking about the scandal I had visited upon the company. I ran out and hid in the stairwell on the floor above and cried hard for a long time.

At noon, when I could expect that everyone except the switchboard operator would be out to lunch, I went back to my office to take a few personal things from my desk and collect my severance check, which had been left in an envelope atop my desk.

I ate a large lunch, the blue plate special at the Wheel Cafe: Swiss steak, with mashed potatoes and gravy and string beans. Then, I spent the afternoon in bed, thinking through my alternatives. There was only one thing to do. I would go home. Almost certainly, I could not expect to find a job in Cincinnati, since any prospective employer would surely check with my previous employer. And I had no desire to stay. The only question was how to explain things to my mother. I settled on a mixture of truth and fiction.

I wrote a letter to her explaining that I had been "let go" because business was slow and the company was cutting back. In the summer of 1940, during the "phony war" period when Hitler seemed to be resting upon his successes in Poland and Western Europe and the war-preparation boom was only beginning to get under way in the United States, stories such as mine were not uncommon. The unemployment rate was still high, and jobs were hard to find and sometimes hard to keep.

Mailing the letter made me feel better. I had done as much as I could do for the moment. I then called Whit, as I had promised, and Rad, as well, and received a call from Jules. All were sympathetic and solicitous. Each asked why I had not come to him for help, a question I could not answer. Each suggested we get together. Whit invited me to spend a few days at his home, and Jules, at his; I accepted the offer from Jules, knowing I could expect comfort without conversation and questions. I spent a peaceful weekend with Jules and Sylvia and their son, Stanley.

Monday morning, a load of coal was delivered, dumped on the driveway near the basement window through which ordinarily an itinerant handy man would have shoveled it into the bin below. Over Sylvia's objection, I insisted upon doing that job. I stripped to the waist and, working for hours in the bright sun, moved the coal into the basement. In the process, I suffered severe sunburn.

For two days I lay in great pain, while Sylvia alternately applied towels soaked in cold water and vinegar and smeared me with ointment. When the burning subsided I felt whole and strong again, as though I had been purified in a ritual by fire.

I was further strengthened by receipt of a letter from my older brother, Harry, declaring that while everyone was sorry to learn that I had lost my job, my return home was being happily awaited. Now, if I could be sure that exposure of my evil deeds would be confined to Cincinnati, I could go home without further pain. After another day of rest, I felt well enough to pack and say my goodbyes.

When I arrived at his office, Rad was busy with a batch of reviews for movies that had opened that week. I suggested that I could help expedite the work by writing one. I had never written a review or any other "official" copy for a daily newspaper, my efforts having been confined to press releases and picture captions. I wondered how it would feel to write something on assignment and have it published under my by-line. To my happy surprise, Rad accepted my proposal as a way of speeding things up so we could have time to go out for a drink.

He assigned me to a review of an unimportant film which I had already seen. The most distinctive feature of this poor film was that seven authors had received writing credit for it. I began my review with the observation that this film was a case of too many cooks having spoiled the plot. Rad was pleased.

"What are we going to use for a by-line?" he asked. "We can't use the name of an RKO employee." I didn't correct him, realizing that my name would be unsuitable whether as a present or former employee of the company showing the film. I offered several suggestions, none of which suited Rad.

Finally, he said, "I've got it. We'll sign it 'T.L.O.' That would stand for 'The Little Outsider.'" Although I would have preferred my own name, I found Rad's proposal acceptable because the chosen signature seemed aptly to describe what my position had been in Cincinnati, though I wouldn't have thought it had been apparent to Rad.

Over drinks I told him that I planned to leave for home the next day.

"Oh, no," he said. "You can't do that. Whit and I are planning to give you a proper send-off tomorrow night."

We met the next evening for drinks, after which we went for dinner to the Netherland Plaza Hotel, Cincinnati's finest in those days, where Whit's stepfather was the wine steward. We were given VIP treatment, a fine dinner, and drinks, including a bottle of champagne sent to our table by Whit's stepfather.

We went on to visit more bars, some that I had never noticed before. And we talked, mainly about how unfair life could be. When we stopped drinking, at a time when more orderly people were preparing to rise and go to work, none of us had enough strength, or sense, to do more than stagger down the street to a cheap hotel, where we flopped on bed and floor to sleep off our fatigue.

Late that afternoon, we awoke warily, each managing his hangover distress as best he could. We said our goodbyes and went our separate ways. "So long, T.L.O.," Rad said as he headed toward his office. Whit went home. I went back to Avondale, to pick up my luggage and exchange goodbyes with Jules and Sylvia.

I had planned to travel to New York by bus. Now, inspired by my unexpectedly grand farewell, I decided that it would be more suitable to spend another three or four dollars and go in style, by train. I resisted the further inclination to buy a sleeper berth and was pleased with my compromise.

Jules drove me to the Union Station for the overnight train, trying to be cheerful but succeeding no more than I. Aboard the train I dined on cold fried chicken, fruit, and cake, which Sylvia had packed for me. In the morning, I shaved in the men's room before going into the dining car for a breakfast of pancakes, eggs, and sausages served on a white linen tablecloth set with china and heavy silverware. Then I was home, where, despite the tensions of the past, I didn't have to feel like an outsider and could still keep to myself the unsharable secret that in Cincinnati I had become a compulsive gambler.

PART THREE

TIME OUT

23.

MY homecoming was as my older brother had said it would be. Any anxiety I might have felt disappeared in the warmth of my welcome. The people to whom I had returned seeking refuge were pleased to have me among them again and were sympathetic about the loss of my job. Ignorant of the truth, they assumed I had made a valiant effort to succeed, and they considered that more important than my unfortunate defeat. Guilt, never more than a thought away, troubled me but could not prevent me from feeling secure, content, whole—as though my return had freed me from some terrible confinement.

Reassured by the welcome, I dismissed the scandal as a bad dream best forgotten. Then, as though by keeping busy I could keep Cincinnati off my mind, I occupied myself energetically with family, friends, work, sex, and politics. Long afterward, I thought of those eighteen months before I left home again, this time to go to war, as a time of sunshine days and nights filled with small, rich pleasures of a kind that mark in memory a particular time in the past as the good old days.

There was one disappointment, however. I had hoped to find work at one of the dozen daily newspapers then being published in New York or with a public-relations organization. But, after almost two months of job hunting, the only work I would find was on the assembly line of a factory which produced gas-fired kitchen stoves. Though it was not what I had hoped for, the job was less disappointing than it might have seemed at the start of my search. I liked working with the kind of people I had known when I was delivering lunches for Uncle Louis, and the pay check I received each week gave me a feeling of entitlement rare for me at that time.

My mother had a new job as a cook, a labor of love, preparing breakfast and lunch for boys, many of them refugees from Hitler's Germany, who attended a Jewish parochial school, a yeshiva in Williamsburg. My brother Rube, a member of the Arista Honor Society at Boys High was waiting to enter the City College of New York in September and had a summer job and the promise of after-school employment in the fall.

Their earnings and my contributions to the family purse, which I swore to myself would continue without default, made us feel we were living on Easy Street, a rich new status most clearly apparent at my mother's table. I do not know how she managed to work eight hours a day preparing breakfast and lunch for the yeshiva boys and then come home to cook delicious dinners for us. We simply took it for granted that we would eat well every night and superbly well on Friday, when my mother took special pains to honor the sabbath in our fifth-floor tenement apartment overlooking the Rheingold brewery behind our building.

Thinking now of that time, I remember with a still-fresh feeling of pleasure the sweetness of my life in the interval before I and then my brother Rube, followed by Harry—by then a father—went off to war. I spent more time than ever before with my mother and Rube, visited favorite aunts and uncles, and, at my mother's urging, made time for unexpectedly pleasant visits with Aunt Mary, who surely would not have been pleased to see me if she had known of my disgrace in Cincinnati. I spent time with Leon and Murray, made new friends, and was invited to join the Bo Cab S.C., a status symbol as highly regarded in my set as being tapped for one of the campus clubs or fraternities would be for an Ivy Leaguer.

Speaking of those prewar months as a sweet time does not contradict the other reality—that this was also a painfully anxious time. The sweetness came, I think, from the courage and strength of the people with whom I shared that time. We enjoyed our pleasures despite a gnawing awareness that we could expect worse to come. World War II was already ten months old when I came home, and, though the United States had thus far stayed out of the fighting, we realized that we could become involved at any time. Meanwhile, we tried to make the best of what there was.

Our tensions may have been eased by talking about what faced us. I cannot previously remember so much political discussion and so much to talk about. Cincinnatians surely were as concerned about the state of the world as the Brooklynites of Williamsburg. But the people I knew there in show business and show-business journalism had spent little time on politics. During the past year they had been interested in a campaign by the film industry, competing against the attractions of radio, to persuade the public that "Motion pictures are your best entertainment"—a slogan supported by a string of impressive movies, among them *Gone With The Wind, The Grapes of Wrath, The Wizard of Oz, Stagecoach, Ninotchka, Goodbye Mr. Chips,* and *Rebecca.*

At home, in July 1940, when all of western Europe except for neutral Switzerland and Sweden and embattled Britain had become German by conquest or alliance, people were receptive to political chat and any of several trigger words could set off discussion or debate anywhere at any time. Sure-fire starters included: *appeasement,* the British and French policy, passively accepted by the United States, which allowed Hitler to take Austria and Czechoslovakia and join with Mussolini in helping Franco destroy democracy in Spain; *non-aggression pact,* the treaty between Hitler and Stalin in August 1939 which was followed days later by Hitler's *blitzkrieg* invasion of Poland, the first act of World War II; *phony war,* the label applied to the half year after Hitler's victory in Poland when no one raised a finger against him, while the Germans rested and reinforced themselves before opening a new offensive in the spring of 1940. With this new assault, they conquered Denmark, Norway, Holland, Belgium, Luxembourg, and—after outflanking the Maginot Line, which was supposed to have kept France safe—defeated the French and captured Paris a month before my homecoming.

The one event that could be considered a victory for those nations opposed to Hitler was the evacuation of three hundred and forty thousand Allied troops from the French port of Dunkirk during ten days at the end of May and early in June. The situation had improved by the fall as the heavily outnumbered Royal Air Force fliers defeated the Luftwaffe in the Battle of Britain, shooting down twenty-three hundred German airplanes while losing about nine hundred of their own. But, as the Nazis made clear with an extended blitz of nighttime terror-bombing against London and other British cities, there was much more horror to come. We talked a lot about that and what to do about whatever might happen.

Representatives of every point of view competed for attention with their ideas about what might happen and how we should react. Of those eligible to vote, as many as ninety percent in many election districts of Williamsburg resolved the issue by voting for Franklin Delano Roosevelt. But more than a few also listened to what the also-rans had to say. I voted for the first time and cast my ballot for FDR's third term, though with reservations. I admired President Roosevelt but had been deeply disappointed by his passive acceptance of the appeasement policy, which got Hitler to Spain, and the fraudulent policy of neutrality, which severely limited aid to the legal government of Spain while allowing Hitler and Mussolini to give Franco what he needed to destroy democracy in his country.

I had been outraged by appeasement and its consequences, but had not fully understood the whys and wherefores. I began to read more seriously than before, to attend meetings, and to speak up on issues of interest to me, until I began to think of myself as a responsible and responsive citizen of the world.

As it turned out, I remained most urgently a horseplayer. It was no easy matter at this point in my life to move back into action. But, after more than three months without a bet, I managed it. I wonder still that, to do so, I was willing to risk endangering all the good things that had become precious to me. But the need to return to action was irresistible.

If asked, I would have said that, apart from my unsatisfactory job situation, I was happy with my life and hopeful that my career prospects would improve in time. I would have said also that I saw no reason to resume gambling. Yet I did resume, and in so doing I have come to recognize an enabling mechanism that converted me from a briefly arrested compulsive to a born-again gambler.

The process seems to have been activated by what I have come to recognize as my automatic compensating reaction to good fortune: the belief that I was undeserving. That seems to have been accompanied by a good deal of guilt and by lunatic logic, which enabled me to dismiss reality with yes-but arguments and to treat rational thought as naive while making self-imprisonment in compulsion seem an exercise of sensible free will.

Although specific issues arose from time to time, the basic, ongoing debate in my mind involved a series of standard arguments and responses. I could tell myself that it was foolishly wasteful to keep losing money which could be put to better uses, that my hopes for a better outcome had been disappointed over and over again, that I had been at it long enough to know that I really didn't stand a chance of winning. Yes, lunatic logic would respond. There is something in that, but what has happened so far isn't necessarily what should be expected to happen in the future, when the law of averages finally should start to work. Besides, with all the losing, I wasn't on my way to the poorhouse so why make such a fuss? Stay with it. One more time. Give it a real chance to happen.

Invariably, the result would be a comforting ambivalence which permitted me to think of self-defeating decisions as reasonable compromises between what I knew I should do and what I felt I must do. Thus armed, as in Cincinnati, I was able to strike a deal with myself to resolve the contradictory family traditions I had carried out of childhood and to balance accounts through the double-entry bookkeeping of my ambivalence, which required debits to offset satisfactions.

The terms of that deal required me to honor the tradition of respectable effort and social concern by working steadily, meeting my household obligations without interruption, avoiding further misbehavior of the Cincinnati kind, and otherwise behaving as a responsible, responsive citizen of the community. Having met these prerequisites, I could then feel free to act in accordance with my understanding of the family's more compelling competitive tradition of moneyed success above all else, depending on gambling to make me a success or help me become successful.

In arriving at my decision, I may have understood that, more surely than with my first bet in Henny's horse room or with my action in Cincinnati, I was choosing a direction for my life. I took my time, weeks, before making up my mind. Then I went back into action, hurrying to make up for lost time, while also holding tightly to all the good things I had found in my new life at home.

The process cannot have worked as smoothly as I have reconstructed it through memory, but it worked. Within six weeks after starting my job at the gas-range factory, I was back in action. It didn't escape my attention that, two years after my departure for Cincinnati, I was back where I had started.

BEING back in action made me feel comfortable and complete, as though something vital to my functioning had been taken away and was now restored. The drain on my energies imposed by the internal debate over whether to do it was replaced by elation over what I thought of as regained freedom. On that high, I moved ahead in a sort of easy, ambivalent equilibrium between what I knew I should do and what I simply needed to do.

To safeguard myself against excessive damage, I adopted what seemed to me two sensible limits. First, I pledged that in no circumstance would I borrow money. That limited my potential overall losses, in case things went against me. In addition, I decided that I would no longer spread myself thin trying to handicap races at as many as half a dozen tracks, but would concentrate my efforts on just one track and the seven races that were then the daily maximum. That would limit the number of times I could lose, if things went against me.

In addition to such fail-safe protection, my purpose in confining myself to one track was the expectation that, by focusing on fewer horses, I would improve my chances of winning. I did not understand, and would have argued against, the first law of probabilities: that each bet is a new opportunity to lose, more probably, than to win. Or, as a nameless wise person put it: you can beat a race, but you cannot beat the races. I didn't think about such things. I simply proceeded to do what I had decided I must do.

Adding action to an already-crowded agenda was no problem. I think one of the "secrets" which explains my endurance as a gambler is the apparent ease with which I managed the gambling without noticeably detracting from my other activities. As before, the calls made on my time and energy by my return to action were easily satisfied.

At work I became a client of Eddie, a nervous, worried-looking man who delivered sandwich lunches from his grocery store, took bets, and made small loans on which he charged interest of twenty percent per week. Eddie tried hard to persuade his clients that he was merely a runner for an anonymous bookmaker and an anonymous lender, but no one believed that. We took it for granted that the lender, the bookie, and Eddie were the same person.

More important to me than the gossip about this one-man conglomerate was the fact that Eddie was reliable. He delivered lunches on time, showed up at the end of the lunch period to take bets for the afternoon, accepted wagers at his store after work from anyone who was still in action at that time, and, when there were winners, paid off promptly—carefully rubbing each bill between thumb and forefinger to make sure that two bills hadn't clung together.

All that was required to prepare myself for the day's business with Eddie was a minor reorganization of my daily travel arrangements. Previously, in good weather, I had walked to and from the factory, which was about two miles from home. Now, in good weather and bad, I went each morning to a newsstand on Broadway to buy the *Morning Telegraph,* then boarded the Flushing Avenue street car for a twenty-minute ride which gave me enough time to examine entries for the first two races. During the lunch break, I studied two or three more races and placed bets before returning to work. If I had the wherewithal and the stomach for further action after work, I completed my perusal of past performances in the locker room, then stopped in at Eddie's grocery to place bets on the last race or two. On my days off, I accomplished what needed to be done in one or two quick visits to Henny's horse room.

Gambling occupied me in other ways. I daydreamed about the big winnings that awaited me at some point in the future and about the grand things I would then do for my mother and others. To fill idle moments, I also did mathematical doodles, calculating payoffs on various betting combinations. I was particularly impressed to find that one way to win a million dollars (actually $1,048,576), starting with one dollar, is to parlay twenty even-money winners.

Having already encountered substantial difficulty in trying to find just one even-money winner, I understood that it might be very difficult, or impossible, to pick twenty in a row. Nevertheless, I continued to believe that I could look forward to a big payoff from the law of averages eventually. For me, the only question was how big. What was reasonable to expect? How much would it take to satisfy me? If not a million, then how much? Ten thousand dollars? A hundred thousand? Something less than a million but more than ten thousand, I would have said, if pressed. I could leave the specific amount to be determined at another time.

Thinking about winning big led me into another problem, a paranoid fear of being denied. I thought about big hits in the future— not millions, but thousands, certainly—and worried that bookmakers unwilling or unable to pay might welsh on me. I wondered whether Eddie would be able to pay off as much as a thousand-dollar hit from the profits of the one- and two-dollar bets he booked. I doubted that Henny could do any better.

Only at the track, I thought, could I find insurance of the kind I wanted. But I had never been to a track. For more than three years as a horse player I had dealt only with bookmakers. I had never seen a race live. Now, it seemed to me, was the time to parlay two curiosities: to see how a race is run and to scout the facilities for big-time betting and big-time winnings.

I made my debut as a race-goer at Empire City—a mouldy ruin just over the city line in Westchester county which has long since been rebuilt into Yonkers Raceway, a track for harness horses. I went on a cloudy Saturday afternoon, on the spur of the moment, after turning down an invitation from Murray to play handball.

My debut as a railbird left me with mixed feelings of a kind I had experienced after my first Chinese meal. I didn't really like it very much; but, on the other hand, I didn't hate it and thought I should give it a chance, try to understand it, and thus might acquire a taste for it. To do that I would have to overcome my first impression, which was that, except for the exposure to fresh air, the Empire City track had much the same feel as Henny's horse room.

A concrete "lawn" between the track and the gray grandstand reminded me of a penitentiary exercise yard in a James Cagney gangster movie, and the unsmiling crowd—almost all men in that time when playing the horses was considered unwomanly—looked like inmates whose applications for parole had just been denied without right of appeal. I had to remind myself that, as at Henny's, I hadn't come for the ambience.

There was an important difference between my first time at Henny's and my debut at Empire City. On the day I became a horse-room horseplayer, I had been helped by the guidance of my mentor, Jackie. For my debut as a railbird, I had come to the track alone. I was without the technical assistance of a friend, peer, or immediate age superior who could have made it easier for me to learn how to bet by giving the bet-taker the post-position number of the horse rather than the animal's name, how to locate the starting gate on the other side of the track (it was moved to different positions for races at different lengths), and how to watch a race as it was being run.

What should have been most attractive about a visit to the track— the opportunity to watch the races—was most frustrating. Standing on the lawn, I found it difficult to see clearly what was happening in races which started and, for most of their course, were run half a mile or more from the grandstand. Across the track, I could see a moving group of hunched figures topped by the colored silk caps which identify the jockeys and their mounts. What I watched was tersely described by the track announcer calling the order in which the horses passed various points in the race. Without that assistance I would have been in the dark.

Technology has improved matters. Now, closed-circuit television monitors in racetrack grandstands provide a close-up view of the running, and some race-goers watch the races on the TV monitors from start to finish. But, for most, this high-tech aid becomes a nuisance, interfering with the special excitement that explodes in a roaring orgasm of hope as the leading horses surge around the final turn and the field comes into full view in the stretch.

Then, all space is squeezed into the final three or four hundred yards remaining in the race, and all time becomes the twenty or thirty seconds it will take the straining horses and their riders, urged on by the crowd, to battle time and space to the finish line. For that brief, throbbing moment, a bettor knows that, no matter the outcome, a supreme effort is being made by man and beast to decide the fate of a two-dollar bet.

Reactions may range from exultation to resignation in the aftermath. But there can no longer be any doubt that there is a great difference between being present, hearing the race called over the bookie's radio, or reading the result in the papers—the difference between taking part in the battle and being told about it afterward.

The sheer exhilaration of that experience weighed heavily in my balancing of accounts for that day. I lost money, which was by then nothing new. But I picked one winner and came close with two other selections, which was encouraging. Also, I welcomed the privacy available among this unseeing crowd, where there was not even a bookmaker to know what you were doing, and I was comforted to know that agents of New York State were present to guarantee that all winners would be paid.

As I left, I knew I would be back. I returned a week later for another losing day. On a third visit, one week after the second, I won seventy-three dollars and assigned the proceeds to finance the printing of a radical community newspaper I had been hoping to organize and edit since my return from Cincinnati. I saw this as a way to atone for my disgrace and earn the right to be considered a responsive and responsible citizen of the world.

At that point, I stopped going to the track and withdrew from action altogether. Without thinking about it, I took a time-out to focus my attention and concentrate my energies on making the most of my experience as a journalist.

Nothing in my life up to that point had pleased me half as much. It didn't cross my mind that this new development demonstrated that gambling was not, or need not be, the most compelling force in my life. I could put it aside in favor of the responsibility to which I now assigned higher priority. And I could do so voluntarily.

I wasn't aware that the established pattern of matching sensible activity with my dependence on gambling was yielding to new and higher priorities. That deprived me of an additional reward, for surely it would have pleased me to know that there could for me be something more compelling than the established pattern of constantly struggling to balance the irreconcilable forces at war in my mind.

25.

It seems strange now to remember that when I entered military service in January 1942, six weeks after the Japanese attack on Pearl Harbor, many Americans of my age thought of World War II as an opportunity to make a fresh start on a new life. I think we needed to feel that. A substantial number of the fifteen million Americans who served in the war had been unemployed before the war or, if employed, had worked only part-time or at jobs beneath their qualifications and their hopes. Few of us had gone to college or had any prospect of ever doing so. And, until the war production boom stimulated American industry, there had been little reason to expect anything more than continued slow economic improvement at modest levels. Now, victory became a synonym for postwar economic opportunity.

At first glance, the military situation might have seemed to offer little reason for optimism about the future. Hitler was in command of Europe. His Wehrmacht had killed millions of Russian soldiers and civilians and occupied vast areas of the Soviet Union in the seven months since his invasion. And the Japanese had strengthened their grip in Asia after humiliating the American navy and air force at Pearl Harbor. But, day by day, all this began to seem less important than what the Allies were doing.

The Red Army and Soviet civilians were holding off the Germans at Leningrad and Moscow. The RAF was ceaselessly pounding German cities and industrial targets in severely damaging night raids. And American naval and air forces, gravely hurt, were recovering and being strengthened by armaments flowing from a vast industrial expansion and the drafting of personnel. I didn't know anyone who thought about the possibility of defeat—only of how long it would take to achieve victory and along with it, a bright new future. I set two war aims for myself. I intended to be a good soldier in behalf of a noble cause, and I hoped in the process to become a more sensible, and therefore a better, person.

Meeting my basic responsibility to do my duty was easy enough. For three years and nine months, like the other Americans in uniform, I went where I was sent and did as I was told.

Too often, that meant playing the old army game of hurry up and wait. I wanted to join what was then called the Army Air Corps, before it became an independent branch of the service as the U.S. Air Force; and I applied to do so in New York. But the quota for that area was oversubscribed; and I had to spend four months elsewhere, at Fort Bragg and Fort Knox, before being accepted as an aviation cadet. That wait was followed by three more months at the Kelly Field classification center near San Antonio, waiting with ten thousand other hopefuls for tests to determine the kind of training to which we would be assigned. I was turned down for pilot training and went to school to become a navigator-bombardier. That used up another year, as I passed through pre-flight training, bombardier school, navigation school, and combat training before, finally, receiving an overseas assignment as a navigator-bombardier with the Fifteenth Air Force at a base near Foggia, Italy.

After all that preparation, my overseas duty lasted just six months, during which I flew twenty-five bombing missions—including a historic "shuttle raid" which involved eight days at a base in the Soviet Union—and spent seven weeks as a prisoner of war in Romania after bailing out of a burning B-17 en route to the oil fields at Ploesti. My luck was good and I survived the war with only minor damage: a slight cut over my forehead from a piece of flak caught during a raid on Ploesti and a much more painful fracture of my collar bone suffered in a lively game of what was supposed to have been touch tackle football.

Under the terms of my enabling agreement, with so much good conduct to my credit it should have been easy to pick up the action where I had left it in the months before the war, but it wasn't. Military life encourages gambling, so I could have gambled more conveniently than before; but I had less desire to do so. Ease of access was made more attractive by a fringe benefit that had never been available before: the knowledge that, no matter how often I might go broke, I would never have to worry about eating money. Room, board, and other necessaries were paid for. The pay I received in cash each month was free and clear. Also, I had arranged to have allotments from my pay sent to my mother automatically, so I could indulge myself without guilt on that score. Still, I had mixed feelings about whether I should be gambling at that point in my life and the world's history.

Reflection suggests that I felt about the GI gambling scene as I had about the wide-open action in Cincinnati. It was reassuring to know that I could gamble whenever I wanted; but I seem to have felt that it should not be so, especially for a responsible citizen of the world at a time when the leaders of the world were rolling the iron dice in the ultimate gamble and the future of civilized society was at stake.

I may have thought commanding officers should prohibit the gambling in barracks. But they may have known that, as American commanders since George Washington have learned, it is impossible to eliminate gambling from military life. Washington, himself an avid participant in card games, dice, lotteries, and horse racing, tried at Valley Forge to end gambling in the ranks by commanding his troops to cease and desist. That order, like a second issued soon after, was ignored by men who had little better to do as they suffered through that bitter winter.

There may have been moments of moralistic fervor when I could have been inspired to think that I would have obeyed orders to abstain from gambling. But the likelihood of my doing so would not have been worth a big bet. Any reluctance I may have felt about gambling was inspired by more realistic considerations and more practical restraints.

If any single circumstance can be said to have dampened my enthusiasm for gambling in the service, it could have been the absence of facilities for horseplayers at the bases where I was stationed. I thought of horseplaying as my true calling as a gambler, but I never encountered a bookmaker or saw a racing form at any military base; and, even if these had been available, crowded classroom and training schedules would not have left enough time and energy to perform the chores required of horseplayers.

Poker, blackjack, and craps were the games preferred in the barracks. But although I did better with these games than with the horses—which meant only that I lost less—that kind of action was not the real thing as far as I was concerned. I considered card games and craps only better than nothing.

One other circumstance made gambling less appealing than it had been before the war. Whether on duty or in social pursuits, after hours I enjoyed what I did when I wasn't gambling.

The net effect of these influences was to diminish but not to eliminate my appetite for action. My dependence was too strong to be put off by these considerations, strong enough to overcome any resistance. I made an effort—out of guilt, I suppose—to call a halt. Then I fell back on the Cincinnati solution, combining good work and gambling, but modifying that pattern to alternate bouts of action with time-outs. The new arrangement worked as well as I could have wished, particularly in one instance when a pleasurable time-out at Kelly Field produced a welcome fringe benefit: my first opportunity to play the horses since entering the military service.

While others gambled and griped about the terrible heat, the awful food, and the tedium of waiting at the overcrowded classification center, good luck enabled me to become the co-author, co-producer, co-director, and co-star of a vaudeville extravaganza I helped put together with Bob, a former hoofer who had played the Loew's circuit. In a spur-of-the-moment response to a morale officer's call for assistance, we volunteered to put on a show to entertain the restless troops. We found a juggler, an acrobat, an accordionist, and a sleight-of-hand artist to warm up audiences for our performance of plagiarized comedy material taken by memory from the routines of the Ritz Brothers, Willie and Eugene Howard, Smith and Dale, and other headliners Bob and I admired. Bob then taught me to help him deliver the material with pleasure that was shared by large audiences—seven thousand at one outdoor performance—whose laughter suggested that we might have helped make the long wait for classification less tedious.

Our work was rewarded with the privilege of passes on request to visit San Antonio, officially to shop for costumes, additionally to consume large quantities of good Texas chili, hotter but not better than Cincinnati chili, and fine Mexican beer. On an early visit, while Bob was busy elsewhere, I located a bookie with the help of a taxi driver and placed some bets. Thereafter, I found other occasions to be alone with the bookmaker, to keep my action shielded from Bob.

After a long layoff as a horseplayer, the San Antonio action was especially satisfying; and the good chili eased the pain of bad losses. But that pleasure was small compared to the satisfactions derived from another time-out activity that began with a piece of bad luck, the touch tackle fracture which sidelined me in bombardier school at Midland, Texas. During the weeks of recuperation, I might have found a bookmaker in town and surely could have found card games or craps on the base. Instead, upon hearing of plans for a souvenir book, I volunteered to spend my time editing one memory book for the class from which my injury had removed me and another one for the class with which I graduated. That experience allowed me to think of my accident as a lucky break.

Good fortune produced a curious reaction. Perhaps because it pleased me so much to work as an entertainer and editor, I began to feel guilty about using time in ways that had nothing to do with preparation for combat. Normally, that old feeling should have triggered the compensating response which would have plunged me back into action. This time I didn't quite plunge, but for several months indulged myself in pay-day binges. Then, as I began final preparations for my overseas assignment, I managed somehow to convert the self-destructive impulse into a source of energy for more sensible work and, thus strengthened, I called a no-exceptions time-out for the duration.

THIS time-out was different. It had not been forced on me by fear and the shortage of funds, as had been the case for a time after my homecoming. Nor was it being accepted for want of something better to do. Though I feel uncomfortable speaking this truth, this withdrawal from action was an act of conscience, something I was doing because I thought it would be wrong not to do it. And the doing brought me an unasked and unexpected immediate reward—a feeling of having been liberated, of being free at last, from a dependency that had been part of my life for seven years. That is how I felt when I arrived for duty as a navigator-bombardier, a first lieutenant with a Fifteenth Air Force Unit near Foggia, Italy, in April 1944.

During previous time-outs, I had never really distanced myself from gambling. I had put it aside, but never beyond reach. This time, although I wouldn't have gone so far as to say that I would never gamble again, I had no wish to gamble, at least for the duration. I felt only the need and desire to do what sensible, serious, responsible citizens should do, until the war ended.

I hope I stopped short of behaving like a zealous convert, though I felt superior to those unfortunates who gambled and was pleased with myself for spending my free time more usefully. I was a prolific letter writer, a loyal reader of the daily newspaper *Stars and Stripes*, the weekly *Yank*, and paperback books. And I was an active participant in discussions about preparations in Congress to pass the G.I. Bill of Rights, with its substantial postwar benefits—especially free college tuition—for veterans. As often as possible, I went to a peasant woman near our base who, for a modest fee, cooked delicious meals from ingredients brought to her by GIs tired of GI chow. And once, in heat and in shame, I patronized a woman in the town who sold sexual favors in a fine home she shared with her stone-silent mother, whom I thought of as the saddest woman I had ever seen.

The guilt I felt for my non-gambling sins saved me from self-righteousness. I believe I understood that I had best concentrate on minding my own business, work on correcting my deficiencies, and leave others to deal with their own self-improvement. Also, I think I may have begun to understand that I was much luckier and far more productive with work that didn't involve playing at games of chance than I had been or was likely to be as a gambler.

That was certainly true of one series of events which, after an unfortunate start, made me feel I was living on a gambler's lucky streak. It began with a piece of bad luck: fire in the right inboard engine of our B-17 en route to Romania's oil complex at Ploesti. After six of my crew mates and I responded to the gong sounding the pilot's bail-out command, he and the engineer put out the fire. They and two others returned to Foggia on three engines, while I and six others found ourselves floating four miles up in the air, untutored in the use of a parachute and uncertain about its workings.

Below, I could see the Danube River twisting between the mountains of Romania and Yugoslavia. My mind filled with a dozen thoughts, first and foremost of which was a terrible fear that I might not be able to make the parachute work. At the one quick briefing about parachute management which I could remember, a supply sergeant had concluded his presentation with a joke. "If it doesn't work," he said, "bring it back and we'll fix it." That's not funny, I thought now. I was sickened by the thought I might be smashed to death on the rocks below.

I remembered the sergeant having said something about a rip cord.

There was a handle at the bottom of the chest pack, and I yanked it away from the pack. "That's it," I panicked. "I've broken the damned thing. Now I'm done for." But even as I worried, the chute started to unfold above me, as it was supposed to do when the rip cord was pulled free.

Now my thought turned to other concerns. First, I remembered that I had some briefing notes and maps in my flight suit pockets. I tore them and let the wind take them. Then, by instinct, as the wind blew me one way and another, I tried to guide my descent by pulling on the cords of the chute. We had been told that, given a choice, we should avoid Romania, which was strictly enemy country, and try to make it to Yugoslavia, which, although also a fascist country, supported a large partisan movement led by a man named Tito.

I tried for Yugoslavia, but the wind took me to Romania. I landed at the edge of a corn field on the outskirts of Basle Herculani, a resort town. As I touched down, a peasant with a lynch look in his eyes and a long scythe in his hands raced toward me at the head of a crowd of civilians and soldiers. I was about to abandon hope when events turned in my favor, and I was off on a winning streak.

Before the man with the scythe could reach me, a civilian—a local landowner, it turned out—raced up between us and held off my would-be-executioner until a detachment of Romanian troops arrived. I took that as a good sign. But as the Romanians marched me toward town, a squad of Germans double-timed into view, bringing with them the prospect of trouble.

Germany had virtually occupied Romania, which, under its dictator Ion Antonescu, was allied with Hitler. These Germans, it became apparent from an angry argument between the captain commanding the German squad and the lieutenant in charge of the Romanian detachment, wanted to take custody of me. But the Romanian held his ground. Livid with frustration, the red-faced German marched off his troops more slowly than they had come, and I was saved from being transported to a Nazi prison camp.

The events which followed what I thought of as my rescue made me feel like an honored guest enjoying a day in the country. My crew mates—co-pilot, radio man, photographer, and three gunners—were picked up around the town and the seven of us were brought together outside the town hall. There a curious and, I thought, friendly crowd looked on as a sergeant compiled an inventory of our parachutes and other gear, which was then dumped aboard a panel truck onto which we were also loaded for a ride to the Romanian headquarters at Orsova, about ten miles down river.

The lieutenant who had taken custody of me in the cornfield, a tall, dark-haired young man who looked years younger than I, commanded our escort of four enlisted men. He rode with us and talked freely in French and German about his distaste for the Germans and his hopes for an early end to the war. He said Romania's King Michael was negotiating an armistice with the Soviet Union. I responded with what I remembered of my high school French and some Yiddish, which he seemed to understand as German.

Five minutes out of town the lieutenant gave an order, and, before we knew what was happening, the sergeant driving the truck pulled it off the road and brought it to a stop under an oak outside a tavern on the river bank. The lieutenant then gave some money to the sergeant who hurried to the tavern and returned accompanied by a porter, carrying a basket of bread, cheese, and sausage and a case of delicious cold beer. It was now noon and we hadn't eaten since our pre-flight breakfast at half past five, so we ate with gusto, but politely declined another round offered by our host, who seemed more reluctant than any of us to have his impromptu picnic come to an end.

At Orsova we were taken to a prison compound—a small, walled, riverside farmhouse—commanded by a fat little major who looked at me in a way that made me uneasy. I need not have been. The major was motivated only by his belief that I was a European soccer star he had seen and admired before the war.

Uncertain what it might mean to be the man he thought I was, I tried to make the major understand that this was a case of mistaken identity. He simply wouldn't believe me. Smiling through denials, made in my limited French—which he assumed to be an attempt to mislead him, since the soccer star he had in mind would have spoken French fluently—the major seemed to want to reassure me. Speaking in French, he said approximately this: We are men of the world. I do not ask to know why you need to wear a mask or what brings you here. I respect your position and will honor your incognito.

It then occurred to me that there might be some value in encouraging him to believe I was whom he thought I was. Thereafter, I responded to him with inscrutable smiles and occasionally let myself be caught off guard making shoulder-jerking and leg-kicking moves I had seen soccer players make in the newsreels.

That evening, about eight hours after our riverside picnic, a guard opened the door of the cell in which we were being held, and two young women—very pretty, as women usually are remembered in such situations—came in bearing trays of food and wine. I recall stuffed cabbage, a pork roast, browned potatoes, string beans, cucumber salad, excellent French bread, and two bottles of good red wine. One of the food-bearers invited me in German either to take a walk or fool around with her. I wasn't sure how to interpret the word she used—shpahtzeeren, to write it phonetically—or what she had in mind, but it didn't matter. At that point I didn't think I should press my luck and declined her invitation with a smile of gratitude.

Apart from telling the enemy nothing more than name, rank, and serial number, we knew little about how to behave or what to expect as prisoners of war, but we knew that our treatment by the lieutenant and the major was exceptional. We could have wished for just one more thing: some way to express our appreciation beyond saying thank you, and the next day just such an opportunity presented itself.

That afternoon, as we were sunning ourselves in the farmyard, the lieutenant appeared at the compound obviously distraught. He merely nodded to us before going into the major's office. When he emerged an hour later, he told me that he was to be court-martialled and faced a possible death sentence on the charge of having stolen ninety-eight dollars from among the things that had been taken from us in Basle Herculani. He swore that he was innocent, and we had no doubt about that. Even if he was guilty, my crew mates and I told each other, execution was an excessive price to pay for stealing ninety-eight dollars.

When I asked the major about the matter, he confirmed that a routine check of our inventory had shown a packet containing ninety-eight dollars, which was part of a survival kit carried by American fliers over enemy territory, was missing. The major said that he, too, faced possible disciplinary action.

It was difficult for us to think of the two Romanian officers only as enemies. In the circumstances, we talked about them as unfortunate men who had shown us consideration above and beyond the requirements of the Geneva Convention regarding treatment of POWs.

We wished them well and pondered ways in which we might be helpful.

Over and over again we analyzed and evaluated the possibilities. We couldn't believe that anyone had stolen the money—not the lieutenant nor any of the enlisted men who had handled our effects—if only because of the fear of detection and the terrible punishment such a crime would have entailed. But we didn't know what to believe. Then, when it seemed that a solution was beyond our powers to discern, the tail gunner said he was willing to bet that the money packet was among our things piled in the cellar of the farmhouse.

The major gave permission to have the jumble of parachutes, flight suits, and other gear brought from the dark cellar into the farmyard so we could sort it out. Each item was unfolded and examined, inch by inch, more carefully than apparently had been the case with the examiners who had reported the money missing. Within minutes, the missing packet was taken from the cords of a parachute in which it had been entangled.

For the next four days, until we were taken by train to the prison camp in Bucharest, the lieutenant and the major heaped rewards on us—food, drink, and cigarettes in abundance. As we made ready to depart, they engaged in a final outpouring of appreciation. The major called a special formation, a squad of his troops lined up on one side and the POWs on the other. He made a speech, looking toward the time fast approaching when we would be at peace, and, at his invitation, I responded in kind. He then kissed me on both cheeks, saluted us, and stood at attention as we marched off.

AFTER Orsova, anything short of going home would have been a let-down, and in Bucharest there were other reasons to feel less content that we had in the prison compound on the Danube. There we had been star boarders, honored guests. In Bucharest, we were just seven more fish in a sea of some five hundred Allied prisoners of war—most Americans, others from England, Australia, and New Zealand, and a handful from the Soviet Union's Red Army. About two hundred officers were held in one compound and three hundred enlisted men in another nearby.

The *lagarul de prizonieri* in which the officers were held had been a boarding school before the war and not a very posh one, presumably, since the two-story building was overrun by rats—creatures as big as people, someone said. Even more distressing was the location of the prison camp. It was perilously close to a major bombing target, the railroad-marshalling yards of the Romanian capital. As a result, we were uncomfortably close to the action when the railroad target was hit, which it was once or twice a week, by our

Fifteenth Air Force in daylight and by the R.A.F. at night.

Psychologists have remarked on the oneness that can develop between hostages and their captors in some situations, and we experienced something like that. After a particularly heavy night raid that had subjected us to several near misses, we were coming out of the meager shelter provided in the basement of the building when a plane buzzed overhead and some of us ducked for cover. A steady-nerved veteran calmed the nervous ones with the observation that there was nothing to fear. The plane overhead, he said, was "one of ours,"—a German or Romanian fighter plane returning to base after chasing the R.A.F. bombers.

Food was another problem. Although we were probably better fed than most Romanians, there wasn't enough food to satisfy me. I never felt starved, but I lost eight pounds during six weeks in the Bucharest prison camp. On the other hand, our menus were well-balanced—heavy on tomatoes, onions, cucumbers, potatoes, an occasional egg, prune jelly, and dark bread—with the result that when we were liberated I was in excellent physical condition, albeit somewhat hungry.

Still, all things considered, we felt reasonably well treated; and, on a quiet night or a sunny day when there were no airplanes overhead, it would not have been impossible to think of the *lagarul* as a holiday camp rather than a prison. The Romanian guards, of whom there were remarkably few, were older men whose chief function appeared to be to announce meal times. And there were various activities to keep people more or less pleasantly occupied.

Many took part in sports activity, shooting baskets at a hoop in the yard, playing catch, doing calisthenics, or jogging around the school yard. Others read from a small paperback collection. A small group busied itself putting together a vaudeville show which was well received. And there were the gamblers.

When I have thought about gambling among military personnel, I have let myself remember that most of the people I knew in the service were gamblers. But that was not so. More careful reflection led me to the conclusion that there were not that many men at any of the bases where I was stationed who could be considered gamblers. However, few as they may have been, they were devoted; and their persistence may have made them seem more numerous than they were.

The performance of the gamblers in the Bucharest prison camp was especially impressive. They played—mainly hearts, bridge, and gin rummy—from after breakfast until after dark, and they played for high stakes, though they had neither money nor playing cards worthy of being so described. The cards were made from bits of cardboard; and play was for credit, with players keeping tabs, which in some cases added up to thousands of dollars. In the end, it could be said that a good time was had by all since, as previously noted, all tabs were destroyed and slates wiped clean on the day we were liberated, leaving no winners and no losers.

Before that happened, when it seemed that great amounts of money were being lost and won, my new-found self-righteousness on the issue of gambling led me to pity the poor souls who were wasting their time and money in this way. But I think I was also impressed by the apparent need of the players, and the ways in which they satisfied their need.

My need was for something else, and that was satisfied in a manner that reminded me again how lucky I could be when I wasn't gambling. I became once more an editor—of a two-page, one-copy, hand-lettered, daily newspaper which, it pleased me to think, contributed to the solution of a morale problem in the *lagarul* while also serving my need to do something useful.

The problem arose from a confusion between the most popular rumor in the *lagarul* and a reality which seemed to cut the ground from under the rumor. The rumor, which we had first heard in Orsova, was that Romania was negotiating its way out of the war, and that we would thus be on our way home any day. The reality was that, most days, the Fifteenth Air Force in daylight and the R.A.F. by night continued to bomb nearby targets. There were those who said that the bombing probably was intended to speed negotiations, but that didn't do much to clear the confusion or relieve the anxiety about getting blown to bits by our own side.

The mission of my newspaper was to minimize confusion and counteract its negative effect on morale. I proposed to do that by printing accurate reports taken from newscasts transmitted by the BBC from London and heard on a clandestine radio which had been smuggled into the compound. Previously, three Americans who controlled the radio had passed along by word of mouth what they heard on the broadcasts, but something apparently was lost in the passage, since different versions of the same events were common and speculation was rife. Printed reports would make exactly the same facts available to everyone. In addition, drawing on my memory of what I had read in *Stars & Stripes* and *Yank,* I wrote news features of special interest to Americans, the most popular of which was a long series of reports on the generous benefits in education, unemployment, and housing to be provided for veterans in the G.I. Bill of Rights.

Without a typewriter, mimeograph machine, or printing press, only one copy of each day's newspaper could be produced by hand; and even that presented a problem because paper and pencils were hard to come by. However, someone managed to scrounge the necessary materials, and everything else fell into place.

Each day I wrote feature articles about the GI Bill and other subjects. Each night I listened to the day's-end newscast of the BBC and wrote a summary of the news.

I worked with another POW, Marv, who, in an isn't-it-a-small-world coincidence, also worked with me after the war at UP. In the *lagarul,* Marv wrote some stories, hand-lettered them all, and occasionally drew a cartoon as well. These were printed on one side of two sheets of letter-sized paper, turning to the reverse side the next day. Then the two sheets were posted on a bulletin board in the lobby of the schoolhouse where our readers gathered to peruse the only source of reliable news available to them. This went on until the story that was, for us, the most important news of all—the armistice and liberation—eliminated the need for the newspaper.

Forty-six days after my arrival in Basle Herculani, the rumor about Romania negotiating its way out of the war through an armistice with the Soviet Union became a fact, and we were liberated, though not yet free to go. German troops resisted as Red Army units moved through Romania, and Luftwaffe pilots at Bucharest used their few remaining airplanes for limited terror bombing: sending aloft one plane at a time to circle the city, dropping single bombs at different points. Curiously, though they must have known the location of the prison compounds, they made no attempt to bomb us.

Before we could leave, the German air force remnants would have to be wiped out. Then we could expect Fifteenth Air Force transports to come in and ferry us to Italy. That process, beginning with a massive strike which eliminated the German aerial threat, took a week. While my fellow-POWs could only wait in place, something more attractive was made available to me.

Once again confirming that I could be much luckier when I wasn't gambling, on the day the armistice was announced the senior officers in our group, for reasons known only to themselves, appointed me Public Relations Officer for the Allied Prisoners of War in Romania. Operationally, the title meant nothing, since few reporters or government officials in Bucharest had any interest in the Allied POWs and all I could tell them was that we were eager to go home. Personally, however, the designation gave me carte blanche to enjoy the *dolce vita* of Bucharest, which prewar Romanians called "Petit Paris" in appreciation of pleasures as plentiful, varied, and rich as anything Paris offered. Those who knew told me that the delights of Bucharest had been little affected by the war, and my experience gave me no reason to doubt that.

The senior officers who had created the pointless post for me also arranged for me to be the guest of two wealthy Romanian families; and my hosts made it their mission to provide me with more than I could possibly eat, drink, or otherwise enjoy. I responded with enthusiasm and appreciation, but I also felt a certain measure of guilt. I reminded myself that, while I enjoyed the sweet life, other POWs waited austerely in the prison compound; and millions of other soldiers, including my two brothers, were still actively engaged in war. Then, having thus paid my dues in good conscience, I gave myself over to a week of various pleasures.

I could have stayed on to enjoy more of the wine, women, and song available to me; and I thought about doing so. But that prospect couldn't compete with the alternative. I looked forward to the immeasurably greater pleasures of going home. I had twelve hundred and twenty-one dollars in back pay waiting for me, and I planned to spend it freely on my mother and others as a showing of my affection and appreciation.

A week after leaving Romania, as I boarded a Navy troop ship at Naples, I felt I had good reason to be pleased with myself. Much had happened in the six months since my departure for overseas duty and, all in all, things had gone well. I was excited about going home, excited about being free from imprisonment, and, although I would have been reluctant to admit it, I was excited also to be free of war, at least for a while.

But, my excitement was tempered by the guilt I felt over having survived when so many had not and others would not. I seem to have tried to close my mind to that kind of thinking and to focus on plans for the happy time I could expect at home but without success. I was terribly tired. Too much had happened too quickly and I had run out of energy. I would have welcomed a long sleep and some peace and quiet, but the home-going ship—active with constant movement, constant conversation, and constant gambling—wasn't made for peace and quiet.

Unable to rest, I roamed the ship, searching—like the man in a story popular at the time with GIs. That man went about picking up scraps of paper which he studied and discarded, muttering, "That's not it." Then he was handed a sheet of paper which was identified as a "section eight" discharge from military service by reason of psychological deficiencies. Immediately, the man's face lit up in a smile. "That's it," he announced, and his search ended.

My search took me miles each day through crowded passageways in the sleeping quarters, up and down gangways, and around decks. I thought of these restless journeys as a way of killing time while also getting some exercise. But I may have been aware that movement was also an attempt to distract me from a struggle with the demons in my mind that were trying to stimulate my self-defeating reaction to good fortune. The outcome of that struggle is easy for me to recall and describe, but it is still difficult to explain in any way that makes sense to me.

On my travels around the ship, I saw more gambling than I had ever seen before in one place at one time. There were more gamblers playing in more games for higher stakes; and they played everywhere: in their bunks, on the floor of narrow passageways in the sleeping quarters, on landings between decks, and in latrines—wherever there was light and a flat surface on which to deal cards or roll dice. For officers, the Navy provided more comfortable facilities, a lounge large enough to accomodate half a dozen games around the clock.

Table-stakes blackjack, in which players could bet in total as much as the banker showed on the table, drew the biggest bettors. The first time I observed the game I was astonished to see almost two thousand dollars bet on one round.

Watching, it occurred to me that it could be possible to double my funds in just a round or two, which would give me twice as much to spend on my mother and the other intended recipients of my generous affection. To think that was, of course, to signal the outcome. Unaware of the struggle or of its already-determined resolution, I resisted for two more days before yielding to this latest attack on my senses. Ten months after calling a time-out of conscience for the duration, I called it off and took a hand in the blackjack game.

Since this was the first time I had played blackjack for table stakes, it may be reasonable to speak of beginner's luck. During four days of play, with interruptions only for eating, sleeping, and survival drills, I tripled my money and added a few hundred dollars more. At the high point, I had almost four thousand dollars, more than half a year's pay for a first lieutenant with flight and combat bonuses. Leaving inflation out of the calculation, that was about one third as many dollars as I had lost during my seven years in action.

In heat, I thought only of winning more, but there was no more to be had. Twenty-four hours later I was broke.

That set the stage for another struggle. Before going overseas, I had opened a savings account which now contained seven hundred dollars. At this point, I could call it quits and still have a good deal of spending money for my home leave. Or, I could try to borrow some money and go back into action. In what seemed to me a reasonable compromise, I allowed myself to borrow up to a limit of five hundred dollars, reasoning that if I lost that much I could repay it from savings and still have a little money to spend at home.

After a frantic search, I found a non-gambling member of my crew who agreed to lend me four hundred dollars, all he had. I promised to repay him before we debarked, if I became a winner again, or to pay him on our first day ashore if I didn't.

Between lunch and dinner, that money, too, had been lost.

When my lender discovered that I would not be able to repay him before debarking, he reported our transaction to the senior officers in our group. They had been generous with their assistance to me in the prison camp. Now, in a scene that I recall as having been more shameful for me than losing my job in Cincinnati, they were very starchy about dereliction of duty and conduct unbecoming an officer and a gentleman. Unless I repaid the debt during our first day ashore, they warned me, I would face disciplinary proceedings.

Repayment as promised removed that threat, but not the stigma. I could not forget that whatever I might have thought during the ten-month time-out when my conscience had been my guide, nothing had changed. I was still, at least as much as anything else, a gambler.

28.

As the first of my family and friends to come home from overseas duty, I was welcomed as a hero and showered with food and affection. After thirty days of such treatment, I forgot how tired and depressed I had been at the end of my long voyage home. When I arrived at Bowman Field, near Louisville, a convalescent center to which returning Air Force prisoners of war were sent for rest, recuperation, and rehabilitation, I had no need of those three R's. I was bursting with energy and needed nothing so much as things to do.

Like me, Bowman Field led an ambivalent existence. It was an operational air base, servicing military transport planes. In addition, it had been chosen as the site for the convalescent center, a new concept in the treatment of Air Force personnel who had been prisoners of war or were recovering from serious wounds. There hadn't yet been time enough to prepare formal programs, so the people in charge left the first arrivals to their own devices. That was no problem for someone with a talent for busyness and a need to be active.

The way in which I responded to this new challenge made me feel like a Johnny Appleseed of journalism, planting newspapers wherever I could. A commendation from the commanding officer notes that during ten months at Bowman Field I organized and edited a two-page daily newspaper and a twenty-four-page weekly. The daily was designed to supplement radio newscasts and help fill a void caused by wartime gasoline rationing which barred delivery of the Louisville newspapers to Bowman Field. The weekly covered news of the base. The commendation also records that I reactivated old photo-offset printing equipment and arranged to have personnel trained in its use, while I instructed others in editorial procedures, served as host of a weekly interview program that featured wounded veterans on radio station WHAS, and helped to produce a radio documentary about America's allies.

Not fit for inclusion in the CO's commendation but critical to my well being was the fact that soon after arriving at Bowman Field I had, without premeditation, gone back into action. As far as I could judge, the new gambling took little time or energy from my work. To the contrary, by providing that peculiar balance of the sensible and the absurd with which I felt so comfortable, being in action may have contributed to the ease with which I got my work done.

Using the scheduling skills I had developed in Cincinnati, I made the gambling an integral part of my daily routine without noticeable effect on other activities. To make it more convenient, two elderly Irish-American brothers who ran a book in their pleasant neighborhood bar just down the road from Bowman Field provided me with telephone privileges and a respectable line of credit. Though I was satisfied with these arrangements, I felt an obligation to visit Churchill Downs, across town, to see the track where the Kentucky Derby is run, but after one visit I concluded that the shabby place wasn't worth a return journey. Thereafter, I confined my action to the bar down the road where, in addition to the other attractions, I could count on excellent barbecue-beef sandwiches and a choice of several draught beers.

More important perhaps than the gambling, but in any case as much a part of my operational equilibrium, was an active social life graced by good companions. They remain dear in memory, although I have stayed in touch through the years with only one of the group,

Bill, a sophisticated New Yorker from Kansas City, who was a public relations officer at the base and went on to make a career in that profession.

With that exception, the relationships which enriched my time in Louisville were laughing friendships—good to enjoy but without enduring value. For that, only I am to blame, if one can be held accountable for an inability to establish real connections with other human beings despite the warmth that might appear on the surface.

It hurts still to recall that, whatever I might have thought then, my time at Bowman Field is most accurately described as busy, cheerful, and empty. The pain of regret over failed connections is only little relieved by the knowledge that it is not uncommon for compulsive gamblers to behave in this way, as self-centered loners, experiencing without feeling, avoiding involvement, constantly looking ahead to the next bet, while ignoring the unrecognized winnings at hand.

The arms-length attitude which held me safe from intimate contact was present with old friends in Cincinnati as well as those I met in Louisville. The proximity of Cincinnati, one hundred and twenty miles from Louisville, had been for me one of the attractions of being at Bowman Field; and I took advantage of it as soon as I could. But the visits I made were unsatisfying, disorienting, and disappointing, except for two evenings with Rad, a dear man with whom I could have had a much richer relationship if I hadn't been blocked by shame over what he knew about me—though he never gave any sign of having been affected by my mishandling of company funds at RKO Midwest Theaters.

Rad said he was disappointed over having been rejected for military duty because of his age, which cannot have been as much as forty. He refused to be cheered up, but enjoyed talking about wartime film making, and he gave me an assignment for two Sunday features about the use of film in military training which I was delighted to write as my first professional reporting assignment under my own by-line.

I went to Cincinnati intending to show off, to demonstrate that, whatever I had been four years ago, I was now an accredited officer and gentleman. I went also in hope of recapturing the good feeling I remembered even from my bad time there. But there was no need to show off to the people who mattered to me—Rad, Jules, Whit.

And from others, in place of good feeling, I received only the formal pleasantries of well-mannered people. There was a deadness about it, as in a still life, a sense that I couldn't feel good again in Cincinnati. I must have known that the reason for it rested with me, as at least one experience helped me to understand.

A chance encounter with a woman who, in the old days, had seemed beyond my station—Lillian, a lovely, sandy-haired girl I had thought of as admirable, desirable, but untouchable—put me to a test of human feeling of a kind I preferred to avoid. Lillian still looked like a teenager, but was three years older than I. She was the daughter of a rich father and had married a rich man. Now, after four years of what people had called a perfect marriage, she had just passed through a painful separation. Her demeanor reminded me of one of the more traumatized returnees at Bowman Field. But she seemed to cheer up as we talked during an unexpected meeting at the home of a mutual friend.

By unspoken agreement we left together, and I accepted her invitation for a drink at a nearby bar. We made small talk until our drinks were served. Then, as though unable to wait any longer, Lillian talked to me about her pain. She said she had been saddened by a separation she had not wanted. She said she hated being alone. She asked if I would like to spend the night with her.

Her voice still sounds in my mind's ear. "Don't make love to me because you feel sorry for me," she pleaded. "Don't do it as a favor. If you come with me, do it because you want me. Do you?" she asked. Unable to contain my excitement and unwilling to trust my voice, I nodded.

When I left her apartment the next day, Lillian thanked me. She seemed pleased, but I felt guilty. I thought I had taken advantage of her. My pleasure in her company reinforced the feeling of guilt. I thought that I should have been able simply to give her the benefit of honest, sympathetic attention, which she obviously needed and wanted. But, unable to manage anything more, I had given her only a night of bodily contact and some thinly felt sympathy before walking away from her need, ashamed of my inadequacy as a friend.

Recall of that encounter reminds me of the great changes in sexual attitudes that have taken place since then. My reaction seems quaint when I think of how sexually liberated men and women today might react in similar circumstances. But my behavior was the order of the day in that time. I behaved as I had been carefully taught to respond to an act for which there was little good to be said.

Until marriage sanctified such bodily contact, sexual intercourse was generally considered to be a dirty act: in some circumstances, illegal, immoral always outside of wedlock, and potentially hazardous to health. Distinctions were drawn among those who engaged in it, but no unmarried participant came out looking virtuous in the eyes of respectable society. If an unmarried woman was not a virgin—the ideal state for a woman—she was categorized as a tease, a tramp, or an outright whore, depending upon how far she allowed men to go and whether she accepted money for what was done. Again with the exception of virgins, men were thought to be of one mind. They all wanted the same thing, which was only to be expected of the male animal.

If "anything happened," which was the language to describe unwanted pregnancy, the blame and the shame were charged against the woman, who was then little better off than Hester Prynne wearing the scarlet letter. That was one of the many contradictions and confusions in the sexual code, which also idealized women as "the weaker sex" who needed to be adored and protected by strong, honorable men, until pregnancy made them victims.

Fortunately for the public health, violations of the crippling prohibitions were widespread and exceptions often were made for violators, but for me there were no exceptions, only unexcused violations and guilt. I don't know how to understand my apparent need to seek out guilt for an act that gave me so much pleasure. I can only suppose that, as a product of my childhood teachings, feeling guilty about making love in the unmarried state was a way of demonstrating my respectability.

One other aspect of my behavior with Lillian is more easily recognizable as the tendency of a compulsive gambler to avoid entangling relationships. I never saw Lillian again after our one night together. I may have thought that if I didn't see her, I couldn't again fail her as a friend.

I considered myself more fortunate with a relationship in Louisville that, free of intimacy or guilt, gave me the female companionship I needed without requiring anything more than I could give in return. My friend Eunice was an unusual woman from whom I could have learned more than I did about being a complete person and a friend. She was a well-bred, devout German Catholic who was also a spunky, assertive young woman with an active sense of humor, some unconventional social attitudes, and a talent for friendship. Although we were together three or four times a week, that was as much as I learned or wanted to know about her, except that she was engaged to be married when her fiancé returned from service in the Pacific.

Her commitment to her fiancé defined Eunice's boundary around our relationship, and I felt honor-bound to respect it. As I have come to understand, at least as important as honor was my own need to avoid the intimate involvement to which a breach of the boundary might have led, even though I continued to find sexual satisfactions with women I thought of as less respectable. As a result, without ever discussing the reasons why, we shared no intimate physical contact, and our friendship was unsullied by anything more than a farewell kiss on the day I left Bowman Field.

Thinking back on the way we were, I recognize a special benefit for me. The undemanding nature of our relationship made it more convenient to attend to the other items on my agenda. I did business almost every day with the friendly bookmaking brothers, met my work deadlines, attended to other social interests, and enjoyed every minute with Eunice.

We drank beer and listened to records of show tunes and big-band music at her house, went to the movies, attended parties at the officers' club, and spent warm days at the country club to which her parents belonged. Once, in a conversation unintended for my ears, Eunice sternly rebuked a cousin for an anti-Semitic remark; and the first time we went to the country club she told me laughingly that, as far as she knew, I was making history as the first to violate the club's no-Jews policy.

Of all I took from the relationship, what has remained in memory as the most practical lesson learned from Eunice is how to drive a car. Once before, I had tried unsuccessfully to qualify for a driver's license and was reluctant to try again just yet. As a result, whenever we went anywhere by car, Eunice drove her father's black 1940 Packard. Until one afternoon, on our way to the country club, Eunice stopped the Packard on a deserted back road and declared that the car would not move from that spot and would never move again with the two of us in it, unless I made it move. She said she would teach me how to move it.

After easily overcoming my weak, shamefaced resistance, Eunice taught me then and there how to drive. She insisted on teaching me as a matter of principle. I learned as a matter of pride and affection. Later that day, when I came within inches of crashing into a store window in a town square where cars were parked perpendicular to the curbs, Eunice calmly explained that I had probably stepped on the accelerator rather than the brake. At her quiet instruction, I shifted gears, backed off, parked properly, and thereafter drove whenever the two of us were in the car.

Guilt of a new kind infringed upon my satisfactions without entirely spoiling them. I was never unaware that while I was enjoying myself, great numbers of civilians and soldiers, including my brother Harry in the Philippines and Rube in France, were still at war. Others I knew who had relatives or friends in combat argued that it wouldn't help our loved ones if we stopped living normal lives, and I heeded their advice well enough to continue enjoying what I had, except for a bad scare during the Christmas season of 1944. A surprise German attack threatened to outflank American forces in the Ardennes at the border of France and Belgium. But the Americans stood fast at Bastogne and threw back the Germans. After that, it was only seven more months before the Germans and the Japanese were defeated.

Germany's surrender on May 8, 1945, V-E Day, was preceded by the death of F.D.R. on April 12. He missed by one month celebrating with the rest of the world the event that he had worked so hard to bring about. Victory over Japan, formalized with V-J day on August 14, followed America's awesome revelation of the existence of the atomic bomb in the most dramatic way, by dropping one over Hiroshima on August 6 and a second over Nagasaki on August 9.

The death of President Roosevelt was universally mourned, even by some of his enemies, in an outpouring of grief reminiscent of the sorrow that was evoked with the death of Abraham Lincoln fourscore years earlier. It seemed to me my tears were shared by everyone I saw on the sunny day at Bowman Field when radio broadcasts reported the unhappy news.

Reaction to the dawning of the nuclear age was also personal as well as political. I was in Louisville on another sunny day when radio announcers reported that the United States had destroyed Hiroshima with an atomic bomb, a terrible new weapon, deadly beyond anything previously imagined. I was alone, on an errand, and heard the news from a storekeeper. I had no wish to talk to anyone. I walked the hot, empty streets aimlessly until I came to a church and went in because it seemed a peaceful thing to do.

Back at Bowman Field, as everywhere else, people talked endlessly about the mysterious and horrifying bomb, about how it worked, what it had done to Hiroshima, and what it might mean for the future of the world. Before many people could fully comprehend the fact of Hiroshima's destruction, the second bomb was dropped on Nagasaki—a name which hitherto had been known most widely as part of a nonsense song with lyrics which included the refrain, "Down in Nagasaki, where the men all chew tobaccee, and the women wicky, wacky, woo."

The atom bomb had made Nagasaki part of history, an involuntary contributor to the beginnings of a new world. During this disturbing time, my friends and I talked about the future of the world and we thought about our personal postwar plans. Rather than return to Missouri, I decided to complete my undergraduate studies in New York, preferably at Columbia University, and then go to Columbia's Graduate School of Journalism, which had a reputation as the best journalism school in the world. With the credits previously earned in evening sessions at Brooklyn College and Cincinnati University, I would need three years, including summers, to earn my B.A. I had expected to be able to start in the fall of 1946. But the early end to the war had put me in position to start a year sooner.

A system had been established to discharge military personnel on the basis of points granted for such things as length of service, time overseas, and time spent as a POW. I had earned enough points to qualify for immediate discharge, but getting into school less than three weeks before the start of the academic year would be much more difficult—a long shot, but worth a bet. I had made no other bets since August 6, but I was ready to bet that I could get into Columbia.

The day it became clear that Japan was ready to surrender, I made my decision. The next morning a sympathetic operations officer arranged a place for me aboard a transport flying to Roosevelt Field on Long Island and returning the following day. I was at the admissions office of Columbia College before noon that morning and was told I could expect to be accepted if I applied for admission.

Since my scholastic record wouldn't normally have inspired approval, acceptance could only be credited to the temper of the times. There was a shortage of students, school officials were sympathetic to veterans and there was the practical consideration that the G.I. Bill guaranteed payment of all school costs and provided a cost-of-living stipend as well. I filed an application before going to lunch.

That afternoon, while exploring the campus for the first time, I visited the Graduate School of Journalism to inquire about admission procedures for the future after I had earned a degree from the college. After talking with me for two hours, the chairman of the admissions committee invited me to join the incoming class as a special, non-degree student. If I accepted, I wouldn't have to take three years to get an undergraduate degree. I would be treated like the regular degree students but, in place of a graduate degree, would get a certificate which could be exchanged for a master's degree if and when I completed the undergraduate requirements.

I accepted on the spot, pleased to be able to move three years closer to gainful employment of my choice. Later, I would have second thoughts about the advisability of having taken this short cut. However, at that moment I felt lucky beyond deserving to have had the opportunity to choose.

I flew back to Bowman Field, arranged my discharge, and went home for yet another fresh start. I tried not to think about the fifty million on both sides, including my Uncle Willie's beloved son Jack, who had died in the war. It just felt good to be one of the millions of Americans who survived to enjoy the benefits of the G.I. Bill of Rights and the fruits of the postwar economic boom. I was too excited to feel guilty about the knowledge that World War II had made me a winner, at last.

PART FOUR

ACTION

29.

IT was the best of times after the worst of times: the most hopeful time Americans of my age had known, a time for dreaming, for thinking big, for planning ambitiously, and for making the most of the government's generosity. People who had considered themselves fortunate to hold menial jobs before the war, now, in the first flush of peace, set their sights on achieving previously impossible dreams. I saw the future as a golden opportunity, the chance of my lifetime to end a terribly long losing streak and make up for all the failures of the past. My deferred plan to acquire a formal education, to work in daily journalism, and then to reflect on my experience at book length seemed entirely realistic now. I marched enthusiastically in the parade moving toward a better tomorrow.

Five days before the start of the school year, ten years after my first attempt to become a regular, full-time student at Missouri, I was separated from the service and flew home to become a not-quite-regular but full-time student at Columbia University. Finally, everything seemed to be falling into place.

An administrative officer tried to delay my departure from Louisville with red tape, but my friend Bill had a friend at higher headquarters who cut through that tangle and set me free. At school, I hoped to find a part-time job to reinforce my classroom work; and within a week, through the efforts of an associate dean, I had been given a job as a rewriteman on the night shift at CBS Radio News.

Happily occupied with work, school, and a busy social life, I did not think about playing the horses. I believe that, if the issue had been put to me, I would have bet that I would never again have to depend on that kind of gambling to do for me anything that I could not accomplish by my own efforts.

But such a bet would have lost for reasons obscured at that time by my optimism. Below the surface of awareness, another internal debate apparently had already resolved that I was incapable of dealing with the competitive challenge facing me, that I didn't have a chance, and that I didn't deserve one. Unaware of what was going on, I moved inexorably toward the most active time of my life as a gambler.

As I have come to understand, my surrender to infantile anxieties in this instance may have been brought about by uneasiness over unanticipated competitive challenges at school. I had arrived with an idealized misconception of a university as a temple of learning where all are selflessly devoted to the search for truth, and I appear to have been disoriented by finding that graduate school also is a competitive arena.

Competition among my classmates was masked by good manners and a warm, active social life which encouraged friendship and produced two marriages between students which have endured to the present. I made friends whom I have continued to value through the years and enjoyed immensely the clubby atmosphere in which socializing was inseparable from our labors. We worked hard, mainly at reporting, writing, and editing news and feature stories in a newsroom large enough to hold desks and typewriters for more than sixty students. After hours, we played as hard as we worked.

As I remember the time, there was seldom an evening without something to do and someone to do it with: to drink and talk shop at one of two nearby bars, to share Dutch-treat dinners, to go out on dates, or to attend school or house parties at the homes of students who lived in or near the city. My mother shared in the festivities as hostess at several Friday night dinner parties which she enjoyed as much as any of her appreciative guests.

In the social competition, my mother's dinner parties probably deserve top ranking in family-style entertainment by a small margin over two other class parents: Larry's mother, whose cooking was almost as fine as my mother's; and Flora's mother and father, for the warmth of their hospitality. In the freestyle class, the winner, without challenge, was another class parent, the father of Emily, an oil man from Oklahoma who paid for a birthday party which included dinner at Nino's—no longer in business but then one of New York's finest restaurants—nightclubbing in Harlem, and hansom cab rides through Central Park.

We lived well and I felt enriched by the social life. But I felt also the competition, which centered on the status of old school ties, the quest for jobs after graduation, and three glittering academic prizes: fellowships for a year of travel, work, or study abroad.

Although no one can have been uninterested in the possibility—however small—of winning one of the traveling fellowships, little was said about them, as though it was bad form to seem interested. But the conspiracy of silence only made the competition seem more intense. Students talked more freely about jobs, and some of their remarks suggested envy over my job at CBS—though the same opportunity could have been available to others for the asking, and there was no assurance that the job would be mine after graduation. My classmates talked most freely, endlessly, I thought, about their alma maters, reminding me—in some cases, at least, without meaning to—that I was one of the sixty-two students who did not have an undergraduate degree, the formal education this symbolized, and the ties to prestigious schools of the kind from which some of my classmates had graduated.

Still, despite some discomfort, I was or thought I was reasonably confident about my future. However, all the positive values, every reason to feel good about myself, already had been outweighed by the invisible baggage of my ambivalence and the self-defeating belief that, no matter how promising things might look to the naked eye, such promise was for me a mirage. Recognizing that now, I am filled with awe by the strength of the unyielding ties which can bind compulsives to the deforming influences of childhood.

What I truly felt about my prospects was unintentionally expressed in a word intended as a whimsical display of modesty about my efforts with the four newspapers of my making, which I thought of as weeklies, though two had been dailies and one a monthly. Asked on a personnel questionnaire to describe previous experience in journalism, I listed my work on four "weaklies," the self-mocking word-play discounting the substantial work I had put into the four publications, which had been quite good of their kind—certainly nothing to be ashamed of.

The lack of self-esteem revealed by my low self-evaluation led me eventually to fall back upon the dependence that had hobbled me for so long, thereby turning the golden opportunity of my life into a curtain-raiser for my most active time as a horseplayer. I have not been able to retrieve from memory the precise thought-by-thought, step-by-step process through which I moved back into action, but the main lines seem clear enough.

Behind the scenes, in the competitive arena of my mind, every obvious plus, every rational argument, was overcome by yes-buts of the lunatic logic that had guided me through eight years of dependence on gambling. Lunatic logic would allow me to say that I had here the most promising opportunity of my life but would then respond: "Maybe so, but don't kid yourself. You're a second-class citizen with a fourth-class chance of making good." Reinforcing that line of thought, guilt helped to persuade me that, although there were half a dozen other veterans in the class no more worthy than I to have been discharged early, I had no right to that advantage or to special admission when these dispensations had not been granted to others still in uniform who were as deserving as I but less fortunate. Fear added a further burden: the feeling that, whatever I might have accomplished, it was not enough to arm myself for the competitive struggles I foresaw. Forced to choose between continuing with my career preparations or dependence on gambling, I don't know what I would have decided. Fortunately, it never came to that. Ambivalence proved to be my saving grace, persuading me that there was no need for an either-or decision.

When once again I returned to action, I made the act more tolerable by adopting a three-point package that emphasized positive values. On the chance that I could make it as a journalist, I would work diligently at school and on the job. To satisfy the more compelling need, I would continue as a horseplayer. At the same time, I would find a way to meet my obligations as a socially responsive citizen and thus honor another childhood tie which remained for me the most attractive asset of my ineritance, the family's tradition of social responsibility.

Conscience restrained me from racing back into action. I am not certain what annoyance, disappointment, or frustration actually triggered the process of return. But the chronology as it has emerged from memory suggests that it may have been a student-teacher competition, another defeat in a confrontation with authority, forced on me by my erstwhile benefactor, the associate dean.

In the fall of 1945, just days after the end of World War II, when I left the service to go to school, the atmosphere was rich with euphoria; and it seemed reasonable to believe that the world could look forward to a lasting, tranquil peace and international cooperation toward general well-being. By graduation day, eight months later, the victorious wartime alliance, reacting to an explosion of conflicting interests, had disintegrated into hostilities intense enough to be called Cold War, and the fallout had reached me in school.

Stalin was said to be planning to take all or part of Iran, and some Americans had begun to talk about resolving the growing differences with the Soviet Union by doing to the Soviets what had been done recently to the Japanese. I was appalled to hear the associate dean advocate the atomic solution and solicit my support.

The associate dean, a decorated veteran of World War I who walked and talked with a swagger, enjoyed talking to the veterans in the class. He and I talked often, during breaks in the newsroom routine, or after hours over martinis at his favorite bar, on Broadway opposite the school.

Generally, we shared shop talk, and the conversation was agreeable. Occasionally, he turned the talk to politics, and, as he expressed what I considered reactionary ideas for which I had no sympathy, I would change the subject or end the conversation rather than continue on a collision course.

But when he started talking about "blasting the Bolshies," as he sometimes put it, there was no changing the subject or ending the conversation. Although he didn't say it that way, he seemed to consider it unpatriotic to oppose the idea of dropping atomic bombs on the Soviet Union.

Out of respect for him and gratitude for his generous assistance,

I tried to side-step with noncommittal evasions a dispute I could not win. Eventually, pressed for a specific response, I told the professor I considered the idea unacceptable. Thereupon, his friendly demeanor turned to icy correctness and our relationship became another casualty of the Cold War.

Reflection upon this episode has called to mind a reference in the psychoanalytic literature which may be apropos, if not necessarily applicable. In evaluating the case history of a compulsive gambler who as a child was scolded and beaten for disobeying "self-righteous" parents, the reporting psychoanalyst comments that the child could have avoided punishment, and should have done so, but chose instead to "provoke" the abuse. "There is," this analyst writes, "something like diplomatic adaptation to an unpleasant reality, with private ideas about changing that reality stored away for the future." That is certainly sensible, where feasible, but I don't think it would have worked for me in this case.

As I have been able to reconstruct the confrontation, there were three options open to me. I could have said I agreed, but that would have been a lie. I could have continued to employ diplomatic adaptation and evade the question, as I tried to do without success since the associate dean pressed me for a response. Or, I could express myself truthfully and accept the consequences, as I did.

The consequences included guilt, resentment, and a malaise which could be relieved only by the frenzy of action. I wondered whether I had been wrong in my response, responsible somehow for causing this private cold war. I resented having been forced into an undesirable encounter I couldn't possibly have won. I seem also to have been comforted by thoughts about the protection against indignity that winning could provide in the future, which may have been my kind of "diplomatic adaptation."

Early in December, I received a delayed check from the Air Force for six hundred dollars of terminal compensation. I waited until Christmas break at school, then went to seek out Henny at the Broadway horse room, only to learn that he had retired to Florida. An old acquaintance helped me establish a working relationship with another bookmaker, Fivel, who granted me a modest line of credit and telephone privileges, presumably as another veteran's benefit.

Given my anxieties over real or imagined competitive challenges, going back into action may have served the same purpose as whistling past the graveyard. It didn't improve my situation, but it made me feel better.

A rich winning day encouraged me to think I might have started the really big winning streak I had anticipated for so long. The size of my bets increased. But the hoped-for streak went into my record as just another one-day wonder, leaving me sadder, if no wiser, after one more lesson in the unpredictability of the so-called law of averages.

As horseplayer's work again became part of my routine, I made time to study past performances in the musty school library and placed frequent calls to my bookie on newsroom telephones which were to be used exclusively for reporting assignments. Classes and field work, consisting of reporting and editing assignments of the kind handled by staff members of New York newspapers, occupied me from nine to five every day. I worked at CBS from midnight to eight three nights a week. Unscheduled time was filled with parties, dates, and family visits I seem to have needed more than before and enjoyed more than ever, since I was received everywhere as a winner.

Afterward, I thought of my year at Columbia as a pleasant and productive working holiday enriched by friendships which have continued to matter to me. My pleasure was undiminished by the falling out with the associate dean and two other disagreeable events which occurred during the final days of the school year.

The first of these involved a botch of my making. Assisted by just enough winners to keep me in action without the need to seek outside financing, I had made my way until the last two weeks of the school year. Then a severe run of bad luck overcame the memory of my last borrowing activity aboard the homecoming troopship and led me to try to float a loan.

For reasons beyond recall I chose to approach a classmate, one of the veterans who should have seemed an unlikely candidate for a touch. We respected each other but had spent little time together socially and normally would have no reason to extend our acquaintanceship beyond school. In response to an unremembered but persuasive story, my classmate loaned me three hundred dollars, the equivalent of almost five months of GI subsistence payments. I promised to repay the loan before the end of the summer. Had I done so, that would have completed an insignificant transaction. It became something more in November, when I received a letter from a lawyer threatening to sue, prompting me belatedly to clear the account.

Later, as my borrowings increased and I felt a need to put my activity on a more professional footing, I devised a screening procedure to assure greater care in the selection of lenders by classifying everyone I knew into one of three categories. First, and most important, were the Sure Things: those I could count on to be forthcoming without hesitation—Murray, for example. Other likely prospects, who might require particularly persuasive pleadings but could be called on when Sure Things were unavailable, I listed as Reserves. In the third category were Untouchables, from whom I would not try to borrow in any circumstances, either because they could not be expected to be responsive, or because I would not have wanted them to know of my need to borrow for any reason. If that system had been in effect at school, I would have refrained from approaching my classmate since I would have classified him as Untouchable—for the reason that I would not have wanted to risk losing his respect, as my handling of his loan had assured.

The most disagreeable event of my year as a full-time but not-quite-regular graduate student was an irregular, nasty little episode on graduation day. On my desk that morning, I found an envelope addressed to me containing an undated, unsigned note which read:

"I believe you deserved one of the traveling fellowships and so did most of the committee. But the associate dean vetoed the decision. I thought you should know."

I can't imagine what good my anonymous informant can have thought I would gain from his dirty little writing. I think I would have liked to believe what the note said, so I could have enjoyed a satisfying excuse for having failed to be awarded a prize I would have loved to have won. But I knew that an atrocious exercise in poor judgment on my most important field assignment was enough to have disqualified me, quite apart from any other considerations.

As for my anonymous informant, whatever he may have intended to accomplish, his note revealed that there had been competition of more kinds than I had previously realized.

AFTER graduation, I made a job change which may have been
intended to do more for me as a horseplayer than as a journalist. I
left CBS for United Press, hoping to find in the larger wire-service
organization greater opportunity to become a foreign correspondent.
But if that was truly my reason, then it might have been better to
stand pat at CBS, since the job I took at UP was as sports writer for
the wire serving radio stations—a far cry from managing a bureau
in London, Moscow, or Paris.

However, in every other way the move was ideal for a Jekyll and
Hyde horseplayer deeply involved in a life combining the goods of
work and social responsibility with the contradiction of gambling.
As a newsman, I would expect opportunities beyond sports eventually. As a socially responsible citizen, I could honor my commitment to help improve the world around me by working as an active
member of the American Newspaper Guild, a union organized to
help improve wages and working conditions for employees of news

organizations. Best of all, as a horseplayer, I was perfectly positioned for the strongest run of my life.

Within arm's length of my desk in the headquarters bureau of UP on the twelfth floor of the Daily News Building in New York was everything I needed. At least four bookmakers serviced horseplayers in the building. Racing papers delivered to the sports department were available to me for perusal between assignments or during long, unquestioned visits to the men's room. A racing wire reporting results from tracks all over the country stood a few feet away. Also, as it turned out, a platoon of potential lenders worked at desks near mine, and I enjoyed the security of knowing that I could count on a pay check each week in an amount that grew each year.

Time also worked for me. My schedule, five in the afternoon to one in the morning for most of my years at UP, provided ample time to study past performances and permitted me, in season, to spend afternoons at the track before going to work. All in all, except for winners, a horseplayer couldn't have asked for anything more, and I made full use of the facilities.

Ever since my first visit to Empire City—which had by now been transformed into a track for trotters—I had preferred to be at the track whenever possible, but I did most of my business at the office out of necessity. In that time, New York tracks, which now run year round, were limited to a season that lasted only nine months, and one of those months—August—was assigned to the resort town track at Saratoga, too far for even the most avid city racegoer. Also, during the season, some of the time that could otherwise have been used to go to the track was used instead for chores to which I assigned a higher priority. On balance, I was content. I went to the track as often as possible and did what I had to do at the office when that wasn't possible.

Off-track betting with the office bookies should have been more attractive than it was, since it offered several advantages over going to the track, among them greater convenience, more betting opportunities, and the saving of time and travel cost. But the need for privacy outweighed these attractions.

Despite my best efforts to shield my activity, I was always concerned about the possibility of being exposed as a ne'er-do-well gambler. I tried to limit open contact with the bookies, but I needed to place bets several times a day and collect winnings occasionally. To minimize the chances of being seen with the bookies, I arranged to meet my bet-takers in nooks and corners of the News building, in stairwells, isolated corridors, a little-used library, and the men's room, hoping these precautions would provide a cover for my unsharable secret. However, I think the surest cover may have been the discretion which sealed the lips of those who observed and understood my comings and going but said nothing about my ridiculous conduct.

Privacy was no problem at the track. I seldom saw anyone I knew, and when I did it was someone who, like me, preferred to keep such encounters secret. But that was only part of the great attraction which going to the track held for me.

I cannot think of a hope stronger than the hope I felt at the start of an afternoon at the track, and in those days I don't think I would have been able to imagine many things more thoroughly satisfying than a winning day at the track. Given three wishes, I would have asked for four: a sunny day; a ride to the track in a private, chauffer-driven limousine, rather than having to go by bus, subway, Long Island Railroad, taxi, or shared limousine; a fine lunch in the clubhouse dining room; and a string of winners. One other satisfaction was guaranteed. Admission was free because I went with clubhouse passes, and that made me feel I started a day at the track ahead of the game.

Less often than I would have wished, but often enough, there were winning days to sustain the hope of more. On one such day at Jamaica during my first year at UP, I hit an encouraging high, winning a little more than a thousand dollars—an amount equal to my take-home pay for three months. For several days thereafter, I went to and from the track by taxi, dined regularly at restaurants which normally would have been a great extravagance for me, and treated myself to an expensive suit and a pair of shoes. Then the cash ran out and that episode went into the archives as, once again, just one of those things. Low points occurred on most days. Still, the prospect of an afternoon at the track was irresistible, and I went as often as I could.

Being at the track, any track meant being in the center ring, not in the side-show kind of action available through the office bookies.

Given my choice of venue, I would have picked Jamaica, my lucky track, where I felt more comfortable than at Belmont or Aqueduct and more business-like in the no-frills red-brick grandstand that looked like a factory.

Seated at a table in Jamaica's clubhouse restaurant overlooking the finish line, analyzing past performances, weighing alternatives, and making decisions, I could pretend to be one of the well-heeled high rollers who, more regularly than I, and more richly, supported the place.

Fantasy was encouraged by the special pleasures of a sunny day and a good lunch, which seem to have been always available. Actually, I may have remembered more sunny days than the weather bureau has recorded for the New York metropolitan area in those years after World War II. But it is impossible to exaggerate the certainty with which a racegoer could expect a fine lunch in a dining room managed by the Stevens Brothers at that time. And that was not only true of the clubhouse dining rooms. Excellent food was also served at lower cost in grandstand lunchrooms and soup bars. At every level, grateful horseplayers knew that, no matter how poorly they might fare on the track, they were winners when they sat down at a Stevens Brothers table or counter in those days before phony gourmet food served by cost accountants drove out honest victuals, just as surely as bad money drives out good.

A meal in a Stevens dining room could not eliminate the hurt of a losing day. But a hearty platter of corned beef and cabbage or an Irish lamb stew, washed down with one of the then-fine New York beers, could go a remarkably long way toward easing the pain of loss.

Whether enjoying the special pleasures of an afternoon at the track or doing business austerely with the office bookies, I have recognized a special connection: a compatibility between my work, which financed my action, and the gambling, which helped make even the most routine or dull work tolerable. Perhaps because of that, my feelings about gambling appear to have been similar in critical respects to those I held about work. I liked doing both, and each gave me a sense of importance. I felt I was part of something significant when I showed up for work in the crowded, noisy, worn-out-looking UP newsroom, which was one of the nerve centers of the world. I felt something like that also when I made my way through the day's racing entries, wondering which of them might change my life by making me rich or at least open the way to life-changing wealth.

Whatever I may have felt about similarities between working and gambling, I knew there was also a vital difference. Work was mandatory, gambling a matter of choice. Work was something I liked and did five days a week because I had to. Gambling was something I felt a great *need* to do and did as often as I could, which was less often than I would have estimated before taking a closer look at the record of memory.

Upon reflection, I have become aware that I didn't gamble as often as I worked—to take that as one measure of my frequency of action. I could play out a rather long string of days in action and often did. But I could not have mustered the emotional stamina to sustain a frequency of gambling comparable to a year-round five-day work week.

One widely held stereotype of the compulsive gambler is of a person who, day in and day out, risks all; and there may be some who behave like that in real life. I have known three men—an editor, an editorial assistant, and a teletype operator—and one woman, the owner of a highly profitable small business, who may have gambled every day or as often as the state of their finances permitted. But I could not rank myself in such company.

Possibly, my need to gamble was not as great as I have thought, or perhaps my need for other connections was as great as the need for action. In any case, I took frequent time-outs for other activities. Occasionally, also, I was shut out of action for lack of funds; and on other occasions I was overcome by battle fatigue or by something very like boredom, usually after a painfully long string of losing days.

However, within that balance of things, one thing was true every day. Each morning the first decisions I called upon myself to make were whether to gamble that day and, if so, whether at the track or at the office.

As important, in its way, as the decisions reached was the routine set in motion by the decisions. I think routine is vital to the well-being of a compulsive gambler. My experience suggests that routine provides stability by creating the illusion that what is being done makes some kind of sense, if only because it is done regularly and in some order. I felt that way from the moment I considered whether or not to go into action, and I took comfort in the procedures which formed my routines.

Circumstances might affect the order in which routines were carried out, but the procedures which moved me into action and kept me going remained constant. As an example, on days when my decision was to be in action at the track, I could be awake by eight-thirty and, without seeming to hurry, would:

• Walk a quarter of a mile to a newsstand on Broadway for the racing papers.

• Stop at Mr. Berkowitz's grocery for fresh, doughy, chewy rolls and some cheese—cream or Swiss—to go with coffee.

• Take time for a breakfast that seldom varied but invariably satisfied.

• Follow that with two hours or more of work on the little numbers of the past performance records at the New York track of the day and at one or two out-of-state tracks.

• Compile a list of proposed bets, as few as two or three, or as many as a dozen or more.

• Review my cash position and, if necessary, call one or more of my lenders.

• Place out-of-town bets by phone with one of the office bookies as a backup for my track betting.

• Attend to last-minute chores, as unimportant as taking a rumpled suit to Mr. Schwartz for cleaning and pressing, as urgent as making a promised call on union business, or as frequent as my regular round of family visits.

• Finally, having done all that, arrive at the track in time for the first race and a bracing lunch—in the clubhouse dining room, cash on hand permitting, or at the lunch counter when it seemed advisable to conserve available funds for betting rather than eating.

My first bet, the most hopeful act of the day up to that moment, tied me into a different kind of routine over which my control was limited to betting on one horse or another. I tried to believe that the outcome of that bet, and of the others to follow, was determined by my skill as a handicapper. After a winning race, I felt no doubt about my cleverness. After a losing race I might, out of scientific curiosity, reexamine the past performance statistics to see which factor in the record of my losing selection I might have exaggerated and which critical piece of information about the winner I might have overlooked. In that way I hoped to sharpen my handicapping skills. But I think I knew that something immeasurable, a force not subject to my control, decided outcomes and the best I could do was try to bet on the horses that were moved by that force.

At that point, routine failed me. The importance of something may best be demonstrated by its absence, and that was the case with my lack of the one routine most needed in action: a consistent betting discipline to determine when to bet, how to bet, how much to bet. I had learned and adopted several rules which could have provided the necessary discipline: don't bet blind, don't bet on more than one horse in a race, don't bet on a horse about which you are uncertain, do bet the same amount of money on long shots as on favorites. Strict compliance wouldn't have improved my chances of winning, but losses could have been reduced considerably if I had observed my rules more often than I did.

Time was my problem, specifically the twenty-five-minute interval between the finish of one race and the start of the next. That might have been no problem if there had been someone to share the time with me. But I came to the track for privacy and I came alone. That left me with time on my hands and the need to be occupied. To kill time, I reconsidered races I had previously passed up for lack of clear-cut prospects and took a second look at selections already on my betting list. Almost always, the result was one or more changes which violated one or more of my rules, seldom profitably.

Violations caused no problems on winning days. There were no problems on winning days. On the other days, the knowledge that I had sinned by violating the rules compounded the agony of losing.

Throughout, I appeared, or tried to appear, confident and hopeful. The winning days were easy to deal with. Ecstasy carried me through the routines. Losing days ground me down. I ended such days discouraged and depressed, yet determined to continue my struggle to make the law of averages live up to my expectations of it.

Winning or losing, I kept at it until the last possible minute then hurried to get to work on time—by taxi if I was a winner, in a limousine shared with half-a-dozen other passengers if not. Most of the limousines parked near the grandstand exit went to midtown Manhattan, but some took passengers, who had just spent the afternoon betting on horses ridden by jockeys, to Roosevelt Raceway or Yonkers, to wait three hours before spending the evening watching horses driven in harness. When I wanted to feel better about what I was doing, I used to think that the real compulsive horseplayers were those who went from flats to trotters—something which, I assured myself, I would never do and didn't.

Few horseplayers I knew thought of the trotters—harnessed horses pulling sulkies behind them—as horse racing. For one thing, we considered it unnatural to hobble horses in that way. For another, that funny kind of racing seemed to inspire race-fixing scandals far more often than the flats.

For me, there was still another consideration. One round of action was as much as I could handle. Whether as winner or loser, the tensions of an afternoon at the track left me drained. Yet, oddly, by the time I arrived at the office on work days I felt renewed and ready for the responsibility that kept me whole. What had happened at the track was done. There might be more action tomorrow, if I decided there should be. Now it was time to clear up loose ends—check results of the out-of-town bets I had placed, clear accounts with the bookmaker who had handled the business, line up a potential lender, if necessary—and get on with the work that made everything else possible.

An afternoon at the track involved eight or nine hours of work and travel time before I arrived at the office for eight more hours of work. By contrast, on those days when I decided to be in action but limit myself to betting with the bookmakers, the work required—mainly for past performance research and phone calls to bookies—was less than half as much, leaving me hours more for activities that were neglected when I was involved in time-consuming action at the track.

Most relaxing, and always welcome, were occasional time-outs which freed me from all the chores imposed by action. I felt free even when I used such layoffs for work that required more of my time and energy than the work I had to do when I was gambling. Non-gambling responsibilities, which were wedged into occasional openings in my schedule when I was in action, expanded during time-outs to fill my days with chores that were dutiful and sometimes even pleasurable.

Least attractive, yet most compelling, were gambling-related financial-planning activities. There were loan applications to be made, loan payments to be scheduled and rescheduled, meetings with lenders and potential lenders, and explanations, excuses, and promises to be made, in person, by telephone, or by mail.

Much more satisfying was the quite different kind of business required of an American Newspaper Guild activist. I met frequently with Guild officials at union headquarters and with committee members at UP, maintained a heavy volume of correspondence with Guild members in UP bureaus around the country, and performed various duties in organizing drives, contract negotiations, and grievance hearings.

Having met my obligations, I felt free to indulge myself as normal people do in their free time. I dated and, for a year, enjoyed the thoroughly satisfying, guilt-free company of Gloria, until she decided that she wanted to be married and decided it would not be with me.

When I wasn't with Gloria, I made my rounds of family visits, saw friends—but less often, as wedding bells for Murray and others began breaking up that old gang of mine—played handball or other games when partners were available, and, usually alone, went often to the movies and to the theater.   It was during these years that Broadway was being graced by *A Streetcar Named Desire, Death of a Salesman,* and *The Member of the Wedding;* and international movie makers were lighting up screens with *Sunset Boulevard, All About Eve, Rashomon, The Third Man,* and *Great Expectations.*

People who knew me during those busy postwar years have told me they thought of me as a cheerfully industrious fellow, and I would have described myself that way, too. But I think I was troubled then, and have been since, to recognize that I did a great deal without enjoying very much.

Routine accounted for the amount of work I did as a journalist, gambler, and socially responsive citizen, but what I did was done without feeling. I have recognized during those years the same arms-length approach that characterized my wartime relationships. I remained at a distance from others, maintaining a safe defensive position, unwilling to risk rejection or defeat, except in action, where I accepted losing as part of a gambler's routine. As I remember now, I rarely felt a sense of joyful anticipation about anything I did and may never have experienced any hope higher than the hope with which I began a day in action.

Others cannot have found their relationships with me greatly fulfilling. It seems to have been a point of honor with me to keep promises but not to promise very much and almost never to go beyond what had been promised. For some, that seems to have been enough. As an example, from time to time my colleagues in the Guild expressed appreciation for the regularity with which I met my responsibilities. Others cannot have been pleased to find that they could not have from me more than the little I could give, mechanically and within careful limits.

To the extent that a single relationship may be taken as typical of one's general attitude, the limits I drew may be seen in a relationship I enjoyed with Louise, a magazine editor who seemed to me everything I could have wished for in a woman. I admired her mind, her voluptuous body, her easy self-confidence, and the straightforward way in which she dealt with people. If I had wanted to be married at that time, I would have wanted to marry Louise, but that thought never entered my mind during the two years we spent together.

However, apparently it was on her mind. As she began to hint at it, I tried to evade the issue, as with the associate dean at school. When that proved impossible, I revealed my unsharable secret, told Louise I was heavily in debt, could see no way out, and would not commit myself to marry in such circumstances. She understood, and we ended the affair with a handshake, leaving me to wonder whether I could ever again hope to be lucky enough to meet someone like Louise at a time when I might be in a position to act more sensibly. In retrospect, it seems to me that although I loved Louise and although she might have accepted me as I was in hope of reforming me, I had no desire to quit gambling and preferred to continue the dependency which had sustained me for so long rather than risk what marriage might entail.

Looking back on broken relationships of that kind, I feel that, whatever others may have lost or failed to find in their relations with me, the greater loss was mine. My sense of loss is deepened by awareness that my reluctance to involve myself fully, which limited or crippled so many of my personal relationships, also hampered me in responding to challenges in the public area of social responsibility. However, here my reluctance to engage myself may have had less to do with my unwillingness to quit gambling and more to do with a self-protective, safety-first kind of cowardice, which may have been not greatly different from my response in personal relationships.

Since my personal encounter with the Cold War at school, the temper of the times had grown increasingly perilous. The Cold War had become a primary factor in international life; and at home—largely through the efforts of the House Un-American Activities Committee and Senator Joseph McCarthy—a situation which many people considered a reaction to the fear of Communist infiltration and others considered a witch hunt and a compaign of thought control had become a primary part of domestic political life.

I was a silent dissident, outraged by what was being done in the name of freedom and democracy. But, though passionate in my dissent, I was passive in my reaction, out of fear of becoming a target and possibly being turned into an unemployed horseplayer. I made modest contributions to civil liberties groups, signed petitions, talked with relatives, friends, and colleagues—most of whom shared my concerns—and wished I could find a way to do something more courageous.

That opportunity presented itself to me as a member of the Guild. Union leaders suspected of being Communists or Communist sympathizers had come under broad attack, and that attack spread to the leaders of the Guild's New York local, to which the UP unit, of which I was chairman, belonged. Supporters of the anti-Communist drive organized a campaign to replace the officers of the local on the grounds that they were Communists or Communist sympathizers.

Their efforts came to a climax in a pre-election meeting attended by more than a thousand people at which former supporters and colleagues of the left-wing officials denounced them. Little was said about the record of the officers regarding their effectiveness under fire in organizing and contract negotiations during the past decade. Instead, speaker after speaker took the stage to say that as guests in the home of this officer or that one, over dinner or drinks, they had heard their hosts express sentiments they described as pro-Soviet or anti-American. Some had been friends or supporters for years of those they were now attacking, but they spoke without apparent shame or embarrassment, inspired, I suppose, by self-righteous patriotism.

I thought of the session as a kangaroo court and was offended in particular by two aspects. For one, perhaps my favorite public pleasure is to serve as host at enjoyable dinner parties, and I think I was disturbed by the thought that a host might endanger himself by inviting a potential spy to his table. More important, the attackers did not accuse their former friends and colleagues of any act more physical than speaking thoughts protected by the constitution.

Following the denunciation meeting, right-wing candidates defeated the left-wing incumbents by a margin of two to one, after which the losers dropped out of Guild activity. The next year, a by-election was called to replace the president elected on the right-wing ticket, who had resigned, and it was said that the left might not be able to field a candidate. Upon hearing that, I went to talk with John McManus, film critic of *Time* magazine, who had been president on the ousted slate. I had met him at Guild meetings and had come to know him as a courageous man of great decency who was admired even by many of those who opposed him. He said he was not available for another run, but would support an appropriate candidate.

I offered to run. I was not widely known in the local, but had been active among wire-service people at AP and INS, as well as UP. I wanted to demonstrate that the kind of people who had taken over were not without opposition and should not be allowed to win in a walkover.

With no better offer in sight, McManus graciously overlooked my presumption and agreed to round up other backers and help raise funds for leaflets and other expenses. I called a time-out from the horses for almost two months and campaigned at every Guild unit in an exhilarating effort which, despite my defeat, left me with two satisfactions. I did better by three or four points than the previous losers, and I enjoyed the privilege of getting to know John McManus, about whom I could have testified that, friendship aside, he did take part in at least one questionable activity. At breakfast in his home he served bacon and eggs accompanied by wine—red wine—which he called fruit juice.

Without interruption, following my electoral campaign I moved back into my more normal routine in which the two constants remained continuing action and continuing losses. My greatest loss was the death of my mother of a heart attack, less than three years after my return from military duty. The doctor who saw her at my Aunt Mary's house one evening, when she complained of pains in the chest and back, diagnosed her condition as a bad cold. Her death the following morning of a coronary thrombosis was a piece of bad luck which might have been avoided if her condition had been correctly diagnosed and properly treated.

Since a primary rationalization for my gambling had been the hope of winning enough to put my mother on Easy Street, I thought of quitting. But I concluded that such a move would have been an empty tribute—too little, too late. Instead, I abstained from betting for the month-long mourning period then did what seemed most sensible to me and went back into action.

DURING the early postwar years, I was in what many would have considered an enviable financial position. For the first time in my life, the percentages favored me. Each year at United Press I earned more than the year before, and my income increased more rapidly than my cost of living. As one example, while my salary almost doubled during the first five years, from sixty-five dollars a week to one hundred and twenty-five, my rent rose at only half that rate, from twenty-eight dollars a month to forty-two. The result was that, after paying for necessities, I had an increasing amount of surplus cash to use as I wished.

Some people my age who took on family responsibilities in those years had a tougher time of it. The Office of Price Administration, which had kept the lid on price increases during the war, was disbanded and price controls were eliminated. The inflation that followed was hard on families of limited means. I had only myself to think about, and my personal economy gave me no cause for complaint.

Few things increased in cost at a rate to match the increase in my salary. The subway fare was doubled, from five cents to ten, in 1947, but most price increases were substantially less than that. In an area of personal interest, would-be gourmets of my generation who couldn't afford deluxe restaurants, such as the Chambord, cut their teeth on French food at the Champlain on West Forty-ninth Street, where the cost of a four-course dinner ranged from only seventy-five to ninety-nine cents.

Given the economic advantages I had acquired, this could have been a good time for me to pack it in as a gambler. When I went to work for UP, I was in my ninth year as a horseplayer, including time-outs. During those years, I had subjected myself to some heavy pounding, financially, emotionally, and physically. I could have withdrawn from action honorably after my good fight and retired to work well, live well, invest my discretionary funds prudently, and watch my capital grow.

Instead, my decision, if that word may be used to describe action taken without thought, was to go for more. Because of the spread in my favor created by my income increasing faster than inflation, I could use an increasingly larger share of my income for what had been, for a long time, the largest item in my budget. There was still another financial advantage. My increasing salary made me more credit-worthy in the eyes of lenders, so I could borrow increasingly large sums if necessary. I suppose it was too sweet an opportunity to pass up. I responded accordingly. I stepped up the size and tempo of my betting, doggedly pursuing my vision of how the law of averages should work for me without giving a thought to the better use I could have made of my present financial edge.

In reviewing the errors which marked my way as a horseplayer, I have found it difficult to determine which was the most damaging of my mistakes. But this decision, or lack of one, surely comes close to that dubious distinction.

Having sinned in haste, I could reflect at leisure. Years later, as I tried to understand why I had done what I had done during my years in action, the question which gave me the most trouble was why, at this promising juncture in my life, I refused, or anyway failed, to choose a more rational course, and why I chose to accept the automatic compensating reaction rather than the good fortune that could have been mine for the taking.

By the time I entered my period of reflection, I was already aware that my postwar situation—gambling more while earning more from normal economic competition—is not at all unusual. Among my acquaintances are three successful and rich business people who are also compulsive gamblers. But they are small potatoes, not worthy of a place on the roster of rich and famous men and women—successful in business, the professions, and other occupations—who are also active in race-track clubhouses and at the high-stakes tables of gambling casinos, regularly contributing to the huge profits of such enterprises.

The ranks of prominent affluent gamblers include many historic figures, among them Nero, Napoleon, and a number of American presidents from George Washington onward; business executives beyond counting, among them oil billionaire H. L. Hunt, who is said to have built his empire on oil leases won in poker games; and a large representation from the fields of show business, literature, and sports that include Woody Allen, Milton Berle, Sarah Bernhardt, Ty Cobb, Feodor Dostoevsky, Clark Gable, Jack Klugman, Lily Langtry, Walter Matthau, Edgar Allan Poe, Mario Puzo, Babe Ruth, Frank Sinatra, Oscar Wilde, and Darryl Zanuck. Few of this variety of men and women may have been as compulsive as I, but all have been active enough as a horseplayer, craps-shooter, or card-player to have made gambling a lively part of their life styles.

By coincidence, as I was becoming aware, name by name, of the affluent celebrity gamblers, my attention was drawn to news reports about Sir Hugh Fraser, a major stockholder in a British chain of department stores founded by his father, chairman of the corporation's board of directors, and a high-rolling gambler who had lost as much as half a million dollars in a night of casino action. The reports said the board of directors ousted Sir Hugh as chairman in 1981 because of the corporation's poor profit performance under his management.

As far as the reports indicated, nothing was said by the directors about the chairman's gambling, and Sir Hugh did not talk in public about the role gambling might have played in his ouster or why he became a heavy gambler in the first place. So only speculation is possible about whether insecurity over his corporate performance, the cost of two divorces, or some other reason drove Fraser to depend so heavily on gambling.

What is known beyond guessing is that Fraser attempted to get more of what most people would consider enough. It is also known that situations of this sort—of respected men and women endangering their competitive gains by making themselves dependent on gambling—are more numerous than common sense would allow most people to believe possible.

As evidence of such behavior accumulated, I couldn't for a long time imagine why anyone already well-fixed should risk wealth, reputation, and peace of mind by gambling. I could easily understand that disadvantaged people depend on gambling in the hope that it will bring them more than they feel capable of winning in any other way, and that desperation could drive some of them to gamble compulsively. In fact, I had thought of gambling as a monopoly of the poor. But for those already well-endowed to risk what they had in pursuit of something they couldn't get seemed to me to fall somewhere between foolishness and insanity, and I was baffled by why anyone should do that.

Understanding eluded me until I realized that obvious answers can be the most difficult to accept. As I then came to understand, the answer to why people gamble, so many compulsively, is the same for all: for the affluent as for the disadvantaged. All are trying to win something more than they have, something more than they can gain, or feel they can gain, in any other way.

In this world, everyone must compete, the affluent and disadvantaged alike. Each is moved by the same kind of needs, wants, and desires. Though on a different scale, each acts in accordance with what I have come to think of as the Law of More, which says there is never enough, no matter how much one has.

The Law of More governs competition, and the ever-present competitive challenges compel compliance. For all, the basic challenge to acquire more comes from the need to try to keep up with, and hopefully to stay ahead of, inflation. For most, there are additional compelling reasons for trying to acquire more than one has. Among the other inspirations are plain greed; the need to try to assure some degree of financial security for the future; the desire to keep up with, or move ahead of, the Joneses; and the underlying competitive-acquisitive challenge to improve one's standard of living as one moves through life.

Many individuals who have not yet amassed what they would

consider wealth like to think there is a point at which they would know that they had enough and call it quits. But the biggest winners know that, under the Law of More, there is no standing pat. The law says: Get ahead or fall behind. As the record shows, the most successful accumulators of wealth never stop trying for more until they die, after which their chips are transferred to their heirs and the pursuit of more continues without pause. The more being sought may appear to be something other than money—more power, more respect, a demonstration of greater skill or cleverness than others, an exhibition of the Midas touch—but it all comes down to money in the end.

For everyone except the idle rich and persons who are physically or psychologically incapacitated, the pursuit of more begins with a competitive gambling decision: a choice of occupation. For most, that is not enough, and dependent gambling becomes an added tool with which to probe for more than can be hoped for through earnings from a job, profession, or business. Surveys indicate that four out of five Americans gamble at games of chance at least occasionally. Most of these men and women manage to keep their dependent gambling within tolerable limits. Many do not.

Those who allow their dependent gambling to get out of hand do so, I believe, as an anxious, uncertain overreaction to the demands imposed by the Law of More. In expressing that understanding, which seems obvious to me now, I feel like someone who has only lately learned what others knew all along. Still, for those who already know what I came to understand over time, repetition may help narrow the gap between knowledge and understanding. In that spirit, I can repeat that to live in a competitive-acquisitive society is to compete, that to compete is to gamble, that this process inevitably produces more losers than winners, and that in an attempt to be on the winning side some competitors, ill-equipped for sensible efforts, then exaggerate their need to depend on gambling and carry that dependence into compulsion.

They begin to behave in ways that are far different from what is generally considered normal, to the point that their behavior leads some people to think of them as freaks, or "sickies." That is a winner's view of losers, and everyone is a winner when ranked against compulsive gamblers. However, while understandable, such an attitude obscures understanding by distorting reality.

It may be more useful to recognize that compulsive gamblers are a natural part of the social and economic mainstream, and that they are like other people, only more so: more needy, more competitive, more uncertain about their abilities, more frustrated, more reckless, and more easily moved to excessive behavior. And compulsive gamblers are not the only competitors who behave like compulsive gamblers.

Prevailing stereotypes tend to emphasize the differences between compulsive gamblers and all others. As I thought through the whys and wherefores of compulsive gamblers, it occurred to me that it might be instructive to look at the similarities, as well as the differences, between compulsive gamblers and another class of compulsive competitors with whom I became familiar during four years as a business editor. These are the corporate strivers aiming at the big prizes in their competitive gambles who are known, respectfully, as "workaholics."

I was drawn at first to this pairing by apparent similarities in the ways each responds to the competitive challenges of the Law of More. Both workaholics and compulsive gamblers are not only highly competitive but, quite often, unusually aggressive. Both work in single-minded pursuit of their objectives, frequently to the point that their tunnel vision obscures the emotional needs of those dependent on them. The result, too often, is damage both to themselves and to their dependents, who are vulnerable to the fallout from their compulsion. That kind of damage—alienation, depression, alcoholism, drug abuse, suicide—is deplored, of course. But, for the successful workaholic, it is also accepted as part of the cost of doing business as a winner.

Most important, I think, is the basic similarity that each is engaged in irrational pursuits. The workaholic is after more wealth than anyone could reasonably expect to use in a lifetime. The compulsive gambler is after more than could possibly be won.

Both place great emphasis, perhaps the greatest emphasis, on the acquisition of money. That is considered entirely normal for workaholics, but not for compulsive gamblers. Several researchers comment on the importance compulsive gamblers attach to money, as though it is somehow odd that people gambling for money should be so concerned. One says compulsive gamblers "libidinize" cash. But if that means assigning to money a value greater than its material worth, then workaholics and compulsive gamblers are of like minds.

To the compulsive gambler, money represents everything desirable: success, respect, approval, acceptance—proof of the individual's worth. Money seems to mean much the same thing to workaholics. Some of them are so careful with a dollar—*their* dollars—as to suggest that they consider it a sin to waste their own money on anything that can be paid for with a company credit card. The most "libidinized" view of money may be that of psychoanalysts who insist on punctual payment of their fees in cash or non-bouncing checks for the patients' own good, as a vital element in the therapy.

Similar as they are in this way, the workaholic and compulsive gambler are also different in ways that are more important. The most obvious difference is the far greater percentage of winners among workaholics and losers among compulsive gamblers. However, the more significant differences are those which account for the vast discrepancy in performance.

As I have observed them in action, successful workaholics, like other successful but less compulsive competitors, share four critical common denominators. They have strong motivation, an efficient sense of organization, remarkable discipline, tons of self-confidence, and, as the source of all of these characteristics, self-respect. By contrast, compulsive gamblers lack all or most of these assets. They may speak of possessing them, but it is only talk, which they don't themselves believe. That is their problem.

As I experienced this problem and as others seem to have dealt with it compulsive gamblers are caught in an ambivalent bind. They want desperately to succeed and would prefer to do so in conventional, respectable competitions. But, even when they have achieved such success, they are unable to recognize and accept it as their just due. Their competitive nerves have been rubbed raw, in many cases by frequent childhood defeats; and, oversensitized by rejection, they tend to magnify challenges and minimize strengths, assets, abilities, and accomplishments.

One of the more poignant cases is that of Clark Gable, product of an unhappy childhood, who grew up to be "king" of Hollywood and one of the richest men in California during the 1930s, with a million-dollar-a-year contract. Despite all that, Gable is said to have been insecure, to have worried about possibly dying poor, and to have relieved his anxieties by gambling, until eventually he managed to find better ways to make himself comfortable with his lot in life.

Some, like Gable, are able to overcome their insecurities eventually. Too many cannot. Naked of self-respect, the compulsive gambler is unable to muster the self-confidence vital to competitive success in what are regarded as the normal fields of endeavor. Uneasy about entitlement to rewards for work well done and uncertain about their ability to hold what they have and add to it, their needs are too great to be satisfied by anything less than excess. In that position, with little of positive value from which to construct a sound competitive position, compulsive gamblers are more readily susceptible to the attractions of lunatic logic, which encourages wishful thinking as a substitute for sensible reasoning and sustained effort.

Throughout my years as a compulsive gambler, I was never sure of myself in anything I ever did. Despite respectable accomplishments, I never stopped needing recognition as a successful—and, therefore, respectable—person, even when others already saw me as what I hoped to become. And I never stopped thinking that money, won as a gambler, would bring me success, respectability, and acceptance—all of which were available to me without winning even one dollar at the races.

Reviewing the process in which I was for so long involved, I am moved to sympathetic despair for those who are still engaged in compulsive gambling. More or less safe from the storm and strife of battle, I think of those others as walking wounded in the competitive-acquisitive wars, sadly brave warriors in dubious battle against an overwhelming, unseen, unrecognizable foe. Lucky ones like me have withdrawn to more comfortable competitions. But the compulsive gamblers stand fast, bleeding but unbowed, ever hopeful of finding the way to acquire the more they seek through dependence on endless, pointless action, unaware of their hurts, not knowing that their only way to win is to quit.

I cannot know how I would have behaved if what I have learned since had been available to me then. With understanding, I hope I would have behaved more sensibly than I did. With nothing more than my unrestrained need for more to guide me, I behaved as a compulsive gambler.

UNTIL I went to work at UP, I had never dealt directly with book-makers, only with their agents, the sheet men who accepted bets and paid winners—Henny, Morris, Fivel. At work, bookmaking was a cottage industry run by small-time bookies who took bets on their own account as a sideline to their regular jobs. I did business occasionally with three of these office entrepreneurs.

My feelings toward two of them were mixed. On the one hand, I recognized that they were performing a necessary service for horse-players who needed to place bets. At the same time, I considered it indecent to profit from one's colleagues, especially from such easy prey as compulsive gamblers, of whom there were at least four among the dozen or so horseplayers in the office.

My judgment of the third, Jerry, a teletype operator, was less balanced. Jerry had come late to his sideline. After learning that there was money to be made from the horseplayers, who were already well served by the other bookies, he had decided to cut himself in on the action with the assistance of a silent partner employed elsewhere in the building. I thought of Jerry as an opportunistic grubber out after a risk-free sure thing. I thought of him also as a parasite. And I thought of him as the kind of bookie who made me worry whether I could expect to collect promptly and fully on a big hit. I knew that my attitude was unfair and certainly unreasonable, yet each move he made led me to score him plus or minus, and I seldom found cause to record a plus.

Whenever possible, I preferred to place my off-track bets with Jimmy Mac—a dapper, street-wise little man who was also employed as a mailer for the *Daily News,* wrapping and loading bundles of newspapers onto delivery trucks, a job which served as a front for his real work. The Mac was a businessman, a professional book-maker, who specialized in serving employees of the *News* and the *New York Times.* He operated a store-front horse room across town, at Forty-third Street and Eighth Avenue, down the street from the *Times,* where he needed two sheet men to write the business; and he employed three runners at the *Times* and two in the *News* building.

Jimmy Mac or his agents could be reached, in person or by telephone, in the mail room of the *News.* There was no other tele-phone connection. But normally that posed no problem, since the Mac or one of his runners was on call during day and night shifts. On occasion, illness or some other reason might leave a period uncovered, but such occasions were rare; and there were balancing compensations, particularly the knowledge that Jimmy Mac was a good man to do business with.

The Mac seldom smiled, for reasons that became apparent to me only after I had known him for a long time, but he paid off winners with a smile. That was his trademark. With it, he seemed to say: Winning is tough to do, so enjoy it. He also gave credit; but unlike other bookies, who limited credit only to bets placed with them, the Mac also loaned out-of-pocket cash for other important, nonbetting purposes such as paying the rent and buying food until payday.

As I knew him, the Mac was an honorable man. He talked out of the side of his mouth, but he talked straight. Although our con-versations dealt mainly with business; now and then when we met, we took time to talk of this and that. The Mac knew his world well; and within that boundary I thought of him as a wise man, until he reminded me that no matter how wise we are we are all only human after all. That unexpected learning came much later. For a long time,

I was simply pleased to do business with a bookmaker who made the act of placing and booking bets seem less sordid than it was.

As I have come to understand, the differences between Jerry and Jimmy Mac were not as great as I thought when I was dealing with them; and their essential similarity was more important. The differences between them which impressed me at the time have come to seem only skin deep, a matter of style which hid but could not change the fact that each was doing exactly the same thing in his own way. Neither could turn my losses into winnings. All either could do was to make me more or less comfortable as I continued to lose more than I won.

As for thinking of Jerry as a parasite, that description of him seems accurate enough still, but only in the sense that all bookmakers—including Jimmy Mac, as well as gambling casino operators, state officials who authorize gambling and take taxes and profits from it, and others who thrive on the losses of gamblers—are parasites. Though that may seem a harsh judgement, I think it fairly describes those who live by encouraging the impossible dreams of others.

Still, I can understand that such a judgment might not find favor with many people, gamblers and non-gamblers. During my time in action, I wouldn't have accepted it either or even cared whether any of the people I did business with were parasites. The only distinction I drew was to prefer doing business with the Mac rather than with Jerry or the other office bookies.

On days when I had decided to confine myself to off-track betting, I made every effort to place my business with the Mac or one of his runners, Maxie, a bewildered-looking, almost toothless fat man. Maxie was a round-heeled compulsive horseplayer who probably wasn't as old as he appeared to be and, despite appearances, exuded more hopefulness than I felt, even though he had been at it much longer than I and seemed to have traveled a rougher road. I felt I was doing a good deed when I placed a bet with Maxie. He earned a cut of his handle and needed all he could get to support his habit. When I was unable to reach Maxie or his boss, I gave my business reluctantly to Jerry or one of the other office bookies.

On one such occasion, having completed some personal chores ahead of schedule, I came to the office early to attend to Guild business and place a bet—actually a combination of four bets of five dollars each on a three-horse win parlay and a round robin of win parlays pairing each of these three with each of the others: Horse A with Horse B, Horse A with Horse C, and Horse B with Horse C. It is a silly way to bet; a sucker's bet. The mathematical odds against picking three winners in a row are very high, even if their names were Secretariat, Seattle Slew, and Whirlaway; and the payoff is very small in relation to the true odds. For example, based on the probable odds quoted for my horses, if all three won, I stood to collect about twelve hundred dollars, sixty to one for my twenty-dollar bet, whereas—depending upon the number of horses in each race—the mathematical odds against picking three winners in three races could be sixty times sixty to one.

However, though small in relation to risk, the actual dollars collected if such a combination wins can be substantial. That's what attracts unsophisticated and hard-up gamblers. That is also why, if I were a bookmaker, I would wish to do business exclusively with players making only such bets. I would give big discounts, fifty percent or more, and I would make big profits.

Just how difficult it can be to win anything from this kind of a combination bet may be judged from the penalty for any single defeat. If just one horse loses, three of the four parlays are lost. If two horses lose, all four parlays lose. So, even if a bettor picks one winner out of three—no mean feat in itself—the entire bet is lost.

Realities of this kind confirm the rule that underlies all the others: the only way to bet the horses is one at a time, and carefully. To combine horses in the hope of multiplying profits ignores the golden rule of probabilities, that the more bets a player makes, the more chances there are of losing rather than winning. Needless to say, that doesn't deter some gamblers.

Among my sins on this day, there was already a violation or another basic rule: don't bet blind, without first examining the past performance data. I had not intended to bet and so had not studied the records of the horses on which I now proposed to bet. Out of idle curiosity, while scanning the entries in the *Daily News* during the subway ride to the office, my attention was drawn to three horses at different tracks who "owed" me, having lost the last time I bet on them.

The fact that a horse lost the last time the player bet on the animal is a ridiculous reason for betting on that horse again, particularly when nothing is known of the competition in the race at hand. That didn't cross my mind and wouldn't have stopped me if it had.

All that concerned me when I got to the office was to find someone to take my bet. The twelve hundred dollars I stood to collect if my three horses won was the equivalent of three months' pay at the time. It would be my biggest single hit ever.

With less than half an hour to post time for my first race, the only bookmaker I could find was Jerry. In response to my eye signal, he arranged for someone to relieve him at his teletype machine, and we met in the stairwell. As he studied my betting slip spelling out the four parlays, his eyes widened in apprehension. Small timer, I thought.

The kind and amount of the bet I wished to place would have been accepted routinely by Jimmy Mac. Jerry hesitated. He examined a scratch sheet he carried in his back pocket, presumably to check the odds and estimate the extent of his potential liability. What he saw seemed to make him more uncomfortable. He hurried back to the office to make a telephone call, to his partner, I guessed. Chicken, I thought.

To be fair, the Mac could more comfortably have accepted the bet because he had many more bets to offset this one. For Jerry, it could well be the only bet of the day, one that posed the risk of heavy loss for small gain, even though the odds were heavily in his favor. At the time, I wasn't being fair and preferred to think that only a piker like Jerry would have to call his partner before accepting a bet.

The call seemed to steady him. Before returning to work, he stopped by my desk and, smiling weakly, said, "Good luck." I entered another demerit against him, for his insincerity and for unprofessional conduct, since there was no need for him to have said anything more than OK.

Whatever else I may have felt about Jerry, I felt also relief and gratitude for having had my bet accepted in the nick of time. Only five minutes remained to post time for the first of my races. But, with the formalities attended to, I lost track of the time and gave myself over to daydreaming about what I might do with the twelve hundred dollars if my three horses won. Mainly, I decided, I would press my luck. I would increase the size of my bets to a hundred dollars or more. And I would limit myself to one horse at a time. I would play by the rules.

Lost in my reverie, I was unaware that the first race had been run until I saw Jerry, with an end-of-the-world look on his face, walk away from the racing wire. He stopped at my desk to confirm what was obvious from his appearance. "Fourteen-forty," he said, glumly, informing me in that way that Horse A had won and paid fourteen dollars and forty cents, a bit more than six to one.

Some psychologists have theorized that compulsive gamblers *expect* their bets to win. I cannot recall ever feeling anything like that. I *wanted* my bets to win. I *hoped* they would win. I thought they had a *good chance* to win. But I never told myself I knew they would win.

Common sense and superstition combined to keep me from going that far. I had been a gambler long enough to know that nothing can be taken for granted in a horse race. And I would have considered it bad luck to believe I had it made and could expect to collect.

But now something new was happening. I began to think it might be possible that my time had come, and that this time the big win to open the way to much bigger things really could be taking place.

I joined Jerry at the racing wire for the second race and watched as the keys printed out the name of Horse B as the winner and the payoff price for each two-dollar bet as eight dollars even, three to one. That completed one of the four parlays and gave me a profit for the day of one hundred and twenty-four dollars—one hundred and forty-four as the payoff on this one parlay, minus the twenty dollars I had invested in the combination bet. Victory for the last of the three horses would complete the other three parlays and increase my take to ten times as much as I had already won.

"Jesus," Jerry muttered. He tried to smile, but it was plain that he would rather have cried. "Christ," he said. "I'll have to get a bank loan if your other one comes in."

Cheapskate, I thought. Then, in a mental exercise I understand now to have been a demonstration that guilt can take strange forms, I found myself feeling sorry for Jerry. He had already lost quite a bit and stood to lose a great deal more. I felt responsible for his obvious pain. I didn't want to hurt him. I just wanted to win and would have preferred to do that without causing any further hurt.

A hit of one hundred and twenty-four dollars was already a good day's showing for me. In what I suppose was an attempt at an odd kind of machismo, I thought that perhaps it would be best if I didn't win the rest of what I was trying to win. Taking my lumps as a loser at this point would somehow make me more of a man than Jerry, who trembled at the thought of having to pay a big hit.

Before I could give it serious attention, that preposterous notion was gone and replaced by outrage. I despised Jerry for trying to get my sympathy, for trying to get me to root against myself, for making me feel guilty. It seemed to me a sleazy piece of work on his part, but just what was to be expected from such a vile person.

To make matters worse, his remark about a bank loan aroused in me the awful anxiety about not being paid or not being paid fully and promptly for a big hit. I had my own problems, I reminded myself. I hated Jerry for putting me into this position. I certainly didn't want to lose to this creep. My business was to try to win. I had bet to win. I wanted to win all there was to win and to be paid in full, then and there.

Having resolved that issue, I would have liked to laugh and cheer and do other things winners do in celebration of one hit and antic-ipation of more to come. But I was paralyzed, torn between the need to let loose and relieve the tension of waiting almost an hour for the final race and the need to avoid making a spectacle of myself.

Throughout the office, people were busy with typewriters, tele-phones, and teletype machines, but I would have bet that many of them also were aware that Jerry and I were involved in something they would have considered disreputable. Jerry's solo performance at the racing desk for the first race and our *pas de deux* for the second surely could not have escaped the attention of people who would have wondered why we spent so much time in an area of the office few others ever visited.

Although I didn't know and might not have believed it then, there was no cause for concern. Years later, former colleagues told me they could not recall having been aware of my activity as a horse-player on that day or any other.

At that time, all I could do was try to hide my agitation from those around me. I waited until the last possible moment; then, with all the nonchalance I could muster, I sauntered past busy desks in the crowded office to the racing wire. With somewhat less aplomb,

Jerry, who had completed his work shift twenty minutes earlier but had stayed on, hastened to join me. I ignored him.

Standing before the teletype printer, in front of the east wall of the office, I prayed as though the machine reporting the results could somehow control what had already happened before the contraption began tapping out the critical names and numbers. I pledged that if my horse won I would do some unspecified wonderful things to repay the blessing. I have remembered the first two winners only as horses A and B. I remembered the last of the three horses by name: War Nurse. I prayed for War Nurse to win.

While I waited and prayed, I turned my back to hide my face from what I thought of as my audience. Suddenly, the machine trembled as it was activated by someone at the other end who was about to transmit the message announcing my fate.

A key struck the paper and left behind the letter W.

Jerry groaned. "Christ, Christ," he said despairingly as A followed W.

A great roaring noise formed in my throat as W A was followed by R. That sound would have been something to hear if it had made its way out. But all that emerged was a wheezing wail I could not restrain as the printer added the letter Y to W A R, and my overburdened brain reminded me that there was another horse in this race with a name which began W A R. That one's name, as the printer now confirmed, was Wary Mary; and Wary Mary had beaten War Nurse.

I felt as if I was drowning, but knew I would live. I continued to think, but felt I had otherwise stopped functioning and might as well be dead. I thought that previously I had lost in every way it is possible for a horse to lose a race. Once, a long shot on which I bet had opened a wide lead in the stretch, only to stumble and break a leg yards from the finish line. Now, I thought without laughter, I had experienced a new way to lose: beaten by typographical error.

For Jerry, jubilation replaced despair as he realized he would have to pay me only one hundred and forty-four dollars rather than the twelve hundred which could have been mine. He laughed nervously. "Bad luck," he said, as he raced off to call his partner with the good news before giving me my winnings.

"Tough break," he said, as he paid me with a flourish, delighted to be paying out rather less than more. Bush leaguer, I thought.

Jimmy Mac wouldn't have behaved that way. That was true enough, though I also knew his different behavior would not have produced a different result. A sheet man, I thought, wouldn't have behaved like Jerry, which was also true, but beside the point. The point, I knew, was that if I wanted to find a scapegoat I need look no farther than the nearest mirror.

Later that evening, as was my custom at the end of winning days, I celebrated my smaller-than-it-could-have-been win with a larger than necessary dinner at Manny Wolfe's, a once-fine restaurant which, like me, is no longer in action. By then I had recovered and was able to enjoy a meal of shrimp, steak, and, for dessert, apple pie with vanilla ice-cream, a taste preference carried forward from childhood.

33.

Losing hurt, even on winning days of the War Nurse kind. But, much as I hated losing, I think I hated more the borrowing made necessary by the losing. For a frequent gambler, losing becomes natural. I could accept that. Borrowing was another matter. That was something I chose to do, and did often, although I felt demeaned each time I did.

Needless to say, I would rather have won. That is always to be preferred. But my losses were not unbearable. No matter how much I lost, I didn't starve or go about in rags. During the worst of times, my needs were attended to and my life was not without its pleasures. With the income-expenditure ratio in my favor, I could say I was reasonably well-off—for a gambler.

Being single, I had only myself to provide for, and no one but I was hurt by my losing. Living alone, I had no need to buy a house. Living in the city, I felt no need to own a car. The one thing I wanted but had not allowed myself was a sentimental journey to the war zones where I had spent time to see how other survivors were managing. I could have done that, too. I could have borrowed or saved enough to pay for the trip. I don't know why I didn't. Perhaps because I was too busy with what I was doing, or possibly because I was ashamed to go back as the kind of a person I was.

For whatever reason, I denied myself that one privilege and concentrated on the action at hand, hoping always that eventually the law of averages would put everything right for me. Then, when my ship came in, I could take the journey that was likely to be deferred for as long as I remained in action.

Meanwhile, I continued to lose and to borrow, until I had built a mountain of debt as big as American Express's. At the peak, when my salary at United Press was $6,100 a year, I owed $12,500—more than two years' pay—to thirty-one lenders. That small army included two banks, two finance companies, and twenty-seven friends and acquaintances, some of whom had been little more than strangers to me until they became lenders.

No matter whom I asked, I was seldom refused—even when, in the absence of Sure Things or Reserves, I felt compelled to call upon people previously categorized as Untouchables. Only relatives were barred from my consortium of lenders, probably because I considered them most untouchable of all, the last people to whom I would risk exposing a vice which confirmed childhood evaluations of my character.

For a time, I felt a perverse sort of pride in my apparent talent for persuading so many disparate people and institutions to respond to my need. Actually, as I have come to understand, all that was required of me was the ability to appear needy. The rest was taken care of by legions of good samaritans who stand ready to help people they like, respect, admire, or pity.

I think pity more than any other consideration is the prime mover for what I have come to think of as a benign competition in which the loser also wins. The big winner is the giver, made superior by the act of giving. That may be what made me feel demeaned each time I asked for a loan. I think the borrowing reminded me that I couldn't make it on my own and thus added another dimension to my dependence on gambling, tying me more tightly into the inescapable, recurring cycle of hoping, betting, losing, then borrowing again to finance another round in the losing game.

Several other considerations contributed to my discomfort, among them the possibility that one or more of the two banks and two finance companies, which together accounted for fifty-five percent of my total debt, might charge me with fraud. My fear came from the fact that I had lied on my loan applications, withholding information about other outstanding loans, information which surely would have barred me from further loans. I understood—incorrectly, I know now—that I could be prosecuted for fraud only if I defaulted on any of the loans. I gave the highest priority to meeting loan payments punctually. But I never stopped worrying that something might go wrong and I might still be accused of criminal acts.

Perhaps more troubling than the possibility of criminal action against me was what I thought of as criminal action on my part in adding a new category to my roster of lenders. My thirty-one lenders included two women, each of whom had been persuaded of my affection. I despised myself for misleading them, knowing that the only meaningful thing about our relationships was the borrowing made possible by their vulnerability.

Every time I asked anyone for a loan, I felt I was exposing a grave defect of character which could not be excused by calling it neurosis. That was especially true of my dealing with the two women.

The banks, finance companies, and men who had individually loaned me money could be said to be smart and strong enough to take care of themselves. Besides, they would get their money: I had never defaulted on a loan. The two women were different. By the male-chauvinist code of the time, as I understood it, women were deemed to be incapable of hard-headed judgement. I felt like a gigolo for having traded on the vulnerabilities of two women who could not have understood what a vile creature I was. My conscience was only little relieved by giving the highest priority to these two loans and repaying them quickly before ending the relationships.

The dishonest stories I told to draw the two women into my financial network were taken from a repertoire of four appeals which served me in just about every situation. I had learned that once I had made myself useful or otherwise attractive to a prospective lender almost any story would do, or even no story at all. In my experience, what seemed to matter most was to establish a relationship in which the prospective lender felt some responsibility for the prospective borrower. It could be a long-running friendship developed over the years—my relationship with Murray as an example. Or, it could be something quicker and more tenuous, a connection of the kind formed with one of my female creditors, Frances. She was a cheerfully bright young woman whom I had seen often in Williamsburg but had never talked to until we met at a party, after which we began to spend time together.

Frances, office manager for a ladies' garment manufacturer, shared an apartment near mine with her mother and a younger sister, Alice, who had been diagnosed as a manic depressive. Alice became fond of me; and when a doctor recommended admitting her to Bellevue for treatment, I was able to help Frances persuade Alice to sign herself in.

As Alice began to show progress in her therapy and Frances began to seem easier about her sister's condition, I began to lay the groundwork for a pitch. Normally, I didn't need a special reason to acquire another lender, but in this case there was one. I was passing through a no-win period and had borrowed to the limit from all my other sources. What I did in this instance, I think, cannot be called merely acting or lying. I was increasingly concerned about a tightening financial bind and made no effort to hide my anxiety when I was with Frances. Within days, she began to ask what was troubling me. After several times denying that I was worried, I let it slip that I did have a problem.

"There's something I have to take care of," I said. "And I don't know what to do."

"What is it?" she asked. In other situations, that would have been my cue for a story. In this case I held back. "It's nothing for you to think about," I replied. "I'm sorry I said anything. Don't worry. I'll work it out."

"I would like to help," she said. "Isn't there something I can do?"

As was my custom, I had already formed an estimate of an optimum tap—not too much, not too little—for Frances. "Sure you can help, if you have five hundred dollars to spare," I said sarcastically, making it sound as though I had said five million.

As I knew she would, she replied, "I can lend you five hundred dollars."

"Oh, no," I said, acting now and lying. "I can't let you do that."

She insisted, and after a suitable show of reluctance, I gave in and accepted her check. For the next two months, I spent more time with her than before. Then I was able to rearrange my finances to pay her back. I told her a story about being sent out of town by UP and never spent time with her again.

However, most of my loan negotiations were based on one of the other three appeals involving stories about unexpected expenses, losses from unfortunate investments, or promising investment opportunities.

Prudent people—for example, Rosa, a department-store executive I met at a dinner party—could understand that an unsophisticated person such as I, unused to the intricacies of the financial world, could make mistakes in money management. Weeks after our meeting, I told her of some unfortunate investment losses, and she seemed pleased to lend me a thousand dollars and give me some sound advice about how to clean up my mess. Once again, I felt like a heel when, three months later, I repaid the loan and ended a relationship from which she deserved more than my thanks for her assistance. I was oppressed by guilt for months after our farewell.

At the other extreme, successful people—as an example, Murray, whose business was prospering—could understand that a promising investment opportunity should be seized and every effort made to arrange financing. When I told him I had an opportunity to get in on the ground floor of what could be a lucrative publishing venture, Murray gladly loaned me twenty-five hundred dollars—my small story having secured my largest loan as a gambler.

Borrowing requirements seemed to have turned my life into a sequence of new lows, the lowest involving descecration of my mother's memory. Shortly after her death, I promoted a loan on the unexpected expenses plea—in this case with the explanation that funeral costs had run beyond my immediate ability to pay. I could take it as a balancing positive sign that I was too ashamed to repeat that ploy, though surely it could have worked again.

But balance was becoming more and more difficult to maintain. During that time I dreamed that I was back in Cincinnati, groveling before Chubby, the unyielding bookmaker, while Aunt Mary looked on, stabbing her finger at me and snarling, "I always said you would turn out like you know who."

Compounding the emotional problems brought about by the borrowing was the sheer weight of details involved in the logistics. Without being able to measure precisely, I think it is accurate to say that during the time of my heaviest activity—a period that lasted about five years—I spent more time and energy on prospecting for new loans, devising new strategies, constructing elaborate Peter-Paul refinancings, filling applications, and making payments than I did on any activity other than sleeping and working. It would be an understatement to say that the process became increasingly disagreeable.

Fortunately, I had an ample supply of the compulsive gambler's basics: strong recuperative powers, a forward-looking vision which obscured the past, and an irrepressible, eternal hope that could make the most unpromising reality tolerable. Thus equipped, I could withstand the wear and tear on body and soul, while I continued to hope for the big hit that would put everything right. Meanwhile, I stayed on my guilt-ridden course, outwardly maintaining my composure, never doubting that I was in control of my affairs. Or, so it seemed.

Among the surprises uncovered during my period of reflection was the revelation that, earlier than previously believed, I had begun to worry that I might be losing control and should think about liberating myself from dependence on gambling. I was rational enough to understand that the only realistic way out of my difficulties was to quit and repay my outstanding debts. But lunatic logic persuaded me that to quit and still have to pay off thousands of dollars of debt would make me a victim of double jeopardy, having paid in the losing and having to pay again for having lost. I wasn't willing to take the pay-and-go way out of my misery.

But the need to do *something* seems to have been on my mind. In a move that may have been a roundabout way of taking corrective action, I entered psychoanalysis during my tenth year as a horseplayer. Since my return from the war, I had suffered severe gastrointestinal distress, which neither my doctor nor two specialists had been able to do much about. Bea, a friend whose understanding of these matters I respected, suggested that my condition might be psychosomatic, and on her advice I arranged to see a psychoanalyst.

My analyst, Dr. Leonard, was a pudgy, blond young man, as new to his trade as I was to the idea of being in psychoanalysis. He was a strict non-interventionist, who did little to explain the process, and I found it confusing and forbidding at first.

Eventually, my digestive problems eased—though a new antacid and modifications in my diet may have had more to do with that than the contributions of psychoanalysis—and I found myself freely associating about the painful cycle of hoping, betting, losing, and borrowing. When I started talking about my gambling, I began to think of psychoanalysis as just what the doctor had ordered, good medicine from which a cure could be expected, sooner or later.

I was encouraged in my optimism by a series of events I interpreted as signs of better things to come. At the office, my request for a transfer from radio sports to general news was granted. In treatment, Dr. Leonard moved from a sparsely-furnished office on a bleak street in the East Thirties to a more cheerful place in Greenwich Village, and he agreed to switch the time for my session from nine in the morning to eleven. That made possible still another fringe benefit. After a session, I could stop for lunch at a *rosticceria* on Sixth Avenue owned by a pleasant young couple, immigrants from Florence, who cooked delicious, inexpensive steaks, roasts, and chicken on a rotating vertical coal brazier and served French fries that I remember as having been well worth an attack of gastro-intestinal distress. Also adding to my euphoria of that time was a run of winning days more numerous than losing days. That, best of all, encouraged me to believe that I could, and should, continue in action until the doctor cured me. In that frame of mind, I thought that being in analysis was the best thing that had ever happened to me.

34.

ALTHOUGH I didn't understand the process, I liked the way psychoanalysis worked for me. Early in our relationship, I asked Dr. Leonard to recommend some reading matter so I could familiarize myself with psychoanalysis, but he declined on the ground that the reading I proposed to do might be more confusing than helpful and could complicate the therapeutic process. I took that to mean that things were going as they should, and that pleased me. I believed, as people said, that talking about problems makes them easier to cope with, and the way therapy worked for me seemed to confirm that. I could go through some awful hoping, betting, losing, and borrowing then talk about my adventures to Dr. Leonard and emerge reinforced to endure more of the same.

Ambivalently, I wanted to believe that eventually Dr. Leonard could cure me, while I also continued to hope that eventually the law of averages would lead me to the big hit that would both cure and enrich me at the same time. I was prepared to accept whichever came first.

For a long time, there was no reason to count on either. Then, in the third year of my analysis, option two—the non-therapeutic solution—seemed to become a possibility. I was in the midst of a bad run. My debt stood at its peak, and borrowing sources had dried up. I was as bad off as I had ever been that Wednesday when I went into a session with Dr. Leonard after two heavy losing days that had left me temporarily disinterested in further action.

Normally, during times of heavy losses, our meetings consisted of a confession by me about the stupidity of what I was doing followed by silent absolution for my sins from Dr. Leonard, who seldom said anything more than "Uh, huh," "What do you think?" and "Why?" This time he pressed me with whys which forced me to look more closely at the wasteful way in which I was using analysis to make continued therapy necessary. I left with what may have been the beginning of an understanding that I myself would have to take an active part in my cure.

After that workout, I needed the kind of lift I could expect from a good lunch. I had the wherewithal, more than five dollars remaining after my two losing days, but had not yet decided whether to go back into action. On the spur of the moment, I chose to eat rather than bet. I went to the *rosticceria* and gorged myself on a thick veal chop, French fries, a large salad, two glasses of Chianti, two cups of espresso, and what may have been pounds of fine Italian bread.

After lunch, I had two dollars and seventy-three cents on hand and two hours to spend before showing up for work. One hour was used for something that always pleased me, a stroll through the city streets, from Sixth Avenue and Waverly Place to Forty-second Street and Third Avenue. I remember also that I arrived at the office an hour before the start of the night shift with a familiar problem—time to kill, money in my pocket, and nothing to do—and I solved it in the familiar way. I decided to make just one bet, win or lose, leaving seventy-three cents for a sandwich-and-coffee supper in case I lost.

To avoid the fuss and bother of research, I decided to bet blind on whichever horse had been selected for the sixth race at Jamaica by Toney Betts, the handicapper for the *New York Post,* who was then enjoying a praiseworthy winning average. I have forgotten the name of the horse, but I do remember it paid twelve dollars to win.

I made five more bets and won three. That gave me funds for heavy betting at the track the next day.

Thursday and Friday were my days off at the time—days, I used to think, just made for racegoing. Without the need to worry about rushing off to work at a critical point, I could relax and stay for the full program.

By Friday night, I had completed three big winning days and began to think that perhaps my time—the time when the law of averages could be expected to start working for me—might finally be at hand. There had been three-day streaks in the past which had come to nothing. But, like a punch-drunk boxer who knows what to expect when he steps into the ring yet hopes this time it will be different, I brought to mind superstitious rationalizations to assure myself that this time it really *could* be different. Among the emotional supports I dreamed up was the notion that since it had begun with a gross violation of the rules, a blind bet, to have come this far meant that there was more to come. I thought nothing of the more significant reality that violating the rules in the past had led to more losing than winning days by a wide margin.

All that mattered was that in three days, starting with a two-dollar bet, I had won almost three thousand dollars: half a year's pay, one fourth of my total debt, a lot of money. And with more to come, I felt confident—indeed, it could be said that this time I actually *expected* to win.

Saturday morning I left my apartment in Williamsburg and set up a command post closer to the action, a room at the Commodore Hotel, down the street from the UP office. Rather than bother with laundry, I went to Brooks Brothers, where my officer's uniforms had been made during the war, and bought a taxi full of underwear, socks, shirts, ties, and a hounds-tooth jacket that seemed appropriate for the business at hand. And I stocked up with pencils and pads for handicapping purposes.

On this fourth day of what seemed to be a kind of Christmas for me, I added almost a thousand dollars more to my winnings from bets at the track and with office bookies. After work Saturday I stayed up for hours, trying to make sense of what had happened during the past four days. I had done just what I had been doing for more than twelve years, in much the same inconsistent ways, yet now with wildly different results.

As in the past, I had bet sometimes by the rules, studying past performance data carefully before making up my betting lists, and sometimes going against the rules, betting by hunch and by hope. I had made my biggest bets at the track but also left sizeable bets with the office bookies, distributing bets among them so that no one would know of all the bets I placed and no one could renege on all my winnings, should it come to that. Most of my money had been bet on individual horses, but I had also bet on various combinations. I had lost many bets, but had won many more. Each of the four days had been a winning day, either at the track or at the office and on three occasions both. And I couldn't imagine why.

There was no rhyme or reason to explain why what had not worked before was working now. I knew it was not because I had become particularly clever as a handicapper or prudent as a bettor. The only explanation that made any sense was that I had simply made enough bets and taken enough chances to reach the point at which the law of averages was arranging a balance favorable to me. But I wouldn't have wanted to have to defend such an explanation.

Finally, given the state of my art as a horseplayer, I concluded that there was nothing more to be gained from asking why. I decided that my best bet was simply to go on doing what had worked so well so far.

I had accepted an invitation from my Aunt Molly for early Sunday dinner before going to work, and I wouldn't have missed her pot roast for the world. I enjoyed the meal and the visit, had an easy time at work, slept well that night, and went back into action Monday hoping for the best, but ready for whatever might happen.

Monday began a week unlike anything in my experience. In my pursuit of winners over the years, I had felt and been moved by all or most of the emotions inspired by desire, greed, and zeal, but this was something more. The word that may best categorize the experience is frenzy.

For six days, I made as many as twenty bets a day, analyzing past performance data over room-service breakfasts at the Commodore, then prowling the *News* building to find bookies among whom to distribute out-of-state bets, before depositing surplus cash in my bank and taking a taxi to the track, where I tipped lavishly for a window table in the clubhouse restaurant, as winners are supposed to do, and where I ate and drank too much while I studied and restudied, considered and reconsidered the betting choices I had already made, switching selections and winning, switching others and losing, never knowing which was more productive, which more senseless, staying as long as possible, then going to the office to check results of the off-track bets and clear accounts with the office bookies, following that with arrangements for extended meal times during which I ate lavish dinners at expensive restaurants, gluttonously, without enjoyment, thinking that when I became rich I would also become obese, twice treating recent lenders, who must have wondered about the sudden turn in my fortunes but were too polite to inquire about it, then finally going to the hotel for a solitary nightcap and, I find it surprising to remember, sleeping soundly until time to rise and start the process over again.

Apart from the action-related activities, I was otherwise disengaged except for two critical responsibilities—work and therapy. These served as reference points, reassuring me that, no matter what else I did, I could be sure of my sanity as long as they remained important to me. I showed up promptly at the office as scheduled and worked well, taking no more breaks than absolutely necessary to deal with the office bookies. I also met as scheduled with Dr. Leonard but said nothing about what was happening, declining for the time being at least to share this secret even with him.

That was one of two problems, or discomforts, with which I had to contend. I couldn't share with anyone the tensions and pleasures of the turmoil to which I had exposed myself. The other restraint was less bothersome. At the track I had to maintain decorum in the clubhouse restaurant, which meant restraining myself from joyous outbursts when I won—big-time high-rollers don't show emotion, winning or losing.

Results made those burdens bearable. Every day was a winning day.

On the tenth night of my run, after work on the second Saturday, I sat in my room at the Commodore, counting over and over again the figures that showed I had won thus far a bit less than twelve thousand dollars—a payoff of almost six thousand to one, counting from the first two-dollar bet. After disbursements of almost one thousand dollars for my purchases at Brooks Brothers, the hotel bill, my spending at the clubhouse restaurant, extravagant dinners, taxis, and miscellaneous items, I still had close to eleven thousand dollars on hand—actually $2,914 in cash on hand and the remainder on deposit in the bank.

There seemed little doubt now that the law of averages was working for me at last. Or, had been working for me for the past ten betting days. Could I count on it to continue working its magic for me? I wondered.

Hysterical with fatigue and excitement, I couldn't eat and wouldn't allow myself to drink, as I debated whether to quit or go on. There were, in my mind, good reasons for either decision.

The fund accumulated by my frantic activity was enough to repay about ninety percent of my outstanding debts. That would free me once and for all from the dreadful burden I had carried for so long, leaving very little for me to repay in order to arrive at a zero balance of a debt.

This was a terribly attractive prospect. In fact, even before opening the debate about which way to go, I had already decided to repay, at the very least, the twenty-five hundred dollars I had borrowed months before from Murray plus an equal amount of my smaller obligations, cutting at least $5,000 from the $12,500 presently due my creditors.

However, by my calculations I had lost much more than I owed and to quit now would leave me with a lifetime record some eight or nine thousand dollars in the red. Lunatic logic argued against that. Lunatic logic argued that the way I had moved in ten betting days was reason to believe there was more to come. According to this argument, even if I lost everything after paying off five thousand dollars, as I planned to do the first thing on Monday, I would still be a winner—for this period of action—by the amount I would have repaid to Murray and lesser creditors.

Once my attention was drawn to that line of reasoning, there was no question about what I would do. I swore to repay five thousand dollars of debt first thing Monday morning and continue in action with the rest. I promised myself to quit when I had won the eight or nine thousand dollars more that would make me even for my years in action.

That exercise in ambivalence seemed to me an admirable compromise. I slept well, filled Sunday with eating, drinking, and movie going—all reinforcers of the competitive spirit—and went back into action Monday.

As promised, my first order of business Monday morning was debt reduction—using cashier's checks from the bank to remove the possibility that I might stop payment on my personal checks. I mailed twenty-five hundred dollars to Murray with a note explaining that the publishing venture for which I had borrowed the money had been scrubbed before any expenses were incurred. To a dozen other creditors, I mailed smaller checks amounting to twenty-eight hundred dollars, adding three hundred to the planned twenty-five hundred as a sign of good faith.

I went back into action with the remaining fifty-seven hundred dollars and lost that in less time than I had taken to accumulate it.

It could have been worse, I tried to make myself believe. I had cut my debt by forty percent and come home, by subway, with enough underwear, socks, shirts, and ties to last for years and a classy hounds-tooth jacket to dress up my wardrobe.

More important, I enjoyed a grand feeling of relief once the pressure was turned off.

But I was also badly frightened by thoughts which forced themselves on me—most terrible the thought that I might be better off dead.

No matter how bad I might feel, even in the worst of times I knew
that saying I would be better off dead was an exaggeration, an overly
dramatic figure of speech signifying I had reached another point in
my life from which I would bounce back, as I always did.

In this case, I was disappointed, but not destroyed. I had, after
all, finished in the money. I would have preferred to be able to keep
the winning streak going, but it had gone far enough to give me my
biggest winning as a gambler: some six thousand dollars. I had cut
more than five thousand dollars from the load of debts which had
reached crisis proportions and could now breathe easier on that score.
And I had spent a thousand on the costs and fringe benefits of my
run up and down with the law of averages. More important in dis-
pelling the mood of gloom and doom that seized me at the moment
when the streak was over, I felt I had shown it could happen, and I
tried to believe that was a reason to hope it could happen again.

The disappointment I felt most keenly came later: the thought that
the trauma had not produced the breakthrough to understanding in

my psychoanalysis I thought it could have done. A breakthrough could have been possible, I believe, if either of two conditions had been present. I could have opened the way by being honest about what I had experienced and what I felt about my losing winning streak. Or, Dr. Leonard might have started the ball rolling if he had recognized and responded to clues suggesting that something significant was afoot.

Neither of us made a move. Guilt kept me from saying anything that might be held against me and, instead of probing, Dr. Leonard held fast to his policy of non-intervention. Any chance of a breakthrough was lost in our conspiracy of silence.

That may have been for the best. Despite my efforts to put the best face on things, I don't think I was up to dealing with the stress and pain an opening to honest understanding likely would have required. In my condition, a breakthrough might have lead to a breakdown. I wanted only the peace and quiet of doing things other than gambling.

Whatever effect other childhood influences may have had on me, at this point I could give thanks for one of the most useful lessons learned in childhood, the value of the work ethic. I called a time-out and got busy.

At the office, I sought out extra assignments. After hours, I caught up on Guild projects which has been put off for the duration of my turmoil. I mended fences with friends and family elders and reestablished relations with a woman for whom there had been no time or energy while I was consumed by a greater passion.

Also, for three months I made somewhat larger than usual reductions in my debt balance, and I accepted an invitation from family friends to visit their lavish home in Coral Gables. Except for infrequent weekends at holiday resorts near New York, I had not taken a vacation in the four years since the war. I looked forward to two weeks in the Florida sun as a well-earned opportunity to clear my head and renew myself.

Days completely free of compulsory activities were strange to me. But I soon learned to enjoy endless hours during which I was required to do nothing more than appreciate sun, swimming, and the delicious cooking of my hosts. I intended to spend all of my two weeks doing only these things. However, after four days I was bored.

Apparently sensing that, my hosts suggested that as a first-time visitor to Florida I might be interested in seeing some of the country. They offered to take me on day trips to the Everglades and other natural wonders of the region. They were agreeable when I chose instead to spend two days sampling the wonders of one of the luxury hotels which had made Miami Beach one of the most popular playgrounds in the world.

On the fifth day of my visit, a gloriously warm, sunny, late September day, I checked into the Versailles Hotel. At the weekend resorts I patronized, it was customary to pay in advance for room and meals, and I followed that practice here, prepaying for two days, though it was not required. That proved to be an act of horseplayer's intuition, for within minutes I was exposed to a temptation I had no reason to expect and no will to resist.

As I walked out to the pool area for a swim, I passed a cabana at which a gum-chewing, crew-cut young man ran an outdoor betting operation as openly as the poolside bar dispensed refreshments. I had never heard of such a thing, and my experience with horse rooms had not prepared me for anything so brazen. I was shocked that a posh hotel catering to a high-class clientele would provide such an unseemly activity.

But I cannot have been completely surprised, or disapproving. I must have understood that not for nothing had I prepaid my bill and brought with me much more than I needed for that purpose—in fact, all my reserve cash, some two hundred dollars, which I had left with the cashier for safekeeping.

After a dip, I rested on a lounge chair, letting the sun dry me while I observed the traffic around the betting cabana. The sheet man was kept quite busy by bettors going to and fro between their chairs and his office. It seemed to me a terrible way to waste the splendor of such a day. But, the more I thought about how foolish it was to be betting away such a grand day, the more I began to think it might not be so foolish to join the parade to the betting cabana— for just a small bet or two, I told myself. I decided to retrieve fifty dollars from the cashier, who did not seem surprised to see me return so soon for that purpose.

Before going back to the pool area, I paused to rationalize what I was about to do. I had done it often enough to know that I would benefit from a booster shot of lunacy to facilitate my return to action. As usual, that was no problem. The justifications for my decision were numerous and, I thought, entirely reasonable.

It was clear that, after my time-out, I was ready to bounce back from my unusual experience with the law of averages. That was bound to happen sooner or later. This was as good a time and place for it as any. I would be prudent with my betting. I would bet only five or ten dollars at a time. If I lost the fifty dollars, that wouldn't be so terrible. Should that happen, I could say I had spent the fifty dollars for some fun in the sun because, really, it was boring to sit around by myself with nothing else to do.

I borrowed a *Morning Telegraph* from the sheet man and found a sprinter who seemed well-placed in a six-furlong race at Belmont. "Beautiful Belmont"—as sports writers called Belmont Park—looked like a well-tended park, prettier than Jamaica or Aqueduct or Empire City, but it had always been an unlucky track for me.

This time there was reason to think my luck could be good. The record of the sprinter showed some excellent times in recent races, and the competition was nothing much. In the circumstances, my choice seemed worth a larger bet than the limit I had intended to maintain. I bet twenty dollars and went to the cabana to listen to the call of the race.

My horse broke poorly but made up ground rapidly, and failed by just a nose to catch the front runner at the finish. Bad racing luck. It could happen to anyone.

I bet the remaining thirty dollars on a horse that, by my calculations, was a much more promising choice than my first selection. This race also was at six furlongs, and my choice was a strong front-runner stepping up in class against horses which had not performed as well as mine, including one which was strongly favored to stage a winning performance in this race.

My horse broke in front and stayed there until the stretch. Then the favorite came on, and the two ran neck and neck into a photo finish, which the favorite won.

I needed no further rationalization to go back to the cashier for another withdrawal of fifty dollars or then to change my mind and retrieve all of my remaining cash, one hundred and fifty-nine dollars—part of which I had planned to spend for a night on the town with my hosts. In an attempt to change my luck, I switched to races at other tracks but with no better results. My stake was reduced to fifty-nine dollars as the betting day entered its final moments.

Frantic now, but struggling to maintain an outward calm, I switched back to Belmont for the last race. Last races are notorious for large fields of no-account horses brought together to stimulate heavy betting at the close of the day. This field was as motley a collection of equine misfits as one could expect to find at a high-grade track such as Belmont. Yet I pretended to find the one horse in the field that seemed to have a good chance to make it home ahead of the rest.

The sheet man's betting line showed my choice at three to one. A winning bet of fifty dollars could make me even for the day. I was reminded of the joke about the compulsive gambler who said he was lucky to have broken even for the day because he needed the money badly. The joke did not cause me to laugh as I bet fifty dollars on the three-to-one shot.

Hoping for the best but ready for the worst, I joined one other die-hard horseplayer in the betting cabana to listen to the call. As expected, my horse held back while others set the early pace until the field turned into the stretch. Then my horse started flying, passing others, until he was neck and neck with the leader. He was a strong, driving finisher. That was the pattern which had attracted my betting interest. This was again a driving finish, but this effort ended in a photo, and the picture showed the effort to have been good enough only for second place.

Losing three photo finishes as I had done this afternoon is not something a horseplayer would accept cheerfully. I tried to comfort myself with the fact that I had come very close three times and the hope that things would improve in the future. There is no substitute for winning; but I had long ago learned to take events of this sort in stride, since in the other way lay screaming madness.

Calmly as possible in the circumstances, I had a drink while taking a leisurely bath, dressed for a gala evening, and went to the bar for another drink before my prepaid American Plan dinner. I was the only customer at the bar until a well-groomed, somewhat older woman with an intelligent face and a friendly smile seated herself on my right, ordered a rum drink, and asked for a light for her cigarette. Neither of us can have expected all that followed.

When it became apparent that she was alone, I suggested out of politeness that we might share a table. I was too depressed to be otherwise interested until, during dinner, she told me how she had worked to finance her husband's medical education and was now in the process of negotiating a settlement for what was for her clearly a hurtful divorce, so the forty-four-year-old doctor could marry a younger woman.

She seemed to need a sympathetic ear, and I seemed to offer that. In fact, her story aroused in me all the worst instincts I knew as a gambler. All I seem to have been able to think as she talked was that I was in the presence of a Sure Thing. Nothing I had done as a gambler troubled me more than borrowing from a woman. After repaying the two such loans, I had vowed never again to demean myself in that way. Yet now I could only think that because of this unhappy woman I might be back in action the next day.

Later that night, in her room, I told her my story. On the spur of the moment, perhaps in penance for violating my vow, I decided to do something I had never done before. I told her the truth. She asked whether a loan would be helpful. I replied that I would like to take another shot at the betting cabana. She asked how much I would require. I said two or three hundred dollars, which I could repay then and there if I won or soon after I got home, if I lost. She said I could have it in the morning, and we went to bed.

Before breakfast, she handed me the money in an envelope. When I excused myself to work over the data and prepare my betting list, I was delighted to find that, in response to my request for a loan of two or three hundred dollars, she had enclosed three hundred in the envelope.

We met for lunch and spent a strange afternoon at poolside. From the first bet, it was a losing day for me. I had two winners, which only extended the agony. Throughout, she was cheerful, encouraging me, reassuring me, comforting me, and ordering rum drinks. Finally, when the money was all gone, I was too drugged to care.

She seemed more cheerful than ever, and her high spirits shamed me into putting aside my grief to share a pleasant dinner and a happy night together. In the morning, as we said our goodbyes, she thanked me, and that seemed to me more strange than anything else that had happened in our time together.

I went back to Coral Gables, made excuses, and left for home a week ahead of schedule, hating myself for having gone back into action, for losing and for making things worse by taking advantage of a vulnerable woman who was in no position to recognize and resist my counterfeit attention. I couldn't wait to repay her.

The morning after my return, to save the extra day or two that would have been required for the same transaction at lower interest in a bank, I went to one of my finance companies and arranged an on-the-spot reorganization of an outstanding loan to raise the cash for repayment. To speed the process further, I sent the three hundred dollars by telegraphic money order, delighted to be free of further liability.

But this time that wasn't enough. Repayment did not have the cleansing effect I needed and had experienced in the past. This time, I felt I had sinned in a way for which there should be no forgiveness.

As it turned out, I was not alone in thinking I was unworthy of forgiveness. Dr. Leonard also had some thoughts on the subject.

For two weeks after my return, I suffered in silence, too ashamed of what I had done to discuss it with Dr. Leonard or anyone else. Somehow, I managed to put a cheerful face on things. Having just come back from a vacation in Florida—an expensive and uncommon thing in those days among the people I knew—I didn't want anyone to think my visit had been anything less than pleasant. But I couldn't hide my distress from myself. I needed to talk about it but couldn't.

Throughout our time together I had thought of Dr. Leonard as a priest or judge, someone hearing my confessions and judging me. I understood that this judging was done with my best interest in mind, for my good. But I couldn't bear to be judged just now. I also understood that a change in my attitude was required to make improvement possible in my situation. But, thus far, I had not been able to change, and Dr. Leonard had done nothing that I was aware of to encourage movement on my part.

Surely, in two and a half years he had made statements more meaningful than "Uh, huh," and asked questions more probing than "What do you think?" and "Why?" However, despite my best efforts, I have been unable to recall anything that seemed greatly significant then or memorable now.

To be fair, that may be my fault. Quite possibly, I wasn't paying attention when I should have been. Still, the fact remains that despite a determined effort I have been unable to bring to mind anything Dr. Leonard said that seemed important to me until, finally, my conduct in Florida came under review.

Without an opening from Dr. Leonard, I had remained silent, drifting. Then, as though one was the key to the other, I ended a brief time-out, went back into action, and hesitantly began to talk about my actions in Florida. Bit by bit, spreading the pieces over three sessions, I doled out the details.

As I began to unburden myself, Dr. Leonard's demeanor, always neutral in the past, began to turn icy. By the time I finished, he was furious. He had always seemed incapable of anger. Now he exploded. I had talked endlessly, he reminded me, about hating what I was doing yet had gone right on doing it. I had made no effort to break the pattern of hoping, betting, losing, and borrowing; and now I had committed the kind of borrowing I had said was particularly abhorrent to me.

"This is impossible," he declared. "I can't help you. You will have to find someone else who can. I just don't understand how compulsive gamblers function, and I cannot go on trying to help someone who refuses to help himself."

I was not greatly upset at first. I must have thought it was a ploy to get my attention and get me moving, the way a teacher of the old school might have rapped an inattentive pupil on the knuckles. But, as his words sank in, it became clear that he meant what he had said and that the only move he had in mind for me was out. Still I seem to have been slow to react.

I glanced at my watch, as I sometimes did when a session seemed to be dragging, though that was most certainly not the case in this instance. There were eight minutes left in what presumably was to be our final hour—not enough time for a meaningful response and exchange but enough for me to try to resolve a conflict between the intense, mixed emotions I felt and the behavior protocol might require in such a circumstance.

Above all, I wanted to be fair, to consider the situation objectively, so I could understand it truly. Now that we were at the break point, I knew that it should not have come as a terrible surprise. There had been warning signs. For some time, certainly since my run with the law of averages, I could have detected impatience on the doctor's part. His silences had been longer, less often punctuated by his neutral questions; and he had been uncharacteristically brusque in turning away some of my questions.

Still, there had been nothing to prepare me for such a drastic resolution of whatever it was that was bothering him. It had seemed reasonable all along to assume, as I had, that we were bound together until he could succeed in curing me. That, I understood, was what the Hippocratic Oath required of him. Yet here he was, breaking what I had thought of as a sacred contract and blaming me for what he was doing.

On at least one point I had to concede that Dr. Leonard had truth on his side. I knew I had contributed little or nothing toward my cure. I had to admit—to myself, if not to him—that I had behaved badly and probably deserved to be punished. But what he proposed seemed excessive—cruel and unusual punishment, as I saw it.

Whether right or wrong, I was frightened. I thought, my God, if my own doctor is washing his hands of me and my problem, then I must be beyond hope of correction. It seemed a terrible thing for a doctor to do. That thought made me angry.

In reading his riot act, Dr. Leonard sounded like Chubby in Cincinnati, telling me he was hurting me for my own good. Or Aunt Mary or the associate dean telling me to play it their way or lose. He had wasted two-and-a-half years to discover he couldn't do what he had been paid to do; and now he was passing the buck, blaming me for his inadequacy. I wanted to hate him but was too full of guilt to manage that. I thought of him as someone who had failed me and shouldn't have. I felt wronged.

It might have been better for me in this situation, I thought, if, despite his disapproval, I had done some reading about the psychoanalytic process. That might have taught me what to expect and how to deal with what was happening.

At that moment, I could only think that there was nothing to be done. I might have tried reasoning with Dr. Leonard. I would have argued that I deserved points for swiftly repaying the Miami Beach loan. But the obvious response was that such an attempt at atonement was nothing new. I had done it twice before. Doing it again was regressive.

Whatever he might think of any arguments I could offer, I wondered whether a softer approach could be more effective. I thought there might be the possibility that Dr. Leonard's declaration was intended to maneuver me into an apology, a promise to do better hereafter, and a plea for another chance. But I declined to test that hypothesis for fear of being rejected a second time in this clash with authority.

On this point, I may have erred. It might have been more useful to try to continue the relationship, because, unproductive as it had been, I had no idea what I would do without it. Certainly, I had no intention of starting over with someone else. Nevertheless, I refused to plead. If the doctor wanted to do something about continuing our relationship, he could say so. Otherwise, I would go on to do without his help what he had been unable to help me do. No matter what happened, I swore, I would not allow myself to think I was a loser. But I think I knew this was a transparent attempt to hide what I truly felt.

Now there was nothing more to be done. My next move would require more thought and energy than I was capable of at the moment. I was too tired to do anything that might be stressful, too tense even to speak. I don't know how long it had taken me to conduct my review of the situation—four or five minutes, perhaps. That time had passed in silence. I had made no spoken response to Dr. Leonard's announcement, and he had added nothing to it.

Finally, I said, "I guess that's it." And he nodded. At that moment, I did feel for him what may have been hatred. Or contempt. But I didn't want to delay his next client.

With two or three minutes remaining in the final hour, I said, "Goodbye."

He said, "Goodbye, and good luck."

I said, "The same to you."

I didn't think about it then, but it seems to me now an odd thing for each of us to have said, except that, consciously or unconsciously, analysts and their clients may recognize that a bit of luck is never out of place even in therapeutic situations—particularly in therapeutic situations where nothing else has worked.

PART FIVE

WITHDRAWAL

37.

ONE of the more popular clichés concerning the compulsive gambler's predicament is the idea that compulsive gamblers can't quit when they are ahead. Actually, few gamblers, compulsive or otherwise, ever get far enough ahead for it to matter whether they quit or continue. The real problem is that compulsive gamblers find it difficult to quit when they are behind. That was my problem. I wanted to quit but not as a loser.

Long before Dr. Leonard dismissed me, I think I knew that my best bet would be to take my losses and get out, if I could find the way. The way was clear enough—simply to pack it in—and the arguments for quitting were all I should have needed to make the move. But, facing the strongest challenge yet to my powers of rationalization, I became once again the agreeably ambivalent host for conflicting forces making a battleground of my mind.

By the time Dr. Leonard and I terminated our relationship, I had been a compulsive gambler for more than twelve years. I was thirty-one, and I didn't want to grow old as a gambler. On days when I could think clearly, I knew that was just the best of many reasons why I should be making my way out of the morass I had made of my life.

No matter what I might have believed in the past, the old urgings to continue were no longer as persuasive as they had been. Some now seemed downright silly—for example, the notion that gambling and borrowing were as natural for me as breathing, which I had allowed myself to believe for a time. I no longer found it comfortable to go on thinking that lightning could strike twice and bring me a really big winning streak, and that next time I would be smarter about making the most of it—if only I would hold on and let hoped-for things happen. By now, I had come to understand that the odds on having the law of averages make me well eventually were much longer than I had calculated, and I knew that reliance on the law of averages already had cost me more than I cared to count.

During my years in action, I had lost approximately half of all I had earned in half a dozen occupations: at the Village Pharmacy, at RKO Midwest Theaters, at the gas-stove factory, in the Air Force, at CBS, and at UP. In actual dollars of the time, after almost thirteen years my losses came to something more than twenty thousand. In purchasing power based on average prices for those years, the money I had lost could have paid for two or three average-priced houses or a fleet of inexpensive cars, free and clear; or it could have fed and clothed a family of four quite decently throughout all those years, if I had chosen to spend my money in any of those ways.

Those were the ways in which respectable people spent money. I didn't see the irony of wasting money as I did in the hope of winning enough to make me a success and, as such, a respectable person. But I believe I had begun to understand that winning big as a horseplayer was not necessarily the only way in which I could hope to gain acceptance in respectable society. When I could ignore lunatic distortions, it was apparent that respectable people I knew thought of me as a decent person who worked well, met his social responsibilities, and was as respectable as they.

More important, now when I thought of respectability, I thought of marriage, of being a husband and a father; and I knew that was impossible as long as I remained a gambler. I had been able to do what I had done for so long because I was the only one at risk. It would have been impossible to subject loved ones to what I had been through. I knew that before I could become a family man, I would have to quit being a gambler.

If I needed a special incentive to withdraw from action, I had it in my desire to show that I could do it on my own, without any help from Dr. Leonard. In the anger that took shape during the weeks after my expulsion, I came to think of curing myself as a particular personal triumph that would also be revenge against him.

Yet, with so many good reasons to quit, I decided to continue in harness. Why I should have done so after all I had been through is a question which led me finally to two answers, which I think of as the romantic and the realistic explanations. Both show the still-considerable force of my powers for rationalization and ambivalence.

In the romantic explanation, my problem was a consideration I hadn't thought of before. Suddenly, after having made it sensibly over all the other hurdles on my way to the finish line, I ran into a barrier I didn't have the strength to clear—the thought that if I quit now, as a loser, I would be conceding that I had been wrong all along about my gambling. I couldn't bear to do that. I told myself it would have been easier to write off all the money I had lost than to accept this much greater loss to my distorted sense of self. I couldn't bring myself to admit that for more than twelve years I had been engaged in an absurdity. In the romantic explanation, compulsive gambler's pride kept me from making it over the final hurdle.

According to the realistic explanation—by which I think I mean the more influential of the two—when I said I wanted to quit but not as a loser, I meant just that. I wanted to try to recover all the money I had lost and perhaps add a little more. Despite all the evidence to the contrary, I continued to believe that what I hoped to do was *possible*. Not necessarily probable. Not likely, it could be said. Just *possible,* and that was enough.

It is painful still to recall that I was willing to continue in error, rather than admit I had been wrong about what I had done for so long. But that was the situation. My decision was made to seem more reasonable by the belief that this latest triumph of infantile reasoning was not an unconditional surrender to my powers of rationalization. In the process of decision, my conciousness had been raised and a new balance of forces was being shaped by the ongoing struggle between my real and imagined needs, between my burdensome dependence and my desire to be free eventually.

Now, when I placed a bet, which I had resumed doing three days after my abrupt dismissal by Dr. Leonard, I was aware of reasons to question what heretofore I had done without thinking, and I could detect some reluctance to continue it automatically. At the same time, I adopted strategies to improve the conditions in which I operated.

I set a ceiling on by borrowings, pledging never to allow my indebtedness to rise above the present level. And I took two other steps to reduce losses and improve the quality of my life.

Often in the past I had bet every dollar I could lay my hands on during losing days; sometimes I had to borrow meal money. Now, at the start of a day in action, I put aside enough cash for dinner to be used on losing days. Though I allowed myself to tap this reserve fund occasionally for betting money, the strategy worked well enough to assure two appreciable benefits. I could be sure of eating well more often than might otherwise be the case, no matter what happened in action, and I could count as winnings the money paid for meals, which otherwise might have been added to losses. In addition, on winning days I put a portion of my winnings into a kitty to finance weekends at nearby resorts.

I expect I would have acknowledged that these fringe benefits and my exercises in rational thinking were intended to shield me from reality. I might have agreed that I was trying to cure a cancer with aspirin. But in the prevailing atmosphere of self-pity, I would have pleaded that I was too weak to take stronger medicine just then. Meanwhile, I could only go on and hope that I would find the way to quit—but not as a loser.

38.

THE first weeks after my unwelcome parting with Dr. Leonard were difficult. Having lost the crutch effect of therapy, I was unsteady on my feet. But, aided by the bounce-back power that had carried me safely through every crisis thus far, in time I got the hang of things and began to enjoy what I thought of as my new life because of the reforms and fringe benefits which had been added to the old.

I took more frequent time-outs and bet less when I was in action. At the same time, my winning average improved a little, with the result that I lost less and could assign a larger portion of my cash flow to debt reduction and to non-gambling activities, which gave me more pleasure than I had known in the recent past. In every way, I felt I was making reasonable progress—more, I would have said, than had been achieved with the participation of Dr. Leonard.

Among the non-gambling activities that gave me special pleasure were weekends in the country at vacation resorts in the Adirondacks and the Catskills. I felt at home in the mountain greenery and invariably enjoyed these brief holidays, but previously had limited myself to one or two a year. In the year following termination of my therapy, I went five times to the north woods and began to feel like a commuter.

Everything about those outings pleased me, especially the feeling of peace and freedom that came with the territory. Once past the city limits, awareness of horses and race tracks and bookies and debts to be paid disappeared. I was not again conscious of gambling until I returned to the city, except to think how pleasant life could be without it. The more often I experienced that feeling, the more often I wanted to.

Meanwhile, assisted by the enabling mechanism of my ambivalence, I continued to maintain a balance between reason and lunacy and was comfortable with the new deal I had worked out to combine my action with sensible restraints and satisfactions. It was a nice way to keep things on an even keel, I would have said, until, to my chagrin, Senator Estes Kefauver upset my balance and my peace of mind.

To the extent that the lanky Tennessean is remembered today, it is often as some kind of a kook who went around wearing a coonskin cap. In fact, Kefauver was a well-regarded liberal Democrat who was seized by a desire to compete with Adlai Stevenson (the man with the hole in the sole of his shoe) for their party's presidential nomination in 1952. As part of his campaign, one day Kefauver put on a furry cap someone handed him to provide a photo opportunity for photographers covering his campaign, presumably intending to present the sophisticated, amiable man as a Davy Crockett kind of Tennessee backwoodsman. To me and countless other horseplayers, Kefauver was, briefly but painfully, something else: a terrible nuisance who became in March of 1951 an obstacle to the orderly process of betting with bookmakers in New York.

Kefauver was little known outside his home state at the start of his presidential drive, despite his defeat of Boss Ed Crump's corrupt machine in Tennessee and his work in behalf of civil rights. But by 1951 he had become chairman of the Senate Crime Investigating Committee and had begun to make a widely recognized name for himself as a crime-busting investigator with a special interest in illegal gambling as a source of funds for organized crime. His image-building campaign reached a climax in March of 1951 with a series of star-studded hearings, carried live on national television from New

York, featuring the testimony of prominent crime celebrities of that time, among them Frank Costello, Joe Adonis, and Frank Erickson.

That event was a small disaster for horseplayers in New York. When it became known that he had chosen New York as the site for his televised hearings, the word went out to put the lid on all off-track action, and it was done.

There had been other shutdowns in my time, but generally these had involved local anti-bookmaker campaigns affecting one neighborhood—Williamsburg, for example—or one borough. Kefauver was using the momentum from one such crackdown which had begun in Brooklyn the year before and was continuing. That one involved a bookmaker, Harry Gross, who would later claim to have paid a million dollars a year in bribes to police—worth a great deal more in 1951 than a million today—for the right to operate twenty-seven horse rooms, a large number at any time. But Gross was small potatoes compared to the stars of the Kefauver hearings; and while he was the subject of investigation, it was still possible with some effort to get a bet down in Brooklyn.

The Kefauver shut-down was different from anything that had preceded it. I don't remember how long it lasted, only that it seemed forever, but it probably lasted no more than a week or two. During that time, New York became a wasteland for off-track bettors. It was impossible to find anyone to take a bet. Bookmakers stayed underground, or, like Jimmy Mac, went on vacation. Those bookies in the office who stayed on the scene behaved as though they feared Kefauver might burst through the door with the FBI to arrest them at any moment.

Though I was inconvenienced by the show, as a UP newsman I wrote about the Kefauver hearings in New York fairly, squarely, and objectively. By coincidence, six-and-a-half years later, my final assignment before resigning from UP was to write the overnight lead, the story to be used the next day by afternoon newspapers, about the murder of Albert Anastasia, who had been the subject of inquiry by the Kefauver committee. Anastasia, a reputed Brooklyn gang boss and murderer, was involved in larger issues concerning ties between government and the underworld in New York. He suffered no apparent hurt from his appearance and continued to prosper until on October 25, 1957, he was shot to death while having his hair cut in a New York hotel barbershop by two gunmen who were never caught.

Like other horseplayers at the time when Kefauver was talking about Anastasia and other figures under investigation, I considered the gambling portion of his hearings a farce which served no better purpose than to harass horseplayers and deprive us of our rights to do with bookmakers what we were given every right to do legally at state-authorized race tracks. Still, there was nothing to do but accept the reality and make the best of it.

I made a conscious effort to avoid looking at the racing sections of newspapers, which continued to publish entries and results from tracks operating legally all over the country. But one afternoon, on my way by subway to attend to some banking chores before going to work, my eyes strayed to the entries in the newspaper I was reading and I spotted an owe-me horse that seemed ready to win. A fever seized me. I postponed my banking errand to get to the office early and try to find someone to book my bet.

Putting aside my distaste for them, I asked Jerry and another of the in-office bookies to handle my action, but they refused. I hurried down to the mail room of the *News,* but was unable to find either Jimmy Mac or Maxie. I had visited the Mac's horse room across town once, out of curiosity. Now I raced there by taxi, only to find the normally wide open, bustling place still and locked. I hurried back to the office, hoping to cajole Jerry to change his mind, but he and the other bookie were adamant. I remembered having filed in a desk drawer the telephone numbers of two horse rooms to which I had been referred some time previously but had never patronized. I called but got no answer at either number.

With less than fifteen minutes to post time, I began to feel per-secuted. Horrible thoughts assailed me. I daydreamed that the race had been run without my bet, and my horse had won—easily and at a fat price.

As I agonized over the frustrating state of affairs, I was accosted by Mike, a teletype operator known in the office as a compulsive horseplayer—a *sick* compulsive, I would have said, to underscore that he was something more than I. People in the office reacted to Mike with scorn or pity. I tried to ignore him, but couldn't in this instance. Mike said he had observed me scurrying about and had assumed that I was in the same fix as he, with a hot horse to bet and no one to book the action. I resented his observation and assumption, but was sympathetic to his obvious misery, which mirrored my own.

I said, "It's tough to be a horseplayer these days."

Mike said, "Yeah, What you gonna do?" His question was intended as a philosophical comment on our plight. But one of us—I remember it was Mike, though it could as easily have been I—answered his question with what struck us both as a reasonable solution to our mutual problem.

Much as we detested the very thought of acting as bookmakers and thus violating our standing as players, we agreed to book each other's bet. We would do it just this once, we said, to take the curse off our action, and we set a limit of five dollars on our bets, though I would have bet at least five times that much with Jimmy Mac or Jerry.

Mike bet his five dollars on an even-money favorite and I bet five to win on a four-to-one shot. We ambled over to the racing wire to await the result of my race, which would be first to go off. Ray, the racing editor, remarked jokingly that his business had fallen off considerably. With the heat on and no one betting with bookmakers, the only traffic around his desk consisted of some few people who had been to the track that afternoon and had left behind a bet on a race for which they would get the result at the office. All this, I thought bitterly, was legal, yet I was stuck with Mike, of all people—two sad sacks playing make-believe.

The tapping of the machine interrupted my reverie. I watched as the moving key wrote and having writ moved on leaving behind the name of my horse in second place. Since I had bet to win, I was a loser, though my horse paid more to place than Mike's horse would pay to win, if that horse won. With the empathy that only one horseplayer could feel for another in the circumstances, Mike said nothing. He wandered off silently, surely sensing the sourness of mind that threatened to drown my brain in bile, searing me with wild, uncontrollable thoughts of self-hatred.

It was not the losing that disturbed me. I had lost too often before despite high hopes to give a second thought to a five-dollar loss. It was losing to Mike, of all people, that made me melancholy. I wouldn't have been at all upset to have lost another bet to Jimmy Mac, or Jerry, or another bookie, or at the track. That would have been normal. But losing to Mike was too much to bear.

My burden was made heavier when Mike's horse won. Again, it wasn't the money. His horse had been bet down to three-to-five, so his victory cost me only three dollars, making my loss for the day only eight dollars—nothing of significance to someone who had lost as much as I had lost. But to have lost in this way shook me as I had never been shaken before. For the first time as a horseplayer I felt *sick*. Before I had thought of myself only as wrong and wasteful. Now I felt *sick* in an unacceptable way. I was overwhelmed by shame for having involved myself in a preposterous charade, which had exposed a need so great that I had been willing to demean myself by taking part in an obscene joke of which I was the butt.

Until then, even when my behavior might be considered hysterical, I had been able to think of what I did as businesslike. But there was nothing businesslike about playing pretend with poor Mike, whom I thought of as an incompetent loner. He seemed to have neither family nor friends, lived by himself in a rooming-house across town, spent much of his non-working time at the office handicapping horses or teaching himself chess, seemed never to have had a square meal, seldom shaved, and even less often changed clothes. I wasn't in any way like Mike, yet he had beaten me both ways in a childish game I had no business playing.

What terrible need, I wondered, could have been served by exchanging five-dollar bets with this person at this stage of my life? There was no comfort in the answers which came to mind.

A major casualty of my encounter with Mike was its effect on my bounce-back apparatus. The system that had worked like a rubber band in the past had lost some of its elasticity. It was clear that I would need more time and greater effort to recover, if indeed I could ever again manage recovery.

Automatically, as in past crises, I indulged myself in an orgy of self-loathing that, as my form of penitence, had in the past absolved me of sin and released me to resume business as usual after a respectable interval. But past practice didn't apply in this instance.

In the past, my misdeeds had been errors of excess—too much betting, too much losing, too much borrowing, too often borrowing from people I shouldn't have imposed upon. These were errors that could be forgiven upon my promise to act with more restraint in the future. My grotesque *pas de deux* with Mike was something terribly more, the most senseless thing I had ever done as a horseplayer, an act too depraved to accept as an exercise of my own free will. I didn't see how I could hope ever to recover a semblance of balance.

And yet, once again, in what might be considered an act of faith in myself, eventually I *did* recover. Within sixty days I was back in action—hesitantly, sporadically, half-heartedly—but back in action. After two more uneventful months, I could consider the prospect of a pleasant weekend in the country, as though the horror visited upon me by Senator Kefauver had never happened. In July, I got permission to combine two pairs of days off back to back and booked a four-day weekend at a resort I had enjoyed on a previous visit.

At the tennis courts the morning after my arrival, I met Jeanette, a graceful brunette who played the game as poorly as I. We did little better with a rowboat, though what I lacked in skill we compensated for with laughter, and we did best with a long walk through the hills. That evening, we rearranged our dining-room seating assignments to be placed at the same table.

In the past, I had avoided any possibility of serious entanglement with a woman. At the first sign that a relationship might become more than casual, my instinctive reaction had been to cut and run. Now, although I could sense that something potentially serious was happening, I had no wish to avoid it.

For the next three days, we made extensive use of the sports facilities; and we spent hours talking—as though to reveal ourselves to each other as fully and as quickly as possible.

Jeanette told me she had been a medical laboratory technician in Maine, Florida, and Oregon and was now working for a busy internist in Manhattan, commuting from an apartment she shared with her widowed mother and younger brother and sister in the Westchester County village of Port Chester.

I said all there was to say about myself, except what was most important to know. I excused my evasive dishonesty on the ground that if she were to learn my unsharable secret our affair would end before it could begin, and I didn't want that to happen. It pleased me to learn that, apart from my most compelling interest, we shared similar interests and attitudes about many things and could conclude on the basis of our getting-to-know-you inventory that we were compatible.

Back home, we continued to meet frequently, which pleased me. However, as I began to realize that we were in love, I realized also that I had allowed myself to become involved in a situation that, whatever else it might bring, certainly would mean great difficulty for me. I knew that if our romance were to continue to its logical conclusion, I would face the need to take two steps, neither of which appealed to me.

First, before long I would have to reveal my awful secret. If I did, I was sure I could expect Jeanette to turn her back on me, as any respectable woman would. On the other hand, if she should be willing to continue our relationship despite that knowledge, then sooner or later I would have to take the second step and withdraw from action. I didn't want to confess or quit and doubted my ability to do either, in any case. Yet I continued to want what seemed impossible to achieve, a lasting relationship with this woman.

Then, by winter, we began to talk around the subject of marriage, and my mind became once again the arena for internal debate that I had experienced in the past but now with much greater urgency. Should I take step one and be prepared to follow that with step two? I argued that I couldn't expose myself as a gambler and risk losing the woman I loved—at least, not just yet. Winning would make a difference. Not big winnings, necessarily, I thought. Not the kind of winnings that would permit me to avoid having to quit as a loser. Not that much, I thought. Just enough to permit me to face the challenge of step one on the upbeat.

I didn't think what continued losing would do to my position. I simply needed to be in action. I responded by breaking into a panic of betting, in my best form, without thinking, and moved into what has come to be remembered by me as the time of the objectionable tip.

A tip is a piece of special, secret, or closely-held information about a particular horse in a particular race which gives reason to expect that this horse will win this race. Sometimes, the basis for the tip is the claim that the race has been fixed. More often, it is likely to be based on alleged "inside" information about special, but legal, steps that have been taken—in terms of conditioning or strategy—to put this horse in a very strong position to win.

Either way, the wisest thing to do with a tip is to ignore it. One of the more rational things I did as a horseplayer was to observe, as rigorously as I observed any rule, a policy of ignoring tips. That is sensible because the winning percentage of tips may be close to zero, and few tips with a better than zero chance of winning are likely to be made available to run-of-the-mill horseplayers like myself. I do not remember ever having bet on the basis of a tip before entering this new period of turmoil.

Then, by accident, one afternoon at unlucky Belmont, shortly after the start of the New York racing season, I ran into Vic, one of the few horseplayers of my acquaintance whom I met at the track from time to time. Normally, upon meeting, we would nod and move along. This time, Vic buttonholed me to say in a whisper that I would be well advised to bet, and bet heavily, on number four in the next race. "He's up for it," Vic said, his language conveying the knowledge that special preparations had been taken to ready the horse for this race.

Normally, I would have shrugged off such advice. Now, desperate for a winner after three losses, I gave it a second thought. Although I knew that the best thing to do with a tip is to forget it, it seemed to me there were other considerations to take into account, such as the source of the tip. If Mike had offered me a hot tip, I would have bet on any other horse in that race. But Vic was different. He had been a war correspondent, he was well-connected in what was then called "cafe society," which included people connected with horses, and, except for being a horseplayer, he seemed a sensible person.

Since I had no better information, I decided to act on Vic's tip. At first I intended to bet only ten dollars, because the odds on number four stood at sixteen to one, and I didn't want to risk more on such a long shot. However, upon reconsideration, having violated one rule, I fell back on another—play the horse, not the odds, and bet as much on a long shot as you would on a favorite. I increased my bet to fifty dollars—more than I had bet on a horse since my up-and-down winning streak.

Number four broke fast for the one-mile race, and I could see the red and white silks of his jockey clearly out in front of the field down the backstretch, around the turn into the stretch, and into the final straightaway. Midway through the stretch, another horse—the favorite, it turned out—came flying up on the outside and seemed to catch my long shot at the finish line. "No, no, no!" I screamed as they approached the finish, until shame at this unseemly display silenced me.

"Don't worry," someone said. "Number four got it." That was the consensus of those around me. But the consensus was sometimes wrong, and I agonized over that possibility for the two or three minutes it took to produce the print of the photo finish. Then the infield data board lit up with number four on top in the winner's position.

Despite my best efforts to maintain decorum, a cheer burst from my throat; but another was choked off by a word that was flashed on the infield board, "Objection," the formal language used by racing officials to announce that a foul had been claimed—in this case by the jockey of the favorite against the unofficial winner, number four.

Previously, I had thought of a horse race as a one-stage event—that is, a race run with a finish clearly visible to the naked eye—or a two-stage event, in which the race is run and then a photo is required to determine the winner, while the bettor carries his anxieties through both stages. Now I was reminded of a third dimension. I had been involved in objections before, but they seldom occur; and I had not experienced one for long enough to make me feel this was happening to me for the first time.

Until this moment I could have said that, except for my quandary over Jeanette, things had been going reasonably well for me recently. Although I continued to lose, I also had managed to continue my program of bit-by-bit debt reduction. The number of creditors had been reduced to four—the banks and finance companies—and the amount of my debt still outstanding had been reduced to thirty-five hundred dollars. If the foul claim was disallowed I would win enough to cut the outstanding balance of my debt by one fourth. That could be the morale booster I needed to take step one and tell the truth to the woman I said I loved.

Lost in thought, I became dimly aware that someone was saying the jockey of the favorite had claimed he was bumped by my four horse. I remember thinking the two horses had seemed to be running close together as they approached the finish. That could mean the foul claim was valid, in which case the number of the long shot would come down and the favorite's number would replace it on the board.

While the judges viewed the film of the race and interviewed the jockeys, a process that took perhaps five minutes, I stood with my eyes fixed on the infield board, hoping desperately that the claim would be disallowed and the numbers would stand unchanged. But, as I watched, my hopes were wiped out by the blinking lights on the board. The first place number was changed from four to two, and that result was declared official.

The apparent victory of number four had raised my spirits marvelously. Winning made me feel I could do anything, especially what needed to be done about Jeanette. With the change in the numbers, I fell from that high to a new low. I felt as though I had lost not just the fifty dollars I had bet but also the eight hundred I would have won except for the objection; and with that loss I had lost all hope.

Black humor may be one of the mind's therapeutic defense mechanisms against grim situations of the kind I now faced. I attempted a small joke. I said they forgot to tell the two horse about the hot tip on the four. In another difficult situation, during the war, while bailing out over the Danube River, I remember bringing to mind the joke that if this parachute doesn't work bring it back, and we'll fix it free of charge. I remember thinking that joke wasn't funny, and I could see nothing humorous in my present situation.

Wearily, I made my way to work, and that helped. I had money for dinner but no appetite. The next day I began a time-out, and that helped. I made excuses to Jeanette to avoid seeing her for the next week or two, and I spent a great deal of time thinking about what I wanted to do with the rest of my life.

Physically and psychologically, I knew that I could not absorb much more of the kind of punishment I had imposed on myself through the years, most recently with my misadventures in Florida, which had been too much even for Dr. Leonard, the demeaning make-believe with Mike, and now with the objectionable tip. That sort of thing was behind me, I swore. I assured myself that I wanted to be an attentive husband and father and a responsible, mature man.

Time had passed. I was thirty-three. I didn't want to become a middle-aged bachelor. I was frightened by the thought that it might already be too late to hope for a decent future; and it would surely be impossible if I continued with my profitless business as usual. I wanted to cry out for help, and that may be what I was doing when, finally, I decided to come clean with Jeanette, to tell her all there was to tell and, on my promise to reform, to ask her to marry me. That decision made me feel good. Second thoughts made me hesitate.

Jeanette's response to my confession could only be negative, in which case I would have gone through the pain of sharing my secret for no useful purpose. I worried even more that, for some unfathomable reason, her reaction wouldn't be negative, and she would look with favor upon my proposal of marriage. In that case, I reminded myself, I couldn't be sure whether—despite all that had happened—I was capable of walking out right now on the life I had led for so long.

Other questions tested my sincerity. Did I have the right to involve her in an uncertain venture? I wondered. And was I using her just to solve this crisis? Those questions, I decided, were for her to answer. I could only speak for myself—honestly, at last. She would then act for herself. Anxious but determined, in a now-or-never spirit, I mustered enough courage to request an audience for my disclosure and proposal. To make the telling easier, I arranged to have the moment of truth take place while we were doing something she enjoyed: walking along the tree-lined streets of her town to Lyon's Park, a quiet, green sanctuary.

I apologized for having been silent about something she should have known sooner. I said I hadn't spoken until now for fear that, knowing what I was about to say, she would have ended our relationship. I said that was something I hoped to avoid, but in any case, I had to speak now. I recited the details of my gambling, the losses, the debt. I said I wanted to quit and make a decent life with her. I said I hadn't gambled for several weeks, which was true; that I didn't miss the action, which was not quite true; and that there was reason to believe I had broken the habit, which I could only hope was true.

She listened without comment and was silent for a long time after the conclusion of my confession. When she spoke, she seemed more puzzled than disappointed. She said she couldn't understand how anyone could get into the position I was in, though she knew it was something that happened to people. She, herself, had never risked a penny on a gamble and considered gambling the height of wasteful foolishness. She said it would be impossible to live with someone who gambled. She said she wouldn't consider marrying me in the hope that I could be healed by marriage. However, she said, she had confidence in my determination to call it quits; and, because she felt about me as she did, she would be willing to marry me after I had quit and she could know I was cured.

Her verdict made me feel like someone who had gone into the boss's office expecting to be fired and had come out instead with a promotion and a raise. I was intoxicated by visions of a grand new opportunity for a bright new future.

Much more would probably be required of me before I could make it over the final fence. But I felt secure in thinking that no matter what might be required or how long it might take, I was on my way out after more than fourteen years.

40.

DAZZLED by the prospect of how serene life could be in the future I foresaw, I began to think of myself as a former gambler. That was a grand feeling. I remember well the elation, optimism, and determination which led me to imagine that magic was being done.

Then it vanished. Within days of the conference with Jeanette, reaction set in. My spoiler mechanism, dormant while I propelled myself in fantasy toward a happy ending, slipped back into operation, reactivating the cancer of lunatic logic eating away at my will.

What had begun to seem the most promising time of my life became the most difficult time of my life as I moved into a new struggle between the best and the worst. Everything that had gone before—all the ambivalent, back and forth, this way and that, yes-but rationalizing—had been only a warm-up for the main event. Now, when it seemed that all I needed to do was what I said I wanted to do, I found myself challenged by the most powerful resistance I had ever encountered in my uneven progress to this point.

Something seemed to have gone wrong, something invisible to

me. I was confused—for good reason, as I came to understand—for I had made myself the victim of an elaborate scam that had boomeranged.

As far as I could tell at the time, my confession and proposal to Jeanette were well meant. I wanted to marry the woman I said I loved, and my presentation was designed to reassure us both. She could see that I was an honest man. I could see that I was sincere. However, more powerful than anything we could see was the hidden, controlling truth that, no matter what I might think, feel, and say, I wasn't ready to quit gambling—certainly not as a loser.

Heard correctly, the true intent of my revelation had been to persuade Jeanette that she would be better off without me. I would then be free to continue as before and could even enjoy the feeling of having performed a noble act by saving her from a hurtful decision.

But she had failed to understand the intent of my declaration and, instead of being free to continue on my errant way, I had placed myself in a potentially embarrassing position. I could break my promise and our relationship, or I could try to make good on my promise and almost certainly fail. Either way, honesty, sincerity, and my self-respect would be casualties. I didn't know what to do or even how to think about it, though I thought about my dilemma constantly.

I had never experienced a more difficult time. I ate poorly, slept restlessly, and dreamed disturbing dreams. I was saved from the worst of my depression by the need, and the desire, to go to work five days a week and to busy myself with preparations for a new season of American Newspaper Guild contract negotiations. I managed to hide my distress from Jeanette when we were together, and eased the strain of that effort by reducing the frequency of our meetings on the excuse of more urgent obligations.

This experience led me to understand that crucial decisions, and the need for change that they imply, are more difficult for compulsive gamblers than for most other people because of the rigidities that build up through the repeated process of the same questions producing the same answers. Time after time for almost fifteen years I had asked myself whether I should quit or continue. Each time, the answer had been the same: there is nothing to lose by going on with it—and there had seemed to be some truth in that.

Going back into action after a crisis of conscience or a time-out had never caused me unbearable pain or irreparable damage in the past. Each time, I had been able to manage my gambling and my real-life responsibilities in a reasonable manner. There was no reason to expect any different result now if I decided to resume my chancy ways.

But I could not fail to be aware of a significant new element in the debate that crowded my mind. Always before, these exercises in irrationality posing as reason had affected only me. This time, another person, someone dear to me, was involved, and the decision would affect her and us. Always there had seemed to be no real choice, merely a contest between gambling or not gambling, without any compelling reason to choose either. Now, for the first time, I could see two greatly different alternatives: a choice between the way things were and the way they could be if, finally, I could overcome the force of lunatic logic.

I dreamed of making a dramatic, heroic decision and sailing off into a bright new future with the woman I loved. But I knew I couldn't easily manage anything heroic. I dreamed also of finding the easy way out—a magic cure—as some people hope when they think of wanting to quit smoking or lose weight or give up drugs or drink or quit gambling. But I knew there was no easy way.

The problem, as I seem to have sensed, was my urgent need to grow up. I had been too long at the childish game of competitive make-believe and was, as military personnel say, over-age in grade—too old to be stuck in the same rut I had occupied for almost fifteen years.

That was the heart of the matter. I might not have found it agreeable to think of my situation in those terms. But I believe I was thinking about having to grow up and asking myself: if not now, when, and if not by withdrawing from action, then how?

As I seem to have understood, the first and surest test of the seriousness with which I viewed my situation was the way in which I dealt with an obvious contradiction between the two issues most important to me: my desire to marry the woman I said I loved and my intention to quit gambling but not as a loser. Realistically, I would have known that to recoup the losses of years and thus change my status from loser was all but impossible. In that case, to say I wanted to quit gambling but not as a loser was tantamount to saying I had no intention of quitting. And, if I didn't intend to quit, that could only mean I didn't want to marry the woman I said I loved. I would have been reluctant to think of my position in those terms but could not have failed to recognize the facts.

Evidence of my maturing consciousness is demonstrated by the determination with which I pursued a resolution of that dilemma. My effort was assisted by what I have come to think of as the Aiken Out, a strategy devised by Republican Senator George Aiken of Vermont in 1971 when, after seventeen years of increasingly costly involvement in Viet Nam, starting with "advisers" in 1954, the United States government wanted to quit but not as a loser. American leaders, acting in a way that some might see as compulsive, preferred instead to continue fighting for an "honorable peace," generally understood to mean clear-cut victory. Since that appeared to be unlikely, Senator Aiken proposed that the United States simply declare itself the winner and withdraw from Viet Nam.

Aiken's proposal didn't get very far. The war dragged on four more years to a painful conclusion, which left the United States no better off than it could have been by adopting Aiken's Out. His strategy worked better for me. He had tried to redefine winner in terms that would save face for American leaders and save further losses for all concerned. I needed to redefine "not as a loser" in terms that would enable me to save face while also saving myself.

Once I put my mind to it, that proved to be less difficult than I might have anticipated. With surprisingly little effort, I was able to make myself understand that marriage to the woman I loved would be a much richer prize than any I might win as a horseplayer and that, no matter how much I had lost to date, *that* prize would make me a winner. To collect, I needed only take the final step and declare myself free at last.

But I was paralyzed. Before I could take one step toward my new life, all my good intentions were swept away by a wave of resistance that turned me around and left me facing backwards. Having arrived at a liberating awareness of my choices, I rejected the newly acquired understandings as unwelcome truth and began to think of how to avoid having to behave as acceptance of the truth would have required.

Recalling this turnabout, I have wondered again and again how it is possible to keep repeating the same damaging errors. One answer, I think, is that—like others, only more so—compulsive gamblers are able to block out or distort disagreeable past experience, so that what is happening again seems to be happening for the first time. Also more than others, compulsive gamblers are well trained in rejecting anything which challenges their prejudices and predispositions and in hiding from themselves the self-defeating nature of their resistance to reality.

I have come to understand at least two other reasons why I was willing to turn what would have been my first victory over lunacy into just another mirage. The reasons involve contradictory attitudes toward the woman I said I wanted to marry.

On the one hand, I felt I was being judged by Jeanette, to see if I was behaving as I had said I would, and I resented being in that position. At the same time, I questioned whether I was worthy of this good woman, whether I was using her to solve my problem, and whether I had the right to endanger her future well-being by exposing her to the risk that I might go on being a compulsive gambler even after seeming to withdraw from action. I remember thinking it might have been better for both of us if we had not met.

Also, although I was willing to take the Aiken Out and consider myself a winner with a desirable marriage as my prize, I couldn't fool myself about the reality. I would always know that no matter what marital prizes I won I would remain the loser of a great deal of money. And she would know that, too.

If all that weren't enough, there was also the issue of freedom to deal with in my debate over whether to go forward or fall back. I wanted to be free of the burdens I had carried for so long, yet I wanted also to remain free to act as I might choose in the future. Honoring my pledge to quit gambling would close me off forever from something I might want to do again occasionally, briefly, without harming anyone, just for fun. Certainly I wouldn't run wild ever again, and I might choose not to gamble at all. But I wanted to be free to do so if I chose to do so, without having someone hovering over me—without having to get permission from my wife, so to speak.

As I have come to understand, these rationalizations, taken all together, would not have carried enough weight to move me. In my understanding, they were window dressing, distracting me from the true reason for the choice I was about to make. I was simply not ready to withdraw from action just yet. I was falling back once again on my automatic compensating reaction to the prospect of good fortune, allowing myself once more to believe I was undeserving of the good I could expect from changing the course of my life.

Had it been called to my attention, I might have been comforted to know that resistance to change, even for the better, is commonplace—only somewhat more common among compulsive gamblers. One doesn't easily surrender the security of the familiar for the uncertainties of a new and different state of things, no matter how promising the prospect of change may seem to be. Gambling was my security blanket, helping me hide from reality. I couldn't afford to discard my shield and expose myself to greater responsibilities than I felt capable of handling.

Retreat seemed the most natural and sensible move. Guilt opened the way out. Throughout my deliberations I had been troubled by the burden of debt, about three thousand dollars now, that I would bring to the prospective marriage. It didn't seem right to saddle someone else with an obligation that was mine alone. If I could find some way to liquidate my debt, I could then feel free to share the responsibilities of marriage with the woman I loved.

Once I arrived at that understanding there was no question which way I would go. It wasn't as easy as it had been in the past to sell myself that fraudulent proposition. But, after a mighty struggle, faith conquered common sense and I managed, with the help of a carefully crafted game plan.

Above all, I assured myself, I would be prudent. I wouldn't go for broke and try to win back all I had lost. My objective would be to try to win just enough to clear my debt, so I could enter into marriage unencumbered. And I wouldn't keep at it forever. If after a reasonable time I saw that things were not working out, I would quit. On the other hand if things went as I hoped, I would quit as soon as I had won enough to clear my debt and would then be ready to start my new life with the woman for whom I was doing this.

In a more reflective time I would understand this compromise as another example of the way in which the churning confusion of my life enabled me to believe I was making progress while standing still. At the time the plan seemed to me wise, if only because it gave me a sense of doing something hopeful rather than wallowing in idle thought.

41.

ALTHOUGH I was ambivalent about the wisdom of my decision to make a last chance try for a limited victory over the laws of probability, I conducted an all-out, single-minded, totally-concentrated effort to make good on the decision. I think of the period that followed as a time of disorganized turmoil, during which I converted a promising growth opportunity into a now-or-never, do-or-die struggle to achieve what might not be possible and clearly was not necessary.

The degree to which I brought my energies to bear on the situation was unlike anything I had done before—except perhaps for my efforts during the up-and-down streak three years earlier. I didn't move into a command post at the Hotel Commodore and I didn't stock up with haberdashery at Brooks Brothers, as I had done then, but I went at my action with the same intensity. Apart from that, there were sharp differences between the two periods, among them my frame of mind as I moved through what I thought of as my final battle.

In that other time, as winnings had piled up, I had been cheerful, hopeful, awed by the wonder of incomprehensible and good things happening to me, at least until the last terrible days, when winning turned to losing. Now, from the first, I went at my work in a high pitch of joyless excitement, making every bet an act of desperation, seeing every result as a decision on my future. Each time I counted out the money for a bet, I felt I was putting pieces of myself on the line. It took all the emotional strength I could muster just to keep going. Still, I persisted, somehow overcoming all the doubt, fear, and guilt.

Guilt of a new kind created a cloud which nothing, not even winning, could dissipate. I suffered from growing awareness that with each bet I was poisoning my well of hope for the future by lying to myself and to the woman I wanted to marry. Legalistically, I could say I had not told Jeanette I was finished with gambling; I had simply promised to quit at some unspecified time. But such quibbling was unpersuasive. Our conference had left no doubt of my commitment to withdraw from action with all deliberate speed. Each bet was a betrayal of our understanding, and I knew that dishonesty was poor material from which to make building blocks for our future.

Nevertheless, racked by guilt, torn by anxiety, driven by despair, I pressed on. I am awed still by my tolerance for so much self-punishment, but it would appear that I still retained enough of the compulsive gambler's fortitude to shield myself from the worst of the torment and maintain a facade of well-being that hid my agony from those around me. A survey of four persons with whom I spent time during this period reveals that none of them was aware of anything amiss.

If Jeanette was aware of anything out of the ordinary, she said nothing. I tried to hold our meetings to a minimum, and when we were together I made every effort to direct our conversation away from anything to do with gambling. I assumed she was content for the time being to wait until I could take step two and declare myself quits.

Meanwhile, I spent every possible day in action—with rare exceptions—at the track. To stay within the debt limit I had set while also assuring maximum cash availability for my betting, I adopted an austerity budget. I no longer spent my afternoons, and the dollars they cost, in the clubhouse dining rooms. I took my lunch more cheaply but almost as satisfyingly at one of the Stevens Brothers soup bars, which each day offered a choice of hearty Manhattan clam chowder or a soup du jour, plus French bread and large, chewy soup crackers, for fifty or sixty cents. I also cut back on other food outlays and drastically reduced all non-essential spending in order to squeeze every possible betting dollar out of my weekly pay checks.

In the office, I spent more time than I should have at the racing wire when I had a bet going. At the track, I watched races in agonized, prayerful excitement, suffering painful depression when I lost, feeling relief when I won, and feeling also something new to me— anger over my predicament, a reaction that became part of the pattern of these days.

The first occasion on which I became aware of this new response to my fortunes involved a go-for-broke bet on a six-to-five favorite in a race at Aqueduct. My horse was a standout in a field of ten. In a smaller field, attracting less diffused betting support, my choice might well have been bet down to four-to-five or less. In that sense, the favorite could be considered an overlay, an added attraction for me.

I had sixty-eight dollars, After due deliberation, I decided to bet sixty-five on what seemed to me the most promising betting opportunity I had found in months, leaving three dollars for transportation to the office and a sandwich supper if, for some unforeseeable reason, the favorite should lose. I regretted not having more money to bet, since the more closely I examined the past performances, the better my horse looked.

This front-running sprinter was, by any standard I could find, lengths better than any other horse in the crowded field for the seven-furlong race. The favorite broke from the starting gate like a sure thing, racing clear of the possibility of a jam, which sometimes takes place when a large field goes off. I was pleased with my good judgement as the favorite steadily widened his lead to four lengths and maintained it into the stretch.

With the favorite comfortably in the lead, I watched the race confidently, counting my probable winnings, calculating the amount at about seventy-one dollars. With little more than five seconds to go to the finish, I was thinking ahead to a horse I liked in the next race. Suddenly, confidence turned to consternation as a horse burst out of the crowded field and began to close in on my horse.

"Oh, God, no!" I prayed. "Oh, no!" I cried, as the oncoming horse caught the favorite and the two crossed the finish line in tandem. The infield board flashed "Photo," and the people around me began debating which of the two horses had won.

While they debated the probable order of finish, I thought wild thoughts about what I would do if my horse lost. Kill myself, I thought. But I knew I would do nothing more awful than go to work, no matter what happened.

The debate was going on hot and heavy when the infield board lit up with the numbers showing the order of finish with the favorite in first place. My reaction surprised me. I felt none of the joy or satisfaction I should have felt. After the torment of the closing seconds of the race and the two or three minutes required to process the photo of the finish, all I felt was anger. I was angry over what I thought of as the indignity of having been required to suffer so much to win a piddling bet on a race that should have been decided more quickly, more easily, less painfully. When the anger had spent itself, I felt also relief to have been saved by a result that, after all, was better than losing. I took a taxi to work without waiting for the last race.

During this run of action, I won quite often though not quite as often as I lost. A curious see-saw, win-lose pattern developed. For weeks I couldn't get far ahead, but didn't fall far behind, either. It was as though God or fate or the laws of probability were toying with me, trying to show me the pointlessness of what I was doing. I responded by stepping up the tempo of my action, as though to force the issue by increasing the size of my bets, until often they were for a hundred dollars or more—but of a value greater than could be counted in dollars.

Watching a race on which I had bet a day's pay or a week's pay or more, I had to struggle for breath in a stratospheric high of uncontrollable excitement and unrelieved terror. Win or lose, I watched apprehensively as my fate was decided several times a day, day after day, and was afraid that at any moment I might die of a heart attack or despair.

Yet I continued to subject myself to this excruciating process again and again for two months. The painful pattern finally was smashed on the good-news day when I lost seven hundred dollars, the biggest bet of my life, at Jamaica, my lucky track. As a postscript that may have more curiosity value than significance, it could be noted that this loss, too, was part of the win-lose pattern. The day before that Tuesday at Jamaica I had turned fifty-five dollars into the seven-hundred dollars I had lost by touting myself off the gray overlay. That switch had cost me the chance to win the three thousand dollars to liquidate my debt, which was the stated objective of the process I had endured during these hysterical weeks.

The terrible, wild bad news day at Jamaica unnerved me. I did not think my body or soul could withstand another such experience. I was, as they say of a horse that has run out of energy and will, used up. I could barely make it back to the barn. I had no desire to go to the post again.

42.

To say I had no desire to bet again was not quite the same as calling it quits unconditionally, but this was as far as I had yet come to withdrawing from action, and the implied decision filled me with pride. I had begun to think of my life as an unkept promise, but now I had made good on what might very well be the most important promise of my life. I had been able to go into this last period of action only by pledging that if after a reasonable time I had not achieved the objective of liquidating my debt, I would withdraw from action. After two months, a reasonable time in my judgment, I had failed to do what I had set out to do and I had given up the hopeless effort, as promised.

However, there appeared to be some doubt whether this was to be merely another time-out or the real thing. In the past, I had thought that when I was finished forever I would know and would be able to pinpoint the time, place, and manner in which I had made my last bet. But I didn't feel any of that after my hysterical seven-hundred-dollar fiasco at Jamaica. As far as my future intentions were concerned, I felt as though only the apparent order of finish had been posted and would not count until the judges declared the result official.

In the circumstances, I thought it might be premature to say anything to Jeanette immediately. Rather than risk an upset, however dim such a possibility, I decided for the moment to treat my decision to really quit gambling as a secret I couldn't share even with her just yet.

Despite precautions that might have suggested something to the contrary, I believe I was confident about making good on my decision to quit, and I know I felt relieved. It pleased me to contemplate a future in which I would never again have to suffer through the torment of hoping, betting, losing, and borrowing. But I had felt relief before, each time I ended a costly run of action with a time-out. I couldn't help wondering whether I was merely tired now and might yet want to return to action when I was rested, as I had before.

Given my history, more than fifteen years of it by now, that was not an idle question—nor were others that filled my mind. Did I truly *want* to quit gambling? If so, should I reveal to Jeanette the details of my latest fiasco? If she were willing to marry me, might that endanger her? As for me, could I do without the routines that had sustained me through thick and thin for so long?

Finally, there was the question of the Aiken Out. I could understand that marriage to Jeanette was a bigger prize than any I might win as a gambler. That was why I wanted to marry her. But I wondered whether I could live with the inescapable knowledge that, whatever I might win in the future, I had worked for more than seven of the last fifteen years just to pay for my losses as a horse-player.

These were difficult questions until I came to grips with them. Then answers came easily—in every case an answer that brought closer the prospect of marriage. A month after my hysterical debacle at Jamaica, I told Jeanette what had happened, assured her that I was through with that life, and asked her to marry me. Not without some reluctance, I think, she agreed. We were married five months later.

During that time I didn't bet or want to, but neither did I feel free. I felt that something was missing. It was nothing vital—a hub cap rather than a spark plug—but still something that had always been there before and was not any longer.

Our married life began with one problem we were aware of from the start and another that became apparent later. We found an attractive apartment in Queens, on the border of Cunningham Park in Bayside, met pleasant neighbors, and prepared to make the best of the problem we knew would be with us for a while, a conflict in our work schedules. As a laboratory technician, Jeanette worked nine to five, with Saturday and Sunday as her days off. I started my night shift at her quitting time and only infrequently had Saturday or Sunday as one of my days off. Although we would rather have had more time together, we regarded the schedule conflict as a temporary inconvenience that would last only until Jeanette became pregnant, at which time we had decided she would stop working.

Not so easily dealt with was another problem to which the conflict in work schedules contributed. Within weeks of our arrival in Bayside, I became aware that the apartment into which we had moved was ten minutes from Belmont Park.

I don't know whether I was aware of the geographic coincidence before we moved in but am inclined to doubt that. In any case, it was not a problem at first. We moved into our apartment in November, at the end of the racing season, and for a long time I was much too busy with other demands on my time to have given any attention to the coincidence. Also, when I called it quits I would have bet that I had cut myself off completely from any connection to gambling, as cleanly as a surgeon cutting away every last bit of cancerous flesh from a sick body.

During the winter I occupied myself with household chores and preparations for new Guild contract negotiations before going to work. When the new racing season opened in March, I was too busy to notice. But within the next few weeks a contract was signed, the burden of household chores was lightened, and I found myself in a position that had proved troublesome before: time on my hands and, for five days a week, nothing to do until it was time to go to work. Then I started thinking about the nearness of Belmont Park.

Our finances had improved to a point at which we could afford to buy a used car, and I used it to extend shopping trips into nearby Nassau county. On those trips I passed often within sight of the

Belmont grandstand, and on one such occasion the thought crossed my mind that I hadn't made or thought of making a bet for months. Even now it shocks me to recall that, after all I had come through, making progress now in a sensible and satisfying life, I should have thought of betting on a horse race again. Yet that was what I was thinking on this occasion as I passed by Belmont on the Cross Island Parkway, continued on toward home, then made a U-turn and drove into the track's parking area.

Obviously, I had not succeeded in removing all cancerous tissue when I called it quits on my career as a horseplayer. Still functioning was the lunatic apparatus of my automatic compensating reaction to good fortune. Go on, it said. This is no big deal. Everything is going well and will continue to go well, no matter what happens. And nothing terrible is going to happen. You might lose a few dollars. So what? You can afford it. On the other hand, you might win. Either way, so what? You will just be passing a pleasant hour or two before going to work. *Do it!*

I made no effort to resist or offer counter-arguments. I don't think I acted so much out of wanting, as of feeling that there really wasn't any reason not to do it—just this once.

Lacking a clubhouse pass, I paid two dollars for admission to the grandstand, rather than five dollars for the clubhouse, and took a seat high in the stands, as though to hide myself from the crowd below. Along the way I found a program and a *Morning Telegraph* left behind by someone who had departed early and was pleased to have saved the half dollar these two items would have cost.

Sitting there, reading the little numbers again, I felt as though I hadn't been away, as though I was doing the most natural thing in my world. I bet five dollars on a horse shown at three-to-one on the board and was delighted to see my selection lead the field home easily by three lengths. I bet the fifteen dollars in winnings on the favorite in the next race; and when that one also finished first, I began to think I might have found the winning touch I never had. I couldn't stay for the last race, but used twenty dollars of what was now thirty-two dollars in winnings to carry away with me two ten-dollar tickets on a four-to-one shot in the last race.

That was something I had often done in the past, when I couldn't stay for a race but wanted to bet. I think I knew that doing it now meant I might be doing it again. I tried not to think of that and tried to tell myself I was pleased when I got to the office and found my bet had lost. Without a winning ticket to cash the next day, there would be no reason to return to the track.

It embarrasses me to remember that, although I didn't return to the track the next day, eventually—more than a week, but less than a month later—I did go back. I felt guilty. I felt foolish. I knew it was absurd. But the thought of doing it stayed with me. I had accumulated from my pocket money a private slush fund of about eighty dollars. I swore I would risk no more than that, plus whatever I could withhold from my personal budget.

When I went back into action, I stayed within those limits. I had also decided that I would not bet with bookies and would not again make betting a regular part of my routine. I don't remember how often I went to the track, except that it was not very often.

On one of my better days, I left the track with a ten-dollar ticket on a horse that paid twenty-two dollars and eighty cents to win the last race, making my ticket worth one hundred and fourteen dollars. Normally, I would have gone back the next day to collect what was almost a week's take-home pay for me. But other obligations kept me away for days.

On one of my nights off during that time, my wife and I were dressing to go out for dinner when my wallet fell from my hands and the contents, including the uncashed betting ticket, spilled all over the floor. Jeanette bent to help me gather the things, and one of the items she picked up was the parimutuel ticket.

"What is this?" she asked, knowing but unbelieving.

I tried to concoct a lie but could think of nothing quickly enough that would make sense. I think I welcomed the horrible scene that followed.

I may have been seeking some formal ritual of exorcism and purification, something like the sunburn suffered while unloading coal in Cincinnati—this time, not merely as punishment for my sins but rather as a cleansing preparation for a wholesome new life. Something like the ritual baths Orthodox Jews take to prepare for the holy Sabbath. What I received was purification by scathing denunciation. Jeanette did most of the talking, as I felt she was entitled to do. I suffered for the most part in silence.

It wasn't what Jeanette said that hurt. What she said was ordinary. She had trusted me, and I had lied to her—before we were married and now again. We couldn't live together without trust, and she didn't see how she could ever trust me again. I was afraid she would carry it to the breaking point, but she stopped short of that. We left it that the next time would be the breaking point.

None of that hurt. In fact, the resolution left me feeling like a winner. But I couldn't escape what had caused the hurt, for me and for her: the knowledge that my infantile behavior had brought us to this terrible crisis. Nothing she could have said would have caused me more pain than the knowledge, not only that I had lied to my wife about a vital matter, but that what I had done by moving backward into action was beyond explanation or excuse.

Recalling now what happened next, I would like to be able to laugh, but it would be unfelt laughter about an absurdity that was in no way amusing. Rather than risk what might have happened if I returned to the track to cash my hundred-and-fourteen-dollar ticket, I asked George, another of the racegoing horseplayers in the office, to do it for me. When he delivered the proceeds, I placed a small bet, two dollars, on a horse chosen blindly from among the entries. And I continued doing that, placing small bets with bookies at the office, while thinking of these bets as tokens of my degradation.

I can recognize these haphazard acts as the final sparking and sputterings of a faulty engine after the ignition had been switched off—a final act of infantile lunacy. But it was brutally painful then to understand that what I was doing was pointless, hopeless, absurd—and to live with an understanding I couldn't avoid.

I don't remember how long it went on, but it couldn't have been very long—perhaps a few weeks. Then fatigue and disgust combined to send me to the sidelines. I couldn't bear the thought of making another bet and of engaging in what I had come to think of as an act of idiocy.

After sixteen years I might have thought I would end my career as a horseplayer with a dramatic flourish. I could have imagined myself flinging a betting slip and some cash at a bookie—Jerry, perhaps—and saying as I did so: "Here's my last bet. It will lose, but that doesn't matter. I'm done." But I don't remember my last bet. I had made too many, like Sir Harry Lauder, the long-ago vaudeville star from Scotland who was more famous for his numerous farewell appearances than for his actual talent.

I like to think my last bet was made on another life-promising spring day, a lucky Tuesday, possibly. But all I remember is that at some point in my sixteenth year as a horseplayer, I became aware, with a sense of awe, that I had not made a bet for some time and had absolutely no desire to do so.

I tested myself with why-not urgings of the kind that always had been effective in the past. But I was surprised to find that these lunacies had lost their compelling force. As I became aware that I didn't have to do as these urgings would have me do, I came to understand how it feels to be whole. I began to think of myself as cured, and that time of my life came to an end, not with a whimper but a sigh of relief.

PART SIX

AFTERMATH

43.

AFTER so many false endings, I was reluctant to believe I had finally liberated myself from a lost weekend that had lasted sixteen years. But as time passed and I became aware of a new texture to my days—a lightness and openness that had not been there previously—I began to believe I was free at last.

I had felt something similar before during time-outs. But those free-seeming moments never had been intended to provide anything more than temporary relief from ongoing pain. This was something quite different, something much more—the difference between a soothing rubdown and successful spinal surgery. There was a sense of permanence in what I felt now, whereas I think I had always known that the time-outs were only brief breaks from action—time enough to catch my breath before returning to the front lines. This, I felt certain, was the real McCoy.

With that understanding, I began to feel like a winner: satisfied, confident, even cocky. I didn't think about it very much, but I had acquired enough faith in myself to believe it would never again be necessary to depend on gambling to do for me anything I couldn't do for myself.

And so it has gone. I have never again allowed myself to become a dependent gambler—counting on horses, or cards, or dice to compensate for my competitive shortcomings. I have gambled eleven times in the thirty-one years since my liberation. But with one exception—actually a pair of engagements on two consecutive days—these widely-spaced bouts of action have not been the kind of serious gambling in which substantial risks are taken in hope of more substantial gains. Rather, my outings have been exercises in the kind of freedom I considered a condition of my withdrawal from action—the freedom to indulge occasionally. With the one exception, I have gambled only in social circumstances or for purposes of research and, in every case, have found pleasure or instructional value.

The one occasion on which there was a real possibility of backsliding took place fifteen years after my official withdrawal from action. I was under heavy financial pressure and seem to have hoped, as in the old days, that gambling might help me resolve this crisis.

It began innocently without any thought of gambling. I accepted an invitation for a junket to the Bahamas as an opportunity to enjoy a few restful days in the sun. I did not think of gambling until our flight from the JFK airport was delayed four hours because of mechanical trouble. Then, as other passengers headed for the bar or coffee shop, I responded—automatically, it surprises me still to recall—by taking a taxi to nearby Belmont Park.

I lost eighty-three dollars but decided not to risk any more on the last two races. The next day I lost one hundred and twenty-five dollars at dice at the Freeport casino but decided against cashing a check to continue in action. In each case, I seem to have sensed that one more bet, win or lose, could carry me over the precipice. I don't know why I didn't take that step. Instead, I left Freeport ahead of schedule to spend two days with friends in Florida before returning home and resolving my financial crisis without the assistance of gambling. None of my gambling ventures before or since that Bahamanian adventure has jeopardized my good-conduct status.

For the first four years of my reformation, I abstained without difficulty. I thought about racing and betting from time to time but cannot recall actually wanting to make a bet. The first time I did, I was in Chicago on a long, hard-working assignment for United Press.

I had done little more than work and sleep for three weeks and was bored. When a colleague suggested spending Saturday afternoon at Arlington Park, I agreed without hesitation.

That proved to be one of the more satisfying decisions I have made in connection with gambling, and that afternoon became a peculiarly pleasurable, satisfaction-guaranteed, no-lose, gambling experience. The racing itself was nothing special, and my handicapping had not improved with disuse. I lost forty dollars. My companion, who bet a winner I rejected as unworthy, lost ten. Our outing became memorable only because a sympathetic division manager persuaded the penny-pinching auditor of UP to approve for payment an item recorded on my expense account as "Entertainment, Arlington Park, $50." If that is what is meant by having fun as a horseplayer, then I agree it is possible to have fun betting on the horses.

However, I was not inclined to press my luck. Six years passed before I bet again; and when I did, it was to place a bet on myself as the result of a strange competition. I had made a career change and was serving as marketing consultant for the owner of a successful small business. He and his wife also raced trotters for tax benefits; and, as the husband told me over a drink one day, he and his wife bet heavily on their horses and others. He invited me to spend an evening with them at Roosevelt Raceway. I declined, explaining I had been a horseplayer but, except for the Arlington Park outing, had been clean for ten years and had no desire to gamble.

Something in my story apparently struck a competitive spark in my client. For weeks, he badgered me with invitations and challenges. To end the harassment, which threatened to affect our working relationship, I agreed to bet fifty dollars that I could spend an evening at the track without betting. I ate an abominable dinner in a garish clubhouse dining room, witnessed my hosts lose more than a thousand dollars, made no bet of my own, but, despite winning the bet on myself, wrote off the evening as a loss—the most boring time I have ever spent in a gambling establishment.

By contrast, I think of the one other outing prior to my Bahamanian misadventure as the most exotic. In 1967, twenty-three years after my incarceration as a POW in Romania, I went back on a sentimental journey to revisit wartime scenes and took a side trip to the lovely Black Sea resort of Mamaia. There, I discovered the most luxurious nightclub I have ever seen, a two-level chamber that looked like a palatial ballroom. Within that stately structure, one cramped room, which may originally have been a pantry, had been set aside for gambling. There was, as I remember, one table for roulette and another for *chemin de fer* or baccarat, high-stakes European versions of blackjack.

The gambling cubicle and the ornate main room seemed out of place in a Communist country, but explanations about this apparent contradiction came easily. Governments everywhere, Communist governments not excepted, try to get all they can out of gambling. Communist governments have a special interest in gambling as a means of accumulating Western currency, and Mamaia attracts many Western visitors. That makes it an ideal setting for a casino and a sure-thing profit maker for the state.

Romanian nationals are not permitted to play. The house wants and wins only dollars, francs, pounds, marks, and other foreign-exchange currencies. I contributed ten dollars at the roulette table then went off to enjoy the splendor of the non-gambling attractions.

Mamaia's gambling nook was too small to have attracted much Western cash. However, I would guess that in the eighteen years since I was there the gambling facilities have expanded considerably—as has been true in so many other countries during the world-wide gambling boom of the 1970's and 1980's.

Compared to the closet-sized room at Mamaia, the Freeport casino in the Bahamas, which I visited in the following year, was gigantic—the largest gambling room I had ever seen. But another comparison may be closer to the point. As a gambler, I would have chosen Freeport for size but might have appreciated Mamaia for class, which may be an odd thing to say about a Communist venture.

The half-dozen outings since my escape from Freeport have been a mixed lot. I didn't gamble at all for seven years. Then, in 1975, I lost forty dollars in the casino at Dorado Beach in Puerto Rico playing blackjack after dinner. Later that year, I enjoyed the races and a trackside lunch at shabby Saratoga on the suggestion of a sister-in-law and her husband who are not gamblers but had been invited by his employer, who was.

Five more years passed before my next outing, a visit to Atlantic City. I had never been in a big-league American casino until 1980 when, on the spur of the moment while driving home from a vacation on the Outer Banks of North Carolina, my wife and I decided to visit the seaside gambling supermarkets. We spent two hours on a sunny Wednesday afternoon in three casinos crowded with gamblers, many waiting patiently in line for a place at one of the gambling tables. When a seat became available without my having to wait, I played blackjack for twenty minutes, accumulating winnings of sixty-five dollars before my luck changed, and I quit even. Few others may have done as well.

That visit stands in memory as my most depressing gambling experience. I think of Atlantic City, which I knew long ago as a pleasant family resort, as being now a place of clashing realities that deny each other: palaces of ersatz luxury floating on a sea of flotsam and jetsam from a festering, decaying dump of a city. In 1984, while the city continued to decay, bettors lost almost two billion dollars in these "play-palaces," a sum larger than the national budgets of many countries. There has been talk about using more of the gambling taxes New Jersey collects to improve things for the residents and about a move to use some casino profits to fund therapy for compulsive gamblers. I find the irony overwhelming. I suppose the slogan could be: "We lure them. We cure them."

Still and all, gambling can be fun, even when losing, particularly in the company of someone like John McCarthy, of Waterford, Ireland—a darling man who is a retired packinghouse worker and a veteran punter who "backs" rather than bets on horses. John and Molly McCarthy came proudly to the United States in 1981 to be present as their son, Jimmy, graduated with honors from the School of Engineering at North Carolina State University.

On the northern leg of their American journey, John agreed that a visit to Belmont Park might be nice. He was awed by the size and grandeur of the place, which is bigger and more ornate than any race track on the Emerald Isle. Otherwise, the day left much to be desired. We lost some bets, which was nothing unusual for either of us. But I was disappointed by what I had expected would be a compensating treat, a good lunch in the clubhouse dining room, which is no longer under the aegis of the long-gone Stevens Brothers.

Inspired by fond memories, I ordered a lunch I thought suitable for the occasion. What we ate was an embarrassment, an atrocious mess which the Sevens Brothers would never have allowed to leave their kitchens: rubbery corned beef, boiled-to-bits potatoes, cabbage cooked to the consistency of pudding, and stale rolls. John ate without comment, except to say he liked the beer.

We did much better four days later, as we watched the 1981 Belmont Stakes on television, while having lunch at a restaurant where a caring, competent family has been serving properly cooked fresh fish for more than half a century. The meal of soft-shell crabs was all one could have asked, and we placed a bet on the winning horse, Summing, with a bookmaker I had never seen before in the place.

I have made one other bet since the official end of my gambling career. In the spring of 1984, I lost ten dollars on a horse of which one of my nephews was part owner.

Those who think of gambling only as dependent gambling— betting on horses, cards, dice, and other games of chance—could consider this summary the end of the story. It would be a happy ending, since by and large I am pleased with the record compiled after my official withdrawal from serious gambling: eleven outings— on the average, one every 2.8 years. But there is the other kind of gambling, the competitive gambling of betting on one's self. That is still another part of the story, and it has its own ending.

NORMALLY, someone with a record like mine would be considered
a reformed gambler, and in that respect I was certainly normal. As
the years went by, I thought of myself as reformed and was pompous
about my new status and my record. I pitied those still dependent
on gambling. However, reflection on my condition has led me to
understand that while my withdrawal from action was all to the good,
even admirable, it was only half the story.

For, as I came to understand, when I liberated myself from dependence on the horses, I did not quit gambling. To the contrary, I then
made the biggest bet of my life—not on the horses or on another
game of chance, but on myself. Acting on the prerogatives of dealer's
choice, I changed the game from dependent to competitive gambling
and became a workaholic in unrestrained pursuit of a good life for
my family and respectable success for myself.

Aunt Mary would have been pleased. She would have said I was
a real hustler, her kind of go-getter. I would have thought so, too—
until later, when reflection clarified my status and enabled me to see

that my single-minded, driving concentration on getting ahead was more respectable but not greatly different from the way in which I had behaved as a horseplayer.

My experience confirms a psychoanalytic finding that compulsive gamblers who withdraw from action tend to switch to more acceptable economic games and continue competing compulsively, for the same reasons that led them to depend upon gambling in the first place. Those reasons, I have come to understand, are continuing uncertainty about how to respond effectively to competitive challenges, when and how to say enough to the insistent demands of the Law of More, and a desperate need to be counted successful and thus respected.

According to the psychoanalytic theory, withdrawing from action is like stopping a hemorrhage so heart surgery can be performed. The only way to complete the process—to learn the right answers and act upon them successfully—is to reconstruct the gambler's personality. I didn't manage a complete rebuilding of myself, though I worked hard toward that end, bleeding occasionally and, despite my best intentions to the contrary, causing others to bleed occasionally as well—though I wasn't aware of that while it was happening.

Understanding has come slowly, in part because of my reluctance at first to rake over the ashes of my misbegotten betting tickets. When my days in action were over, I didn't want to think about what had been. I wanted only to get on with building a future, and I turned to that task enthusiastically.

I began my new life as a winner. During the first three and a half years of my marriage to Jeanette, our union was blessed with two sons who have given me more than my fair share of the joys of fatherhood. To fund the needs of our growing one-income family, I tried to earn more by moonlighting as a freelance magazine writer. But that line of work was less rewarding than anticipated. Too much of what should have been family time was consumed by the additional work, and the fees paid were generally not enough to compensate for the time and effort—especially one major effort that was strangely disappointing.

The disappointment involved an article describing my life as a horseplayer that I wrote for *Sports Illustrated* three years after withdrawing from action. The fee was the largest I received for a magazine article, but my satisfaction was soured by an unusual editorial decision.

Without notifying me prior to its publication, the editors followed my story with another article describing the delights of a non-compulsive two-dollar bettor spending a fun-filled day at the track. This ode to the joys of harmless horseplaying could only be read as an antidote to my story—to take the bad taste of compulsion from the minds of the upscale country-club sports enthusiasts who were then assumed to be the audience of *Sports Illustrated*. To me, it was a slap in the face, a gratuitous reminder that I had been guilty of something foul—as a horseplayer and as author of the offending article.

I would have had no argument with the most unflattering characterization of my life as a horseplayer. But I couldn't understand why the editors reacted as they had to a story about that life—a story they had requested the right to publish. When I inquired about the other article, an editor explained: "We thought it would take the curse off your piece and balance the picture."

His explanation served only to confuse me about why the editors should have felt a need to balance a factual story with what I thought of as a fairy tale. I wondered whether a magazine would publish a story about a cigarette smoker who had recovered from lung cancer and follow that with another article reporting that many people who enjoy smoking don't get lung cancer.

Questions remained, but my attention was already directed elsewhere. I had concluded that freelance writing for magazines was no way to get rich. I felt I had labored long enough in the sideshow and should move into the center ring, where the big money was. I decided to learn about business, so I could get into the business world and make more money than I could expect to earn as a journalist.

That was the first of several chances I took in my search for more, probably more chances that I need have taken. In this case the timing was unfortunate, and the decision may have been the poorest I made in my quest for more. I had been promoted recently to the main news desk at UP and, while I could not hope to get rich in that work, I could expect other promising opportunities to do the only kind of work I enjoyed. I think I would have liked to stand pat, and I have no doubt that I should have held on. But forces not unlike those that had guided me in the old days were in control. I placed the bet and made the switch.

I began my new quest for more with what I thought of as an apprenticeship: a position as a senior editor of *Printer's Ink,* a business weekly specializing in news of advertising and marketing. Armed with what I learned in that work, I moved on to become a marketing executive for a food-sales agency, an ad agency, and a marketing research firm, and a consultant for others.

Although I took a chance with each move I made, I was lucky enough to start off in front and stay there. Within a year of my move into business management, I was able to put aside enough for a down payment on an attractive house in a desirable suburb, and I was earning enough to meet the mortgage and tax payments without strain. Each year thereafter, I was able to add more of the trophies winners bring home from the economic wars. But I was not happy or comfortable as a businessman.

From time to time, I found myself thinking that this was not my game. I liked the excitement of doing business, and in that respect, business was like journalism: there was always something new happening—a plan to design, a problem to solve, a contract to sell—something to respond to. But I was never completely at ease. My position reminded me of Groucho Marx's confession of a loner: "I wouldn't join a club that would have me as a member."

Occasionally, when the rewards seemed inadequate compensation for the effort and the agonies, or when I saw a news story that I thought I could have handled better, I let myself wish that I had not left the only kind of work I had enjoyed and was meant to do. I felt that most keenly as I tried to find time to keep up with the fast-breaking developments that made the 1960's and 1970's a time of frightening violence—actual and threatened, individual and collective—in Viet Nam, the United States, Cuba, Eastern Europe, and Africa.

Two of the major issues of that time—the civil rights movement and the war in Viet Nam—were of ongoing interest to me as a former journalist. As the United States expanded its role in Viet Nam, I could remember writing stories about the first step in America's twenty-one-year involvement: President Eisenhower's decision in 1954 to send advisers to Saigon after the defeat of the French by the Vietminh. Also in 1954, I had written about the Supreme Court decision that inspired the civil rights movement, the ruling that segregated education was unconstitutional.

Observing the consequence of these first steps, I wished that I could be in the middle of things again, but it was too late to get back into that game. Having relegated myself to the sidelines, I could only wonder and worry about the hope and the horror of the changing world.

Meanwhile, my first priority continued to be my competitive pursuit of more. I kept at it, because the money was good and I believed I was working for what my wife and sons wanted and needed.

Oblivious to other considerations, I pressed on with the business at hand while, invisible to my unseeing eyes, I was committing an error common to workaholic competitors. That is the tendency of determined or fearful competitors in the stress and strain of battle to be unaware of, or insensitive to, the emotional wounds their strivings impose on the innocent bystanders—to hurt without meaning to hurt those who are supposed to benefit from the strenuous efforts of the breadwinner.

Whenever I made a career move, I did so like a horseplayer, hoping that it would work out well, as almost always it did. I saw nothing wrong with such moves. I would have been surprised to know that for my wife such risk taking was as bad as playing the horses, a source of anxiety for her. When I worked long hours at the office and often at home on evenings and weekends, I expected my wife to understand my need to do so. I would have pleaded not guilty to a charge of neglect. Except for infrequent business trips away from home, I enjoyed spending time each day with my wife and sons and taking an active part in family chores, whether feeding and bathing infants or doing the supermarket shopping.

Yet, unrecognized by me, my wife and I were working at cross purposes. I might have realized that sooner if I had paid closer attention to something she said to me at a particularly busy time when, under the pressure of extra work, I was unaware of the distress my absences, whether at the office or locked away at home, were causing my family. At a time when I could not understand how deeply she felt about it, my wife had said disconsolately, "I wish you had been a truck driver with an eight-hour day and no homework."

When I did come to understand not only the meaning but the

feelings communicated by that wistful declaration, it was too late to take corrective action. My marriage to the woman for whom I had abdicated my position as a dependent gambler, only to follow another compulsive course, had come to an end after fifteen years. In the final accounting, my efforts had gone simply to accumulate enough capital for a respectable divorce settlement.

Nothing in my life before or since has recalled my childhood with such depressing effect as the knowledge that I had participated in doing to my sons what my parents had done to me and my brothers. I have tried to overcome my guilt with the knowledge that, unlike my unfortunate father, I have been able to do a great deal to ameliorate the pain of my sons. But I know that for children, the divorce of loved parents is a loss for which there is no balancing compensation.

Among the events contributing to a better balance has been my second marriage, to Carol, widowed mother of three daughters. We have endured thus far for fifteen years, enjoying our pleasures, attending to our problems, living a new life, a new story. One hopes the final chapter remains at a distance.

45.

AT the end of my journey down memory lane, I feel safe. I don't
think it is possible for me to go back to the old ways. But, even
after all this time, one never knows. Where gambling and the Law
of More are concerned, anything can happen, any time. However,
should I be inclined to tempt fate, I believe I can count on a lesson
learned by accident from Jimmy Mac to keep me safe.

I admired the Mac, as much as a horseplayer could admire a
bookmaker. I enjoyed our on-the-run chats when we met in and
around the News building. And it was during one of these irregular
encounters that the Mac inadvertently taught me what may be the
most meaningful lesson learned during my lengthy explorations into
the question why people gamble, so many compulsively—particularly people who already would seem to have everything they need.

We met when I was passing through the period after my wild bad-
news day at Jamaica and knew I would have to withdraw soon from
the toils of my compulsion. I had not made a bet for three weeks

and had not seen Mac for longer than that, since my last bets had been placed at the track.

"You been laying off?" Mac asked as we met in front of the News building on a ripe spring afternoon.

"I think I'm ready to pack it in," I replied.

"For good?" he asked.

"For better or for worse," I replied.

Mac studied me for a moment, then nodded in approval. "I hope you make it," he said. He sounded as though he meant it and believed I would succeed.

"If I do, you lose a good customer," I said.

"Not to worry," he assured me. "There's another born every minute."

"There can't be too many," I said.

"Take it from me," he replied. "Sometimes there's too many. I'm worn out. It's like being a doctor to a lot of sick people, and some of these people are really sick."

"You've made your pile, why not pack it in?" I suggested.

"You're right," he said. "It's a good buck. But I can't quit. A lot of people depend on me. If I wasn't around, they'd really be in a bad way." I had availed myself of his generosities often enough to accept his notion without argument, but my curiosity was aroused. Emboldened by the intimate tone of our conversation, I asked, "What do you get out of it?"

Mac weighed the question, deliberating, I suppose, whether to answer and, if so, whether to answer honestly. I don't know why he should have responded, except that under stress, as he appeared to be, he had an unexplainable need to confide in someone.

"In a good week," he said, "I take home three thou." Three thousand dollars a week was almost twenty-five times as much as I earned at that time.

"You must be a millionaire," I exclaimed.

He smiled wryly. "I could be, if it wasn't for the heavy tax I pay," he said. I thought he was talking about payoffs to the police or the mob. "No," he said. "Three thou is after all expenses. The tax is something else. Comes to about one hundred per cent of what's left over."

He smiled at my puzzlement and explained, "When you're in

action, you do the horses every day. With me, it's a floating crap game every Friday night."

"As a player?" I asked, uncomprehending. Mac was at the top of the never-be's in my ranking of compulsive-gambler candidates. Bookmakers were the very opposite of compulsive gamblers, privileged citizens with a license to steal from willing victims, proprietors of absolutely sure things with no need to take chances. Also, they knew better than anyone else the absurdity of gambling, whether compulsive or otherwise. I couldn't believe he meant that he was one of my kind, which was what he seemed to be saying.

"As a player," he confirmed, a rueful smile acknowledging the irony of his earlier self-serving declaration of service to the sick.

We stood wordless for a time—uncomfortable and overwhelmed, I believe, by the enormity of the contradiction and the realization, new to each of us, that in the presence of contagion no one is immune. A nervous laugh forced its way from my throat. Mac raised his eyebrows and twisted his lips in a helpless grimace as though to say yes, well, that's the way it is. There was nothing else to say.

After withdrawing from action and moving on from United Press, I never again saw the Mac, so I don't know how he dealt with his taxing situation. In response to another compulsion, the desire to seek answers to the unspoken questions that hung over us on that lovely spring day, I went on to reexamine my life as a gambler and to explore the reasons why people gamble, so many compulsively, and why in the presence of contagion, no one is immune.

If Mac is in a position to receive the message, I would want him to know that I appreciate the illumination and the inspiration provided by his unintended teaching. I think he would approve of my search for understanding and, perhaps, agree with the result.